MIGRATION
AND
IMMIGRATION

Recent Titles in
A World View of Social Issues Series

MIGRATION AND IMMIGRATION

A GLOBAL VIEW

Edited by
Maura I. Toro-Morn
and Marixsa Alicea

A World View of Social Issues
Andrew L. Cherry, Series Adviser

Greenwood Press
Westport, Connecticut • London

Library of Congress Cataloging-in-Publication Data

Migration and immigration : a global view / edited by Maura I. Toro-Morn and Marixsa
Alicea.
    p.   cm. — (A world view of social issues, ISSN 1526–9442)
    Includes bibliographical references and index.
    ISBN 0–313–33044–1 (alk. paper)
    1. Emigration and immigration. 2. Migration, Internal. I. Toro-Morn, Maura I.
(Maura Isabel), 1961– II. Alicea, Marixsa, 1960– III. Series.
JV603.M54   2004
304.8'2 — dc22   2003060101

British Library Cataloguing in Publication Data is available.

Library of Congress Catalog Card Number: 2003060101
ISBN: 0–313–33044–1
ISSN: 1526–9442

First published in 2004

Greenwood Press, 88 Post Road West, Westport, CT 06881
An imprint of Greenwood Publishing Group, Inc.
www.greenwood.com

Printed in the United States of America

∞™

The paper used in this book complies with the
Permanent Paper Standard issued by the National
Information Standards Organization (Z39.48–1984).

10 9 8 7 6 5 4 3 2 1

Maura dedicates this book to *mis amores*, Frank and Carlitos

Marixsa dedicates this book to her migrant parents, Ana and Manuel, and to her young nephews, Diego and Adrian

CONTENTS

TABLES

SERIES FOREWORD

Why are child abuse in the family and homelessness social conditions to be endured or at least tolerated in some countries while in other countries they are viewed as social problems that must be reduced or eliminated? What social institutions and other factors affect these behaviors? What historical, political, and social forces influence a society's response to a social condition? In many cases, individuals around the world have the same or similar hopes and problems. However, in most cases we deal with the same social conditions in very dissimilar ways.

The volumes in the Greenwood series A World View of Social Issues examine different social issues and problems that are being faced by individuals and societies around the world. These volumes examine problems of poverty and homelessness, drug and alcohol addiction, HIV/AIDS, teen pregnancy, crime, women's rights, and a myriad of other issues that affect all of us in one way or another.

Each volume is devoted to one social issue or problem. All volumes follow the same general format. Each volume has up to fifteen chapters that describe how people in different countries perceive and try to cope with a given problem or social issue. The countries chosen represent as many world regions as possible, making it possible to explore how each issue has been recognized and what actions have been taken to alleviate it in a variety of settings.

Each chapter begins with a profile of the country being highlighted and an overview of the impact of the social issue or problem there. Basic policies, legislation, and demographic information related to the social issue are covered. A brief history of the problem helps the reader better understand the political and social responses. Political initiatives and policies are also discussed, as well as social views, customs, and practices related to the problem or social issue. Discussions about how the countries plan to deal with these social problems are also included.

These volumes present a comprehensive and engaging approach for the study of international social conditions and problems. The goal is to provide a convenient framework for readers to examine specific social problems, how they are viewed, and what actions are being taken by different countries around the world.

For example, how is a problem like crime and crime control handled in Third World countries? How is substance abuse controlled in industrialized countries? How are poverty and homelessness handled in the poorest countries? How does culture influence the definition of and response to domestic violence in different countries? What part does economics play in shaping both the issue of and the response to women's rights? How does a national philosophy impact the definition of and response to child abuse? These questions and more will be answered by the volumes in this series.

As we learn more about our counterparts in other countries, they become real to us, and our worldview cannot help but change. We will think of others as we think of those we know. They will be people who get up in the morning and go to work. We will see people who are struggling with relationships, attending religious services, being born, growing old, and dying.

This series will cover issues that will add to your knowledge about contemporary social society. These volumes will help you to better understand social conditions and social issues in a broader sense, giving you a view of what various problems mean to different people and how these perspectives impact a society's response. You will be able to see how specific social problems are managed by governments and individuals confronting the consequences of these social dilemmas. By studying one problem from various angles, you will be better able to grasp the totality of the situation, while at the same time speculating as to how solutions used in one country could be incorporated in another. Finally, this series will allow you to compare and contrast how these social issues impact individuals in different countries and how the effect is dissimilar or similar to your own experiences.

As series adviser, it is my hope that these volumes, which are unique in the history of publishing, will increase your understanding and appreciation of your counterparts around the world.

Andrew L. Cherry
Series Adviser

PREFACE

This book brings together a number of topics that interest us both personally and intellectually. For both of us the topic of migration has been an important component of our personal and intellectual lives. Maura migrated to the United States from Puerto Rico in the 1980s, and Marixsa is a daughter of Puerto Rican migrants and has lived in Puerto Rico at different points in time. At the professional level, Maura has studied the class and gender dimensions of Puerto Rican migration to Chicago while Marixsa has studied the transnational community experiences of Puerto Rican women. Our conversations about the complexities and contradictions that make up our notions of "home" inspired us to interview second-generation Puerto Ricans to examine the ways in which children of immigrants construct their lives across multiple national spaces. In working collaboratively to co-edit this volume, we continued to build our friendship and professional relationship based on a shared passion for understanding the human experience as it is expressed in people's migratory movements. This book furthers our commitment to educate others about the sometimes unjust and inhumane treatment immigrants and refugees encounter all over the world.

In keeping with the objectives of the series, our goal is to provide a global perspective on migration. We were excited by the opportunity to bring together an international and multidisciplinary group of scholars that could help us create a volume addressed to a nonacademic audience. Too often the literature that is published in the United States concerning these issues tends to neglect nonacademic audiences. Further, as Puerto Rican feminists, we have always been attentive to understanding the migration experiences of U.S. Latinas from a gender perspective. For this reason, this volume is attentive to the issues migrant women face and to how race, class, and gender intersect to shape migratory movements and immigrant lives. We hope that those who read this volume will grow to understand and appreciate the difficulties of immigrant lives in the global economy.

ACKNOWLEDGMENTS

We would like to take this opportunity to thank several individuals and institutions that have helped us in completing this project. Maura would like to thank the lifetime support and devotion of her husband, Frank Morn, who over her professional career has patiently taken on family and household responsibilities above and beyond what she expected. Marixsa would like to thank Maura for inviting her to co-edit this volume. Marixsa would also like to acknowledge the support of her parents, Ana and Manuel Alicea; her siblings, both real and fictive, Carmen, Manny, Diego, and Lisa; and her nephews, Adrian, Diego, and Savannah. Kara McKinney and Laura R. Johnson helped us edit and format the chapters and create the index. The skills, patience, and support they provided were invaluable and are greatly appreciated. Also, the secretaries of the department of Sociology and Anthropology at Illinois State University, Doris Jennings and Joan Geigner, helped in the printing and formatting of the chapters. Thanks also to our colleagues in the department of Sociology and Anthropology and the School for New Learning for their support and collegiality. We want to acknowledge DePaul University's Research Council for awarding us a grant that allowed us to hire individuals to assist us in the preparation of this manuscript. Finally, we would like to thank Greenwood Press and those who conceived and supported this series on world views of social issues. Special thanks to our editor, Wendi Schnaufer, for her assistance, patience, and support in completing this manuscript.

INTRODUCTION

Migration has always been a part of human life. Whether we consider ourselves the descendants of different cultures that developed parallel to one another or, as the most recent research indicates, we come from a small group of Africans who first left Africa some 100,000 years ago, migration has characterized the behavior of humans for centuries. Today, however, we are no longer nomadic hunters and gatherers. Now, nation states attempt to control how and where people move. Although migration has been a constant for most of human history, social scientists have observed that since World War II the movement of people around the globe has intensified in proportions that have surpassed earlier population movements (Castles & Miller, 1993). In fact, social scientists have called the post–World War II movement of people around the globe "the age of migration." In this volume, we have assembled an international group of scholars to offer readers an overview of migration movements around the globe.

Migration and Immigration: A Global View aims to capture the historical, social, political, and economic consequences of migration for a sample of countries involved in both sending and receiving immigrants. We offer a group of contributors representing a wide range of disciplines. As a collective, their analysis defies the simple characterization of migration as a choice of people seeking better income opportunities. They do so by challenging us to be attentive to the specific historical context that frames the migratory movements depicted in each country. In addition, our contributors have been sensitive not only to the ways that race, class, and gender dynamics influence the composition of migratory flows, but also to the reasons why people migrate and the outcomes of population movements. Scholars in this volume also challenge us to reconsider our notions and, in some cases, stereotypes of the "traditional" actors involved in the process of migration. They draw out the human cost of migration for the people involved through carefully selected personal vignettes that alert us to the new conditions and forces that shape the complex processes of contemporary migratory movements. Finally, each chapter aims to offer readers a better understanding of the social issues underlying the process of migration for a selected group of countries at the turn of the twenty-first century.

The 14 countries chosen for this volume represent larger geographic areas that have historically been tied to important past and present migratory movements. In the first part of this introduction, we offer a short historical overview and analysis of the three major periods of world migration in order to understand the ties that exist between past and contemporary migratory movements. Then, we move on to discuss the importance of the chapters selected for this book within the context of the following regions: North America, Latin America, the Caribbean, Africa, the Asia-Pacific Region, and Western Europe.

WORLD MIGRATION: A HISTORICAL OVERVIEW

There is widespread agreement among scholars of migration that migration patterns, though diverse in scope, are the result of specific historical conditions produced by what has been commonly known as globalization. Although globalization has become a convenient catchword to describe a wide range of political, economic, and cultural processes, it frequently refers to the growing economic integration and interdependence between countries in the world economy. Scholars have traced the beginning of this globalization process to the European colonization efforts of the sixteenth century that led to the conquest of the Americas. The development of sea routes via Africa and India allowed Europeans to trade the riches mined in the New World of the Americas for the silks, spices, and products of Asian empires. In the 1600s a network of sea-lanes developed which made possible migration routes for centuries to come. Indeed, the trade and migration of people that we observe today can be seen as a continuation of that historical legacy. The second major period of migration took place during the industrial revolution in Europe, when displaced peasants moved to industrializing cities of Europe and North and South America. The third major period of migration, known as the post-industrial period, began after World War II and it has been characterized as more intense and diverse than other periods of migration. During this period migration has become truly a global phenomenon and the line between sending and receiving economies is difficult to draw. In the next pages, we describe more fully these migration periods in order to provide a backdrop to the country case studies presented in this book.

Colonization Period of Migration

The movement of thousands of Europeans to Africa, Asia, and eventually the Americas during the sixteenth century represents one of the most important population shifts in the history of the world. Social scientists have characterized this movement as emanating from a core region (Europe) and spreading to the periphery (Africa, North and South America, and Asia). Although there are important differences among colonizing migrations, colonizers extracted the wealth of the new lands by using the labor of both subjugated indigenous populations and that of the displaced and enslaved African populations. This wealth supported lavish lifestyles of European aristocracies and the consumption needs of a rising bourgeoisie (Acosta-Belen & Bose, 1995). According to one scholar, during the period of colonization emigrants fell into four classes: (1) a large number of agrarian settlers; (2) a small number of administrators and artisans; (3) a small class of entrepreneurs who founded plantations to produce raw materials for European mercantile economies; and, (4) nearly 10 million Africans who were transported to the Americas by force (Massey, 1999, p. 34). The colonization of the Americas has been seen as the first time in world history that different races were combined in class structures on a large scale (Russell, 1994). The migration of Europeans, African slaves, and indentured workers, transformed countries in North and South America into complex multiracial societies.

During colonization, a racial ideology developed to rationalize and justify the exploitation of non-Europeans. European colonizers reduced indigenous people and African slaves to biologically inferior and savage "red" and "black" races that needed to be civilized. Nobuko Adachi's chapter in this volume, "Brazil: A Historical and Contemporary View of Brazilian Migration," for example, describes the massive slave trade that took place in the sixteenth, seventeenth, and eighteenth centuries in Brazil. As in other countries in the Americas and in the Caribbean, black slaves were used as the main source of agricultural work in sugar and other plantation fields. The Portuguese, Spanish, French, and English colonized the Americas to expand their economic and political power. When gold and other precious metals and resources could no longer be found in the Americas, and when native groups proved insufficient to meet the labor demands of an ever expanding plantation and agricultural economy, Africans were enslaved and brought to the Americas to meet the labor needs of European enterprises. The treatment of these slaves regardless of their destination was harsh, inhumane, and unjust. As Adachi notes, racist ideologies developed to legitimize the inhumane and exploitive treatment of African slaves. For example, Africans were characterized as being less than human and heathens. It was only in this manner that their enslavement could be justified. Unfortunately, the racial ideologies that developed during the colonial and slave trade era have left their legacy, as blacks throughout both continents continue to be the victims of institutionalized racism and exploitation.

Although historical accounts tend to depict the colonization of the New World as an enterprise of men, recently historians have begun to call our attention to the role that women played in the colonization process. Women were both members of colonizing groups as well as the colonized. In Latin America, for example, Spanish and European women migrated to the New World as part of the colonizing elite. Their migration furthered the needs of the state and, more importantly, their marriage to colonizers and the subsequent birth of their children reproduced the next class of landowners.

On the other hand, in North and South America colonialism was (and continues to be) devastating for the indigenous people of the Americas, and in particular to women. As an economic system, colonialism often entailed the introduction of wage labor, performed mostly by men who were taken away from their communities of origin and transported to labor hungry sites. Wage labor among men eroded the importance of the family economy and women's role in it. At the turn of the twenty-first century, descendants of Mayan and other indigenous groups in the Americas continue to feel the impact of colonization in their lives as oppressive conditions in their homeland force them to migrate.

Industrial Period of Migration

The industrial revolution in Europe served as the precursor for two equally significant population movements during the nineteenth and early part of the twentieth century, namely: (1) massive internal labor migrations within Europe; and (2) the Great Atlantic migrations to the United States and other parts of the Americas. As industry developed, it gave rise to large urban centers such as Liverpool, Milan, Moscow, and Berlin, among others. These urban centers attracted a massive migration of men and women in search of work. Irish men and women worked in the mills of Lancashire; Belgians manned the looms of northern France; Polish women went to Germany; Italian women were recruited to work in Swiss textile towns; rural Swedish women went to Stockholm to work as domestic servants; Czechs and Slovaks moved to Vienna and Budapest, also to work as maids (Gabaccia, 1992). Migration and the changes brought about by industrialization had profound implications for people and their families. For example, industrialization and urbanization not only changed the location of work, but most importantly they also led to an increase in the number of women working for wages and had an impact on the allocation of women's time to do housework.

The same economic processes that produced internal labor migrations within Europe also helped develop transoceanic population movements to the United States and Argentina, countries that were undergoing rapid industrialization at the turn of the twentieth century. For example, when Italians and Poles could not find work in Europe, they moved to Argentina and the United States. Foreign immigrant labor was critical to the industrial development of the United States. While slaves had been a major source of labor in the U.S. plantation economy, freed black slaves could not meet the needs of the industrial revolution. Instead, it was the mass migration of European immigrants that offered industrialists a ready-made supply of cheap labor. The peak period was from 1861 to 1920, when more than 30 million European immigrants came to the United States. From the mid-nineteenth century to the 1920s, most migrants came from Ireland, Italy, Spain, and Eastern Europe. Scholars of migration—in particular, historians—have studied this period with great interest. In the United States the mass migrations from Europe sparked important debates about racial diversity that continue today.

The chapter by Rogelio Saenz, Maria Cristina Morales, and Maria Isabel Ayala, "The United States: Immigration to the Melting Pot of the Americas," offers an overview of the magnitude of European migration to the United States and reminds us of the harsh reception and treatment that many of these immigrants received upon arrival. Like the Irish before them, southern and eastern Europeans were perceived as intellectually inferior to the Anglo-Saxon people and culture that dominated American life prior to the 1900s and were therefore considered unworthy of the label "American." Saenz et al. point out that the prejudice and strong anti-immigrant sentiments led to the passing of restrictive immigration laws that halted immigration from southern and eastern Europe for several decades. For example, the Immigration Act of 1917 introduced a literacy test for immigrants and expanded the number of people to be excluded from entry on the basis of physical, mental, moral, and other standards. Immigration laws severely restricted the movement of people to the United States for several decades, until the 1960s when the United States became the recipient of an impressive number of immigrants from Latin America and Asia. This migration wave coincided with the next major period of global migration, the post-industrial era.

Post-Industrial Period of Migration

The post-industrial period of migration came after World War II and has been characterized as increasing the international economic integration between different regions of the world economy. During the post-industrial era of migration a global assembly line has emerged in which research and management are controlled by the core, or developed countries, while assembly line work is relegated to semiperiphery or periphery nations that occupy less privileged positions in the global economy. Globalization has fostered a growing consolidation of global financial institutions, regional trading blocks, and financial resources. As producers and consumers, we have become participants in a global capitalist market. Our national-political identities as consumers often cloud us from seeing the political and economic realities of this increasingly integrated and transnational world. For example, the label "Made in America" misleads U.S. Americans to feel national pride in products that more than likely have been assembled by other workers throughout the world.

At the turn of the twenty-first century, globalization has expanded the boundaries of the developed and developing world and widened the gap between rich and poor countries through the increasing concentration of capital encouraged by foreign direct investment (FDI). Foreign direct investment is controlled by the major players in the global economy, such as the United States, Japan, and Europe. Alongside the geographical concentration of wealth there is also a corporate density, with corporations headquartered in the United States, Europe, and some parts of Asia. In 1995, these corporations accounted for two-thirds of total global outflows, with the United States spending $96 billion in FDI. Global cities such as London, New York, and Los Angeles have emerged as command points in the organization of the world economy (Sassen, 1994). These global cities are key sites for the advanced services and telecommunications facilities critical for the implementation and management of global economic transactions (Sassen, 1994, p. 19). The links between global cities and the Third World create paradoxes wherein wealth and highly skilled professional employment coexist with growing low-paid and unskilled service industry employment in the developing world.

Globalization has also created new conditions for the mobilization of different sectors of the world population into unprecedented population movements. For example, there has been an increase in the migration of people from developing to developed countries. In 1960–1964, the United States admitted only 42 percent of its immigrants from the developing world (Zlotnick, 1995). For the same time period, Canada admitted 12 percent of its immigrants from the developing world. However, from 1985 to 1989, immigrants from the developing world coming to these countries had increased to an astonishing 88 percent and 71 percent respectively, an issue that is addressed in this volume by Saenz et al. In Europe there seems to be a great deal of variation in the number of immigrants coming from what is commonly referred to as "the Third World." Between 1985 and 1988, Belgium admitted about 29 percent of its immigrants from the Third World; Germany accepted 48 percent; the Netherlands accepted 39 percent; and Sweden accepted 45 percent of its immigrants from developing societies. Women represent an important component of this new migration. For example, in 1981, women outnumbered men among the foreign born population in the United States (Zlotnick, 1995). Women have increased their participation in rural-to-urban movements in Africa, Latin America, and Asia (Tienda & Booth, 1991; Zlotnick, 1995). Women also comprised a large share of international migrants around the globe. Women from Latin America and the Caribbean, particularly Mexico, Cuba, Puerto Rico, the Dominican Republic, and San Salvador, make up a large segment of the "new migration" to the United States, as documented by Saenz et al. in this volume. It is also well known that women make up a large segment of current refugee movements in Africa, the Middle East, and Europe (Indra, 1999).

In the post-modern global village, a gendered division of labor has emerged where women from poor and underdeveloped countries in Asia, Africa, Latin America, and the Caribbean moved from the rural countryside to work in the "global assembly line" making clothes, shoes, and computers. Middle and upper middle class families with disposable income across the world have sought the reproductive labor of African, Latin American, and Asian women domestics. Labor shortages in the private and public sector have also attracted a share of professional and educated immigrant men and women. Finally, on the frontiers of the global economy is the trafficking of women sex workers and mail-order brides, the equivalent of the modern slave trade.

Still, it is clear that we cannot reduce all contemporary migrations to the differences in the standard of living between industrialized and less-developed economies (Castles & Miller, 1993). Though accurate, the north-south gap explanation does not allow us to capture the complexities of current migration patterns partly because the demarcation line between "sending" and "receiving" countries is no longer a clear-cut line between the core and periphery. For a long time southern European states like Greece and Italy were considered "sending" economies, but they are now the recipients of new immigrants from Asia and Africa. Similarly, Turkey, which has been for a long time a zone of emigration, has now become the recipient of Iranian and Kurdish refugees. Latin America has also become a region of complex migratory movements. Mexico, for example, has received a growing number of Guatemalans and Salvadoran immigrants. The Asia-Pacific region is yet another example of these new migration patterns. In the past, the Asia-Pacific region traditionally supplied a great deal of migrant labor to industrialized nations in the West. Today, these "tiger economies," as they are popularly known, attract a share of the region's migrant population. In the next pages, we present an overview of how different geographic regions of the world have become part of this worldwide migration process.

NORTH AMERICA, LATIN AMERICA, AND THE CARIBBEAN

Since World War II, migration to and from Latin America and the Caribbean has taken many forms, but the most pronounced movements in terms of direction and size have been: (1) internal migration from the rural countryside to urban centers; (2) massive out-migration from Latin America and the Caribbean to the United States, and to a lesser extent, Canada and Europe; and (3) refugee movements brought by civil wars and revolutions. In addition, as with other movements around the world, since the 1980s there has been an ever growing number of Latin American women on the move. The Latin American migratory experience can also be characterized by the transnational ties that immigrants maintain across borders between their home and host communities.

The internal migration of people in most of Latin America and the Caribbean has been produced by the increasing integration of these regions into the global economy. Between 1950 and 1980, over 27 million people in Latin America left the countryside for the cities of the continent (Chant, 1999). Yet, despite the large-scale internal rural-to-urban migration taking place in Latin America, it is the massive out-migration of people from Latin America and the Caribbean to the United States that has captured the attention of scholars across a range of disciplines. Migration has been both legal and illegal. In addition, migrants have moved as contract workers, as part of families, and as refugees. Return and counterflows have also been an important part of the transnational movement of people in Latin America and the Caribbean.

Between 1981 and 1997, some 14.2 million Latinos were admitted legally into the United States and many more entered illegally (Toro-Morn, 2002). According to the U.S. Census, by 1995 there were 26.6 million Latinos in the United States. If one includes the hundreds of thousands of Puerto Ricans that the INS does not count because they are U.S. citizens, the numbers rise to about 30.4 million. The U.S. Census of Population projects that Latinos are the fastest growing ethnic population in the United States. They also predict that by 2010 Latinos will be the largest racial/ethnic group in the country. In California and Texas, one of every four residents is Latino. Latin American and Caribbean immigrants tend to concentrate in the nation's largest urban areas: New York, Chicago, Miami, and Los Angeles.

It is the historical, cultural, and economic ties between the United States and Latin America, in addition to its wealth and proximity, that has made the United States the preferred destination point of many Latino immigrants. At the turn of the twenty-first century, Latin American and Caribbean men and women continue to play an important role in the global economy. While the migration of many groups from Latin America can be tied to the United States' colonial rule in the region and to the current nature of the global economy, the migration histories and experiences of the various Latin American groups have been diverse. Several chapters in this volume capture the complexity of migration patterns found in Latin America and the Caribbean.

In his chapter on Cuban migration, Felix Masud-Piloto explores the movement of Cuban refugees to the United States from the 1950s to the early part of the twenty-first century. While there had been a sizable presence of

Cuban Americans in the United States from the late 1800s, it was not until after the Cuban Revolution and Castro's rise to power in the early 1950s that there was a mass exodus of Cuban Americans to the United States. The Cuban Revolution was largely a response to the United States' neocolonial rule of Cuba and the terrible economic conditions and poverty rates this economic and political relationship fostered in Cuba. As Masud-Piloto describes, the rise of Castro and communism led to the departure of large numbers of middle and upper class Cuban elites who had supported and indeed benefited from the U.S.-backed Batista government in Cuba. Forty years after the Revolution, the movement of Cubans to the United States, mostly to the Florida region, continues to be strong.

U.S. colonial rule in the Caribbean has also shaped the migration of Puerto Ricans to the United States, as documented by Jorge Duany's chapter, "Puerto Rico: Between the Nation and the Diaspora — Migration to and from Puerto Rico." Duany argues that the migration of Puerto Ricans to the United States was part of a larger economic plan for Puerto Rico designed and carried out by U.S. and Puerto Rican officials. After being ruled for centuries by the Spanish government, the United States took possession of Puerto Rico in 1898. Over several decades, the United States developed an agricultural economy that was unable to sustain and meet the needs of the people on the island. By the 1950s, poverty rates and the misery experienced by Puerto Ricans equaled or surpassed that of poor countries in Africa, Asia, and other parts of the world.

As Duany describes in his chapter in this volume, to improve conditions in Puerto Rico, the United States and Puerto Rican officials sought to transform the island's agricultural economy to an industrial one. However, it was never thought, and indeed it never happened, that the industrial economy created a sufficient number of jobs for Puerto Ricans. People were thus encouraged to leave Puerto Rico. Indeed, throughout the 1960s and 1970s, hundreds of thousands of Puerto Ricans migrated to the United States, sometimes with the assistance of the Puerto Rican government as contract workers or on their own.

The history of U.S. colonial rule in Mexico as well as the global economic relationship between these two countries has also shaped the migration of Mexicans to the United States, as documented by Patricia Zamudio's chapter. It is important to note, for example, that the presence of Mexican Americans in the United States is not solely the result of the migration of Mexicans to the United States, but also the result of the United States' conquest of what was formerly northern Mexico. Mexicans who lived in what are now known as the states of New Mexico, Arizona, California, and Texas were colonized and therefore were not immigrants to this country. Mexican Americans have supplied the labor force for U.S. agri-business for decades. They have also worked in canneries and in other industries related to the processing of food. Together with other immigrant groups, Mexican Americans were recruited to work in the development of the U.S. railroad industry. Mexican women comprise a large share of recent immigrants to the United States, as many come to fill labor shortages in child care and domestic service.

The experiences of Mexican American immigrants can be characterized by the harsh and exploitive conditions they face, and the very little pay they receive in almost all of the U.S. industries and fields in which they work. As Zamudio describes, the Mexican American migration experience has been shaped by the United States' contradictory and incoherent immigration policies. While it has actively recruited Mexican immigrants to work in the United States in times of labor shortages, at other times it has deported and repatriated Mexican immigrants during periods of high unemployment.

The long history of migration from the south to the north means that there is now a strong and intricate social network that contributes to the ongoing migration of Mexicans, Cubans, and Puerto Ricans, as well as several Central and South American groups. Indeed, migration and the constant flow of people and resources between Latin America and the United States have become a way of life. As Jorge Duany puts it, these are nations on the move. People in the Americas live their lives across large spaces and social networks that transcend national and political borders. As Duany and Zamudio both explain, at the family and community level, immigrants and those who remain in the home countries exchange resources and offer assistance to one another. For example, Zamudio explains how over 1 million households in Mexico depend on remittances sent to them by relatives living in the United States. Latin American and Caribbean immigrant groups have also formed organizations and work to influence U.S. foreign policy toward their home country and to play a role in homeland politics. For example, it is in no small part due to the lobbying efforts of Cuban Americans in Congress that the United States has maintained an embargo against Cuba.

AFRICA

Like in Latin America and the Caribbean, increasing urbanization and economic development of urban economies have led to a massive internal movement of people from the rural areas to the cities throughout Africa. Initially, men tended to predominate in most rural-to-urban movements. But recently, demographers have noticed a marked increased in the internal migration of women. In addition, scholars have documented that international migration from Africa has been to former colonial powers: Zairians emigrate to Belgium, Senegalese to France, and Nigerians to the United Kingdom (Castles & Miller, 1993). Since the 1960s, France, a former colonial power in Africa, has also admitted immigrants from its other colonial outposts such as Algeria, Morocco, and Tunisia. In addition, sizable populations of Moroccans can be found in Belgium, Germany, Italy, the Netherlands, and Spain. Another type of migration found in Africa is the movement of agricultural workers and contract workers from underdeveloped, poverty-stricken countries to more prosperous neighboring countries. Demographers call this movement circular migration. For example, in western Africa the movement of agricultural workers to the Ivory Coast has dominated migration. From 1975–1988, the number of foreigners in the Ivory Coast doubled from 1.5 million to 3 million, most of them citizens of Burkina Faso and Mali (Zlotnik, 1999). South Africa, one of the most prosperous countries in Africa, has been a magnet for migrants from neighboring countries for several decades. Gender selectivity has also characterized international and intraregional movements in Africa. Until recently men tended to predominate in the international and intraregional movements found in Africa, but recent studies have begun to document the international migration of African women to Western Europe as domestics. This new pattern of migration has been linked to the changing needs of the global economy.

Africa has also come to be known as a continent of refugees, another important category in defining the global and regional movement of people. After many centuries of colonial rule, numerous African countries experienced and continue to experience political and economic instability. Left with few economic and natural resources, countries in Africa have found it difficult to build economic and political systems that can sustain their people even after gaining freedom from colonial rule. The ongoing internal conflict and civil unrest as well as general warfare in Africa have led to massive refugee outflows (Zlotnik, 1999). In 1985, there were 3 million refugees in Africa. By 1995, the number of refugees had more than doubled to 6.8 million (Zlotnik, 1999, p. 38). In 1980, the number of refugee flows was concentrated in six countries, most of them in eastern and central Africa. By 1995, there were major refugee flows in 13 African nations, and "women and girls comprised over 80 percent of displacees" (Matlou, 1999, p. 129).

Two chapters in this volume capture parts of this evolving migration saga in Africa. Cassandra Veney's chapter, "Tanzania: To Carry a Heavy Burden in the Heat of the Day—Migration to and from Tanzania," captures the dimensions of the refugee problem in Tanzania, a country that has been the recipient of hundreds of thousands of refugees from South Africa, Rwanda, Burundi, the Democratic Republic of Congo (formerly Zaire), and Somalia, who have been escaping civil war, ethnic strife, and general warfare. During the 1960s and 70s, for example, Tanzania provided refuge to people active in the liberation movements of racist and colonialist states such as South Africa and Mozambique. After the April 1994 genocide in Rwanda, 250,000 Rwandans entered Tanzania within a 24-hour period. In addition, people from Zaire, Uganda, and Malawi, for example, experienced gross human rights violations and sought refuge in Tanzania. Indeed, prior to 1990, Tanzania served as a beacon of hope in East Africa due to its political stability.

The Tanzanian government welcomed these refugees because they were viewed as freedom fighters for democracy, justice, and an end to colonial rule. However, with the ever growing economic problems in Tanzania, as residents have grown less tolerant of refugees as resources in the way of jobs, and with food and health care becoming increasingly scarce, Tanzanian officials have been forced to reevaluate the country's generous refugee policy. Refugee policies have also changed because the Tanzanian government believes that refugee camps are being used to train soldiers of oppressive regimes. These factors, coupled with a lack of assistance from the international community, mean Tanzania is not only less willing but also unable to support large groups of refugees. As a result, the Tanzanian government is less likely to admit refugees and is actually forcing refugees to return to their countries without following international refugee human rights protocols.

Joseph R. Oppong's chapter, "Ghana: Internal, International, and Transnational Migration," reminds readers that although the developed and underdeveloped worlds are geographically miles apart, in many ways, Africa, in this case Ghana, has become the village while the developed world—the United States, England, and Germany, among others—has become the colonial city or urban area. Ghana is one example of the ties that exist between former colonial powers and their colonies. Beginning in the 1970s, large numbers of Ghanaians left their homeland largely because of serious socioeconomic difficulties at home. While initially Ghanaians migrated to neighboring countries whose economies were relatively strong, many are now migrating to countries in Europe as well as to the United States and Canada. Educated and professional Africans are attracted by the promise of better opportunities abroad. For example, most Ghanaians who migrate to Canada can speak both English and French and are highly educated. While their advanced education and multiple language skills make the transition to new host societies easier, the exodus of highly skilled and trained individuals from Ghana leaves the country with fewer and fewer professionals.

Besides the ever increasing movement of people from rural areas to urban centers and to international sites, African migration, like that of other migrations around the world, can also be characterized by the growing number of women and children on the move. In the case of East Africa, for example, many of the refugees in Tanzania have been women, children, and the elderly. Veney describes in her chapter that once they are in in host countries and unaccompanied by male relatives, refugee women and children often experience sexual abuse, rape, harassment, and physical abuse, as well as economic exploitation and manipulation. In the case of Ghana, while once it was largely men who left Ghana, now there is an ever growing number of women migrating in an effort to meet the needs of their children and other dependents. As Oppong discusses in his chapter, today women migrate over longer distances and for longer periods.

THE ASIA-PACIFIC REGION

The Asia-Pacific region has long been an area of trade and migration. Before European colonization, Asia was a region of empires, immense wealth, and great civilizations. By land, the silk route was an important thoroughfare of trade and commerce between Europe and Central Asia. By sea, the Persian Gulf route to and from Asia made Baghdad one of the earliest global cities of trade. The colonization of Asia by Europeans led to the movement of Asian workers as indentured workers to replace freed slaves in labor hungry plantations in Latin America, the Caribbean, and other parts of Asia (Chin, 1998; Northrup, 1995). Historically, the region supplied migrant labor to colonial and postcolonial countries well into the first decades of the twentieth century. These early migrations need to be analyzed within the framework that saw Asian men as expendable and easily exploitable workers and Asian women as their subordinated appendages. Colonial racist policies were imposed onerously upon Asian men and women both at home and abroad. It has been argued that the recruitment methods and labor conditions of indentured labor need to be seen as an extension of slavery; thus the social construction of race in destination countries placed Asian workers at the bottom of the racial hierarchy (Northrup, 1995). Colonized Asian men and women were exploited as immigrants and workers, while women also faced gender exploitation. The legacy of these early migrations can still be felt today in the sizable communities of Asians in the United States, Canada, the Caribbean, and Latin America (see Nobuko Adachi's chapter in this volume), as well as ethnically diverse Asian nation–states, such as Malaysia and Thailand.

At the turn of the twenty-first century, Asian men and women continue to play an important role in the global economy. The post–World War II movement of capital, commodities, and culture, and the creation of regional and subregional trade zones have created conditions that favor the transnational flow of people throughout the world. Asia is no exception to this rule. Popularly known as the "tiger economies," the Asia-Pacific region has become a major economic player in the global economy. Once considered a poor region that could only make articles of poor quality, the Asia-Pacific region is now a leader in the production of high-quality products such as automobiles, electronics, and clothing, among others. In fact, some Asian countries have sufficient currency to invest in their own countries, in neighboring Asian countries, and in other regions of the world. The Asia-Pacific region contains half of the world's population and close to two-thirds of the world's workforce (Castles & Miller, 1993).

As we have seen in Latin America and Africa, an important manifestation of the post–World War II restructuring in the global economy is the migration of mostly rural women to work in export-processing zones and in the booming service sector of Asian cities. The development of free trade zones and tourism mobilized, for example, Thai, Filipino, and Indonesian women to enter the workforce. Across the region these "working daughters" are among the most exploited workers in the global economy.

James Stanlaw's chapter, "Japan: Immigration In, Out, and Back and Forth," captures the complex history of immigration to and from Japan in this changing global economy. Although sizable numbers of Japanese workers left the country at different points in history (see also Nobuko Adachi's chapter in this volume), Japan for the most part was a society that was relatively untouched by migratory movements until recently. As Stanlaw points out, today Japan is one of the most powerful nations in the world and, like other post-industrial nations, finds itself in desperate need of workers. Consequently, Japan has become an important destination point for desperate Asian men and women in search of work. According to Stanlaw, a steady influx of both legal and illegal men and women arrive yearly in Japan to do what the Japanese have labeled "dirty work," namely, menial jobs in the economy that are difficult, dangerous, dirty, and offer little remuneration. Thai and Filipino women represent an important segment of this population.

Australia is another important destination point for immigrants in the Asia-Pacific region. Graeme Hugo's chapter, "Australia: The Continent of Immigrants," describes how since World War II labor shortages in agriculture and newly expanding manufacturing sectors have pulled immigrants from non-English-speaking nations to Australia. For example, displaced persons from Eastern Europe, Germany, Italy, Greece, and the Netherlands are among the Europeans found migrating to Australia. Since the 1970s, a substantial flow of Asians and people from the Middle East, in particular Afghans, have sought to make Australia their home. Although most of this migration is legal, undocumented migration has become a source of concern.

Australia has a curious immigration history. As Hugo points out, a "White Australia Policy" prevented non-Europeans from immigrating to Australia. Consequently, prior to the postwar period most immigrants to Australia were mostly from English-speaking nations like the United Kingdom and Ireland. But changes in Australia's immigration policies have led to significant population movements of diverse people to Australia, and today this melting pot in the Pacific region is confronting similar social and political problems found in post-industrial economies in the West. For example, areas of considerable political debate revolve around the way in which immigrants are selected under the immigration program and the detention of all asylum seekers.

At the other end of the spectrum, in Asia's highly stratified market are underdeveloped economies such as the Philippines, Vietnam, Laos, Cambodia, and Indonesia, with considerable social problems, high fertility rates, and a tremendous surplus of labor. It is in the context of such regional disparities that a new migration pattern has unfolded in the region: the intraregional movement of men and women from the Asian periphery (i.e., the Philippines, Sri Lanka, India, Myanmar, and Indonesia) to work in the region's high growth economies (i.e., Japan, Hong Kong, Singapore, and Malaysia). James A. Tyner's chapter, "The Philippines: The Dilemma of Philippine International Labor Migration," captures how one country has turned its citizens into labor commodities in the global market place by institutionalizing employment abroad through the Philippine Overseas Employment Program. In a country with rampant poverty and unemployment, international migration has become a way for Filipino men and women to provide for their families. While Filipino men are recruited to work as contract workers in the Middle East, women are contracted to work in the "entertainment" sector of booming global cities throughout Asia. Women are employed as dancers, singers, and musicians, and as sex workers, as illustrated by the opening vignettes in Tyner's chapter. The concentration of Filipinas in one of the most dangerous sectors of the global economy presents a political predicament to the Philippine government: How can the Philippine government protect its overseas workers when the country does not have that much leverage on the global political stage?

Educated Asian men and women have joined low-skill workers in the international movement of labor from the region to the West. Although seemingly different in class composition, these two types of migrations are two sides of the same coin in the global economy. Global restructuring has led to a global division of labor, where periphery economies have become the source of production and assembly lines while core economies such as the United States, Canada, and Europe have become centers of high finance and technology. Ironically, core economies continue to lack the population base to fill their changing labor needs. Thus, migration continues to provide the much-needed labor for old sectors of the economy and new ones being created as a result of global restructuring.

Although China is today a major global economic power, migration has been part of its history since its beginning. The opening vignette in Yu Zhou's chapter, "China: Chinese Immigrants in the Global Economy," for example, illustrates how one country has supplied both working class and educated workers to the global economy, in particular to the United States. Although there is a long history of Chinese immigration to the United States, most of the recent migration goes back to the liberalization of immigration laws in the 1960s. Zhou describes how post–1960s immigrants differ significantly from their earlier counterparts in terms of their place of origin and social characteristics. Earlier immigrants were mostly men, with little education, recruited from the regions of Guandong to do menial work in the mining industry and to build the transcontinental railroad. Contemporary immigrants are far more diverse in terms of origin (China, Hong Kong, Taiwan), gender (both men and women), and language (most speak

Mandarin as well as local dialects). Indeed, such diversity makes the experiences of Chinese immigrants in the United States complex and multifaceted. Zhou captures such complexity by comparing the experiences of garment workers in New York to the educated, professional transnational immigrants who find themselves in Los Angeles and other cities in the Pacific Rim.

WESTERN EUROPE

As has been described in this introduction, throughout the colonial period and into the 1900s, Europe was primarily an exporter of people to such diverse regions as Africa, Asia, Latin America, and the United States. One chapter in this volume, "Ireland: A Historical and Political Interpretation of the Irish Diaspora" by Sean Kenny, provides an example of this history of migration and the consequences massive out-migrations had for those leaving and for the families and communities left behind. Kenny describes Irish migration at various points in time. For example, Ulster Presbyterians migrated to the American colonies and played a significant role in the American War of Independence. In the midst of the European industrial revolution, the Irish, like other Europeans, left their country of origin for urban centers in England and other cities in Europe in search of work. However, the most studied and well-known Irish migration movement took place in the nineteenth century when a mysterious disease attacked potato crops across Europe and led to widespread hunger, poverty, and mass migrations to the United States. In the United States, the Irish were perceived as a religious and cultural threat and faced widespread prejudice and discrimination.

Although historically we have come to view Europe as a sender of immigrants, at the turn of the twenty-first century Europe has become a recipient of immigrants from every region of the world. In 1991, the foreign population in the European Union (EU) numbered about 16 million, representing about 4 percent of the population in the EU (Messner, Hormats, Walker, & Ogata, 1993). After the fall of the communist block and the USSR, massive unemployment and political instability pushed significant flows of people from former communist countries in Europe to post-industrial economies in Western Europe, the United States, and Australia. In 1989, 1.2 million people left Warsaw Pact states in search of new lives in Western Europe (Messner et al., 1993). A quick glance at current newspaper reports shows that immigration is indeed a major political issue in the region. Every major European Union (EU) summit that has taken place in the last 10 years has raised the issue of immigration.

Two chapters included in this volume, one on France and another on the Netherlands, provide an excellent overview of the different types of migration patterns found in the region since World War II. Labor shortages in the Netherlands, France, and other countries in Europe were filled by guest workers from neighboring southern European countries, Yugoslavia, and Turkey. The "guest worker system" provided war-torn European countries with the necessary labor to be able to rebuild battered economies. Under this program, workers were tied to specific jobs, had no right to family reunion, and could be easily deported for minor infractions. Although the receiving country heavily controlled admission and residence, over time several European countries became heavily dependent on foreign workers. The need to attract and retain workers eventually led to relaxations on family reunions and residence status. The relaxation of rules for family reunification in turn led to the admission of women as incoming migrants. The guest worker programs came to an end in the 1970s due to rising unemployment in the wake of the 1970s oil crisis (Messner et al., 1993), but by then sizable ethnically and racially distinct populations had taken root in advanced European countries (Castles & Miller, 1993).

Twanna A. Hines' chapter, "The Netherlands: The Myth of Ethnic Equality," traces the beginning of postwar immigration to the Netherlands to the guest worker program. Similarly, Jeremy Hein discusses in his chapter, "France: The Melting Pot of Europe," how France too became dependent on guest workers, mostly Portuguese men, to meet labor shortages. Hein points out that France, like other countries in Europe, is in a peculiar predicament with respect to immigration. Severe population loss after World Wars I and II coupled with recent population decline due to declining fertility rates have meant that France has come to rely on immigration as a way not only to maintain its labor force, but also to generate taxes that support its growing elderly population. When the guest worker program came to an end, immigrants from Europe's former colonies filled labor shortages. As Hines and Hein document in their respective chapters, the Netherlands drew immigrants from Surinam, Indonesia, the Antilles, and Aruba, while France drew immigrants from Algeria, Vietnam, Cambodia, and sub-Saharan Africa.

Europe has also been the recipient of refugee flows from neighboring war-torn European countries, Asia, and Africa. In France, the right to political asylum has been guaranteed by the French constitution since the Revolution of 1789, but as documented by Hines, the Netherlands has been second to Switzerland in accepting refugees in Western Europe. In the Netherlands, refugees tend to come from African nations such as Ghana and Somalia, whereas France has accepted refugees from Vietnam, Cambodia, and Africa.

As shown by both Hein and Hines, each immigrant wave in Europe has raised serious political and cultural questions about the reception of immigrants in this region. Although both the Netherlands and France belong to strong liberal immigrant traditions, anti-immigrant political parties have become firmly embedded in their respective political systems, calling into question both countries' commitment to and tradition of welcoming immigrants.

For France and the Netherlands, immigration has come to test their ability to assimilate and integrate racially, ethnically, nationally, and religiously diverse minorities.

BIBLIOGRAPHY

Acosta-Belen, E., & Bose, C. E. (1995). *Women in the Latin American Development Process*. Philadelphia: Temple University Press.

Castles, S., & Miller, M. J. (1993). *The Age of Migration: International Population Movements in the Modern World*. New York: Guilford Press.

Chant, S. (1999). Population, Migration, Employment and Gender. In Robert N. Gwynne and Cristobal Kay (Eds.), *Latin America Transformed: Globalization and Modernity* (pp. 226–261). New York: Oxford University Press.

Chin, C.B.N. (1998). *In Service and Servitude: Foreign Female Domestic Workers and the Malaysian "Modernity" Project*. New York: Columbia University Press.

Gabbacia, D. (1992). *Seeking Common Ground: Multidisciplinary Studies of Immigrant Women in the United States*. Westport, CT: Praeger.

Indra, D. (1999). *Engendering Forced Migration: Theory and Practice*. New York: Berghahn Books.

Massey, D. (1999). Why Does Immigration Occur? A Theoretical Synthesis. In C. Hirshman, P. Kasinitz, & J. Dewind (Eds.), *The Handbook of International Migration* (pp. 34–52). New York: Russell Sage Foundation.

Matlou, P. (1999). Upsetting the Cart: Forced Migration and Gender Issues, the African Experience. In Doreen Indra (Ed.), *Engendering Forced Migration: Theory and Practice* (Vol. 5, pp. 128–145). New York: Berghahn Books.

Messner, D., Hormats, R., Walker, A. G., & Ogata, S. (1993). *International Migration: Challenges in a New Era*. A Report to the Trilateral Commission, 44. New York: The Trilateral Commission.

Northrup, D. (1995). *Indentured Labor in the Age of Imperialism, 1834–1922*. Cambridge: Cambridge University Press.

Russell, J. (1994). *After the Fifth Sun: Class and Race in North America*. Englewood Cliffs, NJ: Prentice Hall.

Sassen, S. (1994). *Cities in a World Economy*. Thousand Oaks, CA: Pine Forge Press.

Tienda, M., & Booth, K. 1991. Gender, Migration, and Social Change. *International Sociology*, 6, 51–72.

Toro-Morn, M. (2002). *Migration, Gender, and Latino Studies: Challenges and Future Directions*. Paper presented at the Latino Studies Conference, University of Illinois, Chicago.

Zlotnik, H. (1995). The North-to-South Migration of Women. *International Migration Review*, 29(1), 229–254.

———. (1999). Trends of International Migration since 1965: What Existing Data Reveal. *International Migration*, 37(1), 21–47.

1

AUSTRALIA

The Continent of Immigrants

Graeme Hugo

INTRODUCTION

Profile of Australia

Australia's population has reached 19,386,700 and is growing (2001) at 1.2 percent per annum (ABS, 2002), making it one of the fastest growing of OECD (Organization for Economic Cooperation and Development) nations. Despite its large geographical area, Australia has a highly concentrated population with 86 percent living in urban areas in 1996 (ABS, 1996 census). A particular feature is the concentration of population in cities with more than 100,000 residents (62.7%) and especially in the two largest cities of Sydney (18.3%, 3,276,207 people) and Melbourne (16.0%, 2,865,329 people) (ABS, 1996 census). The population is strongly concentrated along the eastern, southeastern, and southwestern coastal areas. Despite the large size of the continent, 83 percent of the population live within 50 kilometers of the coast. In 91.2 percent of the surface area of Australia, the population density is less than 1 person per square kilometer. Some 69.6 percent of the land area contains 0.8 percent of the population at a density of less than 0.1 persons per square kilometer (ABS, 1996 census). This reflects the fact that much of the country receives very low rates of rainfall. This has led some to designate it an underpopulated nation, but the ecological reality is that there are severe environmental constraints that limit Australia's potential to absorb population increases without jeopardizing sustainability (Cocks, 1996).

Australia is classified by the World Bank (2000, p. 229) as one of the world's high income nations, ranked 24th with a Gross National Product per capita in 1998 of US$20,300. It was first colonized by the British in

1788 when it had an indigenous population of around 300,000. Until relatively recently the country was largely Anglo-Celtic in composition and orientation, but in the postwar period it has become more closely integrated with the Asia-Pacific region and its population has become more diverse.

Australia has experienced an extended period of economic growth since the recession of 1990–1991, with an average annual growth of 3.5 percent over 1990–1995, 4.2 percent in 1996, 3.7 percent in 1997, 4.5 percent in 1998, 5.3 percent in 1999, 4.3 percent in 2000, and 1.8 percent in 2001. It is a developed market economy dominated by its services sector, which accounts for around two-thirds of its GDP. Its agriculture and mining sectors account for only 7 percent of its GDP but 57 percent of exports of goods and services. The relative size of its manufacturing sector has declined over the last three decades and now accounts for only around 12 percent of its GDP. Approximately 65.7 percent of Australia's population is of European ancestry, predominantly with origins in the United Kingdom (ABS, 2001 census). This reflects its settlement by the British in the late eighteenth century and its development as a group of British colonies until 1901, when it became a federation. It is a democracy with a Westminster system of government and a member of the British Commonwealth of Nations. Its indigenous population numbered 410,003 at the 2001 census. (ABS, 2001 census). They occupied Australia for at least 40,000 years before European settlement and numbered around 300,000 at the time of European settlement. Australia has a high standard of living, with extremely high rates of literacy and a life expectancy at birth of around 76 for males and 82 for females.

Vignette

Phung Nguyen left Vietnam in 1978 when he was 28 years old. He traveled overland through Cambodia and applied for refugee status in a camp near Aranya Pradet in Thailand. After eight months in the camp he was interviewed and accepted for resettlement in Australia. Upon arrival in Australia he was placed in a hostel in the city of Adelaide where he began an intensive course in English. After several months of unemployment he was able to get a job in a motor car manufacturing factory. He moved in to share a house with a Vietnamese family in a suburb near the migrant hostel. After three years he was able to bring his wife and child to Australia under the family migration program and he rented a house nearby. His wife got work almost immediately on a mushroom farm in the outer suburbs and his son began school. His wife had a daughter in 1986. Phung became a prominent member of the small Adelaide Vietnamese community, which was an important focus of the family's social activity. In the late 1980s the family decided to move to the larger city of Sydney. This was partly because several family members had settled in the western suburb of Sydney and both Phung and his wife found work in Vietnamese-operated businesses in the city. Phung worked as a storeman for his cousin who was developing an important business in Sydney while his wife did piecework for a clothing manufacturer. Their son attended a public high school in Sydney and achieved very high grades so that he was able to enter university to study medicine; he recently graduated as a doctor. Phung's daughter is still at university in Sydney and she is also studying to be a doctor. Phung and his wife speak Vietnamese at home and almost all of their friends and acquaintances are Vietnamese. They live in a part of Sydney in which there are many Vietnamese-run shops and businesses. Their children, on the other hand, have friends mainly from outside the community, although both still live at home with their parents.

Overview of Migration Issues

Postwar Immigration to Australia. The post–World War II period was clearly an exceptional era in Australia's immigration history in terms of its scale. However, the country saw for the first time in its national history a large-scale movement of immigrants from outside the United Kingdom and Ireland. The United Kingdom remained the main source of immigrants, but its share dwindled from being the overwhelming majority in the prewar period until the 1990s, when in some years it lost its place as the largest single source of immigrants.

In fact, for much of the postwar period, the United Kingdom/Ireland remained the major underlying source of immigrants during a series of successive waves of immigrants from particular non-English-speaking regions. In the late 1940s and early 1950s there was an influx of Displaced Persons (DPs) from Eastern Europe. This was followed by waves from the Netherlands, Germany, Italy, Greece, and the Middle East, and finally, in the late 1970s substantial flows from Asia commenced and still continue.

These patterns reflect some significant shifts in immigration policy over the last half century. In the aftermath of World War II there were major labor shortages in Australia's newly expanding manufacturing sector as well as in traditional areas like agriculture. This, combined with some continuing notions of "population or perish" associated with perceived threats of invasion from the north, which were strengthened by the Pacific War, led the government to press for increased immigration. When this demand could not be met by traditional British sources, the government assisted over 300,000 DPs from Eastern Europe in settling in Australia, breaking down a previous, almost exclusive orientation toward the United Kingdom and Ireland. The success of the DPs led to an extension of the immigration program to other parts of Europe.

The 1970s saw several major shifts in the immigration policy. First, for the first time since World War II, Australia began to experience substantial levels of unemployment with structural change in the economy, the movement of manufacturing offshore, and the entry of the baby boom cohorts into the labor force. Immigration policy moved from an emphasis on the recruitment of semiskilled and skilled workers for manufacturing to a more complex program containing the following components: economic migration—attraction of people with skills in demand in Australia; family migration—relatives of Australian residents (the specific regulations of this part of the program have changed over the subsequent years); and refugee and humanitarian migration. The government introduced a points system to assess applicants for economic migration. In the 1980s a system was introduced whereby each year the government sets the number of immigrants to be allowed into the country.

A second shift in policy during the 1970s was the final abolition of the White Australia Policy originally instituted in 1901. This policy had effectively prevented non-Europeans from immigrating to Australia. With its removal Asians began to compete equally for places in the immigration program. The influx of refugees from Indochina was the first wave of a continuation in movement from the region.

Permanent Versus Nonpermanent Migration. For almost the entire postwar period there has been bipartisan agreement in Australia that permanent settlement of a significant number of overseas immigrants is desirable and, accordingly, each postwar government has had an active immigration program while the nonpermanent labor migration encouraged by some other OECD nations during the 1950s and 1960s was strongly opposed. There has, however, been a change (Hugo, 1999a). Nonpermanent migration of workers to Australia has greatly increased. Thus, Australia's international migration intake has become more diverse compared with a total focus on settlement immigration for the bulk of the postwar period. At present, this nonpermanent intake is limited only to groups whose skills are in demand in the Australian economy. The linkages with permanent migration are important, however, since the numbers applying to immigrate to Australia as "onshore" applicants have increased appreciably.

Emigration from Australia. Although Australia is one of the world's major immigration countries, it also has a substantial diaspora of Australian citizens living abroad, estimated to number 858,866 at the end of 2001 (Southern Cross, 2002). A major element in emigration out of Australia has been former settlers, about a fifth of whom leave Australia, most within five years of their arrival. Recently, however, there has been an upswing in the numbers of Australian-born persons leaving Australia on a permanent or long-term basis (Hugo, Harris, & Rudd, 2001).

Undocumented Migration to Australia. Since the late 1990s two types of undocumented migration to Australia have become a major focus of attention. First, people who enter the country legally and overstay; there is quite accurate data indicating around 60,000 overstayers in 2002 (DIMIA, 2002). Second, people who enter without documents. This includes persons who enter by sea or air as asylum seekers and, in fact, seek to be identified, and others who seek to enter clandestinely. The numbers of asylum seekers increased to over 4,000 in 2000 and 2001 but decreased to almost nothing with the introduction of procedures to intercept asylum seekers before their arrival.

DIMENSIONS OF MIGRATION ISSUES

Political Dimensions

Immigration issues have loomed large on the Australian political scene for more than a century, dating from the White Australia Policy introduced by the first national government in 1901, which confined immigration to Europeans. In the postwar period, however, political discussion concerning migration has largely revolved around the following issues: the scale of immigration; the composition of migration in terms of origin; the basis on which immigrants are selected; and the response to asylum seekers.

While debates about these issues have waxed and waned throughout the postwar years, for most of the period there has been bipartisan agreement between the two main political parties in the country over immigration. This is because both parties (conservative and socialist) contain substantial pro-immigration and anti-immigration subgroups. Accordingly, government policy has tended to steer a middle course between those groups lobbying for large-scale migration and those espousing low or zero migration.

Although Australia has higher levels of fertility than many OECD nations, it is substantially below replacement level; the outlook is for natural increase to slow down and cease in around 25 years. Moreover, the population is aging so that the ratio between the working age groups and the dependent, older population is becoming less favorable. While the situation is by no means as dramatic as in European nations, the issue of whether immigration can be used as "replacement migration" (United Nations, 2000) to help achieve a more balanced age structure once population stability is attained is gaining increasing attention.

The annual numbers of immigrant settlers entering Australia has varied between 68,810 in 1983 and 145,320 in 1988–1989, and these are likely to remain the outer limits of migrant intake in the foreseeable future. Nevertheless, groups with vested interests in areas such as the housing industry, as well as groups who see that an increase in population would enhance Australia's regional and global position, lobby to increase the scale of settlement. Others point to the important ecological constraints on population growth as arguments for lower or even zero immigration levels. This is very much tied up with the debate about an "optimum" population size for Australia, and there are wide differences between ecologists like Flannery (1994), who argue for a population of around 8 million, and others, like

6

MIGRATION AND IMMIGRATION

former Prime Minister Malcolm Fraser, who wish to see Australia achieve a population of 50–60 million (*The Australian*, 20 December 1995, 13). However, recently there has been substantial agreement around Australia's achieving a stable population of 24–25 million by around 2025 (McDonald & Kippen, 1999). This assumes an average annual intake of immigrants of around 80,000 to 120,000 persons.

Like the other "traditional" immigration nations, for much of the twentieth century Australian immigration deliberately excluded nonwhite populations. The policy was dismantled gradually during the three decades following World War II, and by the 1970s immigration to Australia was no longer selective at all on the basis of race, religion, creed, color, or ethnicity. As indicated earlier, the result has been a dramatic change in the characteristics of immigrants; Australia has moved from being dominated by Anglo Celtics to becoming a genuinely multicultural nation. One of the distinctive features of immigration policy in recent decades is that it has not been dominated by a small number of national origins. Hence, at the 1996 census there were 53 birthplace groups in Australia with 10,000 or more members born and 111 with 1,000 or more residents (Hugo, 1999b). While this policy is accepted wholeheartedly by the two major political parties, there are minority parties that have arisen from time to time to push for Australia to return to an exclusionist immigration policy. The strongest of these has been the One Nation Party, which arose in the 1990s (Jones, 1998) but received only 4.4 percent of the first preference vote in the 2001 national elections. As in the other traditional migration countries, racism remains an issue in Australia despite its being outlawed through a large range of legal and other measures that punish it.

A third area of political debate regarding immigration in Australia relates to the way in which immigrants are selected under the immigration program. There is a substantial bureaucracy in Australia that administers immigration and settlement issues. The government sets targets for each of the subcategories of immigrants, and these are selected as indicated in Table 1.1. There is debate, however, as to the balance of the various categories in the overall immigrant intake. For example, since 1995 the government has sought to put a more economic edge on the immigration program so that the skill stream increased from 28,000 to 33,000 per annum in 1999, while the family intake fell from 39,000 to 23,000 and the humanitarian program fell from 14,000 to 9,000.

In the late 1990s a fourth political issue emerged in the debate over immigration in Australia, and this has surrounded the treatment of asylum seekers. In the period since World War II, Australia resettled around 600,000 refugees as defined by the United Nations High Commissioner for Refugees (UNHCR) and others with humanitarian needs. Of the nine major global offshore resettlement countries, Australia has the third largest intake of refugees after the United States and Canada (8,000 in 2000) and the

Table 1.1
Australia: Program Management Structure, 2000–2001 (Non-humanitarian Program)

Skill	Family	Refugee/Humanitarian
Skilled Independent and Skilled-Australian Sponsored • Points tested • Planning level adjusted subject to demand in Business Skills and Employee Nomination Scheme (ENS)	*Parents and Preferential Family* Can be capped subject to demand in all other Family categories	*Humanitarian* Selected by DIMA from UNHCR-designated refugees
Business Skills, ENS, and Distinguished Talent Demand driven	*Fiancés and Interdependents* Can be capped subject to demand for spouse and dependent child places	*Special Humanitarian* In-country program
Contingency Reserve To be utilized if states and territories, business employers, and regional authorities generate additional demand	*Spouses and Dependent Children* • Demand driven • Exempt from capping	*Special Assistance* Groups not fitting the UNHCR definition but who have real need
	Contingency Reserve Legislation defeated in Senate in October 2000	

Source: DIMA (2000a).

second largest per capita of residents (.043 in 2000 compared with .046 in Canada). Australia has a significant and sustained record of support for the UNHCR, the acceptance of refugee and humanitarian settlers to the country, and the provision of special services to support those settlers in adjusting to life in Australia. There has been a bipartisan approach to immigration and settlement issues in Australia for most of the last half century. Refugee policy has enjoyed widespread community support, even among many anti-immigration lobby groups. However, until recently, due to its island-continent nature, Australia has not had to deal with significant numbers of asylum seekers from other countries who arrive on its doorstep without first having passed through UNHCR formalities in an overseas country. The arrival in the past few years of several thousand undocumented asylum seekers predominantly as "boat people" on Australia's northern shores has confronted policy makers with a new set of challenges and created division in the community about the policies and programs developed to cope. There has been a significant difference between refugee and humanitarian settlers on the one hand, and asylum seekers on the other, in both the way they have been treated by the government and attitudes taken toward them by the broader community.

There is a broad positive consensus regarding Australia's offshore refugee resettlement program. This is a comprehensive program of assistance available to persons who obtain a visa offshore under the Refugee and Humanitarian Program. In most cases refugees have their medical costs and travel costs to Australia paid for by the Australian government. There is a range of services provided to assist refugee and humanitarian settlers in the process of adjusting to life in Australia. Most are eligible for various general and specialist services to help them establish themselves during their settlement period. These include services such as English language tuition for adults, translation and interpreting services, accommodation support, health services and information, and referral services. Offshore refugee and humanitarian settlers are also eligible for the full range of income supports and job search assistance. This is important because they experience high rates of unemployment, especially in the early years of settlement.

The situation is quite different with people who arrive on Australia's shores as asylum seekers. The numbers have increased dramatically in recent years, but still only amounted to 4,141 in 2000–2001 (DIMIA, 2001b; Ruddock, 2001). People smugglers in the last five years have become more active in Australia in facilitating undocumented migration. Upon arrival in Australia, unauthorized arrivals undergo a screening interview to determine whether there is a *prima facie* case, in which instance Australia would have an obligation to consider offering protection. Where there is a case, people are placed in detention to await a formal determination of their status. Others are returned to their place of origin. People can also be returned to a third country where they had been before coming to Australia.

Australia's treatment of asylum seekers has attracted some criticism from international organizations, refugee lobby groups, church groups, and human rights groups. These criticisms have included the following: persons who are unauthorized arrivals are treated differently from overstayers, who are generally not put in detention centers; there have been allegations of poor conditions in the detention centers, including reports of sexual abuse, which have received attention through hunger strikes, protests, demonstrations, and breakouts from the camps; delays in determining whether people are genuine refugees; the treatment of asylum seekers is a breach of fundamental human rights.

Attention has focused, too, on the fact that the bulk of unauthorized arrivals who are formally approved and granted entry are being given a Temporary Protection Visa (TPV) that is valid for three years. This has in effect created two classes of refugee settlers in Australia, although the TPV holders can apply for permanent settlement before their visa expires if repatriation is not possible. The granting of TPVs rather than full refugee status is part of the government's policy of deterring more onshore claimants for asylum, especially those associated with people smuggling. TPV holders do not have access to the same rights as those granted full refugee status and allowed to settle in Australia. While they do have the right to work, access to health care, and access to a special benefit for income support, they do not receive the full package of benefits available to refugees settling in Australia under the offshore program. They also have no automatic right of return to Australia if they leave the country.

The issue took another turn in August 2001 when the Danish ship *Tampa* picked up several hundred asylum seekers who were headed for Australia from Indonesia when their vessel began sinking. The Australian government refused the ship permission to enter Australia and ordered it back to Indonesia. After a prolonged standoff, the government took the asylum seekers to several Pacific island countries to process their applications for refugee status. This ushered in a new "Pacific Solution" whereby all vessels containing asylum seekers desiring to enter Australia will be diverted to Pacific island nations for processing. This policy has gained majority support in the Australian community but has attracted strong criticism from abroad and from many Australians, including some of its most prominent citizens. The government stresses the involvement of "queue jumpers," people smugglers, illegal migrants, and possible terrorists in the movement, while critics point to the large proportion of boat people who have been assessed as having legitimate asylum claims.

Australia has controversially adopted a policy of detention of all asylum seekers while their claims for refugee status are being considered. This practice has come under attack from both within and outside Australia, especially because it has involved women and children, and several of the centers are in remote locations (Mares, 2001). It needs to be pointed out, however,

Table 1.2
Australia: Boat People, 1999–2000, Status in 2000

	Number	Percent
Granted Refugee Status	1,212	13.6
Temporary Protection Visa	2,802	31.5
Entry on Other Grounds	55	0.7
Total Granted Entry	4,069	45.8
Released on Bridging Visa	24	0.3
Escaped from Custody	6	0.1
In Custody	1,541	17.4
Total Remaining in Australia	1,571	17.7
Departures	3,252	36.5
Total	8,882	100.0

Source: DIMA (2000c).

that there is bipartisan support for the policy in both of Australia's main political parties. The government argues that the asylum seekers are "queue jumpers" and that they have been able to get to Australia by virtue of being able to pay people smugglers. Opponents of the policy recognize that there are nonrefugees among the arrivals but argue that the majority of asylum seekers from Iraq and Afghanistan had no chance to access the regular channels of refugee migration to Australia. The status of the 8,882 boat people who arrived in Australia between 1990 and November 2000 is given in Table 1.2. A substantial number have gained refugee status, and many are awaiting determination of their application for asylum.

Social Dimensions

Unlike the United States, Australia in the postwar period has adopted an approach of providing an array of postarrival services to newly arrived immigrants to facilitate their adjustment to Australian society. In the early postwar decades, this was an assimilationist policy but in the 1970s it moved toward a multiculturalist approach; the latter remains the bipartisan approach of recent federal governments. The assimilationist policy of the 1950s and 1960s assumed immigrants would "melt" into the national population and within a couple of generations become indistinguishable from the majority. The multiculturalism policy, however, encourages immigrants to retain their cultural heritage while also becoming full members of Australian

society. Accordingly, the federal government has developed policies and programs of cultural maintenance, language maintenance, and federally funded
multicultural television and radio, as well as institutions to protect fully the
rights of all migrants. The multicultural policy has not met with the full
approval of the community, as some minority political elements, such as the
One Nation Party, see it as encouraging separatism. The policy has been
given less financial support in recent years compared with the 1980s and
early 1990s.

Social cohesion remains an important issue in Australia (Holton, 1994).
Australia has been transformed from being overwhelmingly Anglo Celtic at
the end of World War II, despite the existence of its indigenous population,
to being one of the most multicultural of global populations at the turn of
the century. A total of 32.2 percent of Sydney's population is born overseas,
and 48.2 percent are first- or second-generation immigrants. These represent
a major change and continue to be an area of debate.

Australia's multicultural transformation has been achieved largely without
conflict, despite the fact that many of the incoming settlers have differed
substantially in culture, language, and religion from the dominant population. The reasons for this are partly that immigration has involved people of
very diverse origins so that there has not been a chance for single birthplace
groups to be very large. Moreover, the intake has been steady and consistent,
and to some extent it has "taken the community with it," rather than in
volving massive intakes of immigrants who must suddenly confront the prej-
udices and attitudes of the majority population.

One area of debate that has arisen relates to the patterns of settlement of
immigrants in Australia, especially the degree of spatial concentration of
some non-English speaking origin groups. The issue of the development of
ethnic enclaves has been at the center of debate, initiated by Blainey in 1984,
about modern Asian immigration to Australia (see also Blainey, 1993). Blainey argued that the development of Indo-Chinese concentrations in certain
suburbs of Australian cities jeopardized social cohesiveness and harmony.
This view was opposed by commentators such as Jupp, McRobbie, and York
(1990) and by way of a comprehensive study of Indo-Chinese households
in Brisbane by Viviani, Coughlan, and Rowland (1993), which stressed the
positive roles played by the spatial concentrations.

During the postwar years' debate two models of immigrant social mobility
have been put forward in Australia. The first model suggests that immigrants
experience considerable upward mobility, especially between generations.
While they may begin on low incomes, through hard work, thriftiness, education, and other factors they improve their position. Considerable evidence
has been assembled to show a substantial degree of social mobility between
generations (Birrell & Khoo, 1995). The second model that has been put
forward and has gained some empirical support suggests that immigrants
get trapped in an underclass from which they and their descendants cannot

escape. Immigrants experience considerable barriers to mobility in the shape of language problems, lack of education, lack of recognition of qualifications, and discrimination; they get trapped in low-income and low-security occupations and generally low well-being situations. In fact, both of these models apply to different groups in Australia, there being considerable contrast in the experience between and within different birthplace groups. Existing migration policies tend to result in a bipolar distribution of immigrants with respect to income and well being. The increasing skill orientation of policy has meant that immigrants are well represented among the better-off segments of society. On the other hand, some groups, especially some refugee groups, experience great difficulty in entering the labor market and are strongly represented among the poor.

Economic Dimensions

Much of the research and policy interest in international migration in Australia has centered around its effects on the national economy. There has been a substantial body of research that indicates that the overall economic impact of immigration has been, at worst, benign and has had, at best, a small net positive economic effect. It has been concluded from an exhaustive analysis of Australian research that immigration does not lead to an increase in aggregate unemployment; immigration has relatively little effect on both prices and wages; in the long run, at least, immigration has very little impact on external balance; in the long term, immigration gives rise to government revenues that more than pay for its expenditures (Wooden, Holton, Hugo, & Sloan, 1994, p. 153).

There has been a particular focus in recent years on the labor force impacts of immigration, and Australia has placed increasing focus on the labor market influences of immigration. As with other OECD nations, immigration is increasingly being seen as an important mechanism to recruit skilled labor into areas of the economy that are currently constrained by a lack of locally trained labor resources. There are a number of issues relating to this that are currently being debated in Australia.

First, the balance between family and humanitarian elements of the nation's immigration program, on the one hand, and the skilled/economic part of the program, on the other hand, is a controversial issue. There has been a major shift in the last five years toward skilled migration. This is not only evident in the Permanent Migration Program, but also in the explosion of temporary migration to the skilled side of the balance. There are strong lobby groups in Australia for this change (e.g., national and state governments, employers, etc.) but there are also groups who believe there needs to be a shift back toward family and humanitarian migration (ethnic lobby groups, nongovernment organizations, etc.).

Second, there is a debate as to the extent to which an emphasis on skilled migration and an increase in the proportion of the skilled labor force who are overseas-born migrants are being used as substitutes for training the native workforce to adapt to the human resource needs of the economy. Ideally, skilled migration should be combined with appropriate expansion of training activities in government policy, but many argue that too often skilled migration is used as a substitute for training.

Third, there are important issues relating to recognition of qualifications obtained in other countries. There is a longstanding problem among permanent migrants settling in Australia of people not having their qualifications recognized in Australia by employers, professional associations, or governments (Iredale, 1997; see Kunz, 1988).

A fourth issue of debate is that there has been discrimination against immigrant workers in the labor market. Australia and its states and territories have a strong battery of antidiscrimination legislation. Nevertheless, it is clear that such discrimination can still operate in an informal way so that it is not readily detectable and able to be directly addressed. As Australia has become more multicultural, it would appear that the extent of discrimination has declined.

Fifth, there are some concerns that under the Temporary Entry Program, workers are tied to the employer who sponsors them. Indeed, there is some evidence that employers are turning away from the Employer Nominated Scheme (ENS) element in the Permanent Settlement Program and using instead the 457 Temporary Entry category to attract skilled workers; under the former workers are not tied to employment with their sponsor, but under the latter they are. There is a danger that tied workers can possibly be exploited by employers.

Sixth, there is an emerging area of concern in Australia that relates to the emigration of skilled workers. A recently introduced Innovation Program announced by the federal government has stemming the flow of skilled young Australians overseas as one of its objectives. It has been argued (Hugo et al., 2001) that there is little value in governments attempting to stop recent graduates from seeking work overseas. Indeed, it is argued that young Australians should be encouraged to broaden and extend their expertise and experience, and indeed expand and strengthen Australia's global linkages, especially in the economic sphere. On the other hand, there may be value in the nation having policies that encourage overseas skilled Australians to maintain strong linkages with Australia and return later in their careers to contribute to the economic development of the nation.

A final issue relates to the relationship between temporary migration and permanent migration. In Australia there can be no doubt that there has been a policy shift toward nonpermanent migration in attracting skilled workers. Certainly to some extent, this reflects the fact that many skilled labor markets are international, and a temporary migration program in many ways is better fitted to competing globally for skilled workers in these international labor markets than the longstanding Settlement Migration Program. Moreover, it is clear that some of the nonpermanent entrants under the 457 Program eventually decide to stay in Australia and apply for permanent entry. This is certainly the case in the United States where gaining temporary entry can be part of a deliberate strategy of migrants to eventually achieve permanent settlement (Martin & Lowell, 2000).

However, there are those who suggest that the expansion of the Skilled Worker Temporary Entrant Program has undermined the skilled worker part of the Permanent Settlement Immigration Program. There are definitely perceived advantages to the Temporary Migrant Worker Program in that Australia does not have to pay for the training of the worker and workers who are not needed at the end of their contract can be returned to the place of origin. However, the nation may have other goals in its immigration program other than to fill gaps in the labor market and the temporary movement may not contribute toward achieving those goals. Do temporary skilled workers lack commitment to national development? Do they invest in housing and other elements of social infrastructure? Do they repatriate their earnings to their home area? This issue becomes of particular importance when nations have "replacement migration" (United Nations, 2000) goals in their migration programs. That is, in the face of declining and aging populations in many OECD nations, they may be anticipating that migration can offset some of the detrimental effects of a declining workforce and a dependency ratio between the working age and nonworking elderly population. Temporary skilled migrants are unlikely to have a major impact in this area, although they certainly will pay taxes while working in Australia and hence contribute toward the support of the older generation. Nevertheless, the bulk of these workers will not bring families with them and will not contribute toward affecting the aging of the population.

THE FUTURE

In the 2001 federal elections in Australia, immigration and population issues loomed larger than in any other election of recent times. There is an increasing debate within the country of the population levels that Australia should have and the role of immigration in reaching those levels. Some environmentalists consider Australia already overpopulated and favor a reduction in population size and the ceasing of immigration. Other groups, especially some business lobbies, favor the Australian population expanding to 50–70 million within the next century, with immigration being a major factor in that growth. The most likely scenario, however, is for immigration levels to continue at the current level of a net migration gain of around 80,000 persons. If this is combined with a small decline in fertility, the pattern of population will likely see an increase between 24 million and 25 million in around 50 years and thereafter achieve population stability. This scenario of population change would result in a workable balance between dependent and nondependent age groups, although the proportion of those age 65 years and above would be twice what it is currently. In achieving such a pattern, it would be necessary to invoke a range of population policies in addition to immigration, including policies relating to fertility and increasing workforce participation, especially at older ages.

Immigration to Australia in the twenty-first century will be influenced by a range of influences within and outside Australia. The location of Australia within the Asia Pacific region, which has more than half of the world's population, will have an influence. Trends in undocumented migration, the growth of the immigration industry, the internationalization of labor markets, the aging of the Australian population, trends in forced migration, globalization, and the development of transnational family networks will be as influential as developments in Australian immigration policy.

BIBLIOGRAPHY

Australian Bureau of Statistics (ABS). (1983–1994). *Overseas Arrivals and Departures, Australia* (various issues), Catalogue no. 3402.0. Canberra: ABS.
———. (1995–2001). *Migration Australia* (various issues), Catalogue no. 3412.0. Canberra: ABS.
Birrell, B. (1993). Ethnic Concentrations: The Vietnamese Experience. *People and Place, 1*(3), 26–32.
———. (2000). Informational Technology and Australia's Immigration Program: Is Australia Doing Enough? *People and Place, 8*(2), 77–83.
Birrell, R., & Khoo, S. (1995). *The Second Generation in Australia: Educational and Occupational Characteristics.* Canberra: AGPS.
Blainey, G. (1993, July). A Critique of Indo-Chinese in Australia: The Issues of Unemployment and Residential Concentration. *BIPR Bulletin,* No. 9, 42–45.
———. (1994, August 30). Melting Pot on the Boil. *The Bulletin,* 22–27.
Cocks, K. D. (1996). *People Policy: Australia's Population Choices.* Kensington, NSW: UNSW Press.
Department of Immigration and Multicultural Affairs (DIMA). (n.d.). *Australian Immigration Consolidated Statistics* (various issues). Canberra: AGPS.
———. (2000a). *Locating Overstayers in Australia* (DIMA Fact Sheet 80). Canberra: DIMA.
———. (2000b). *Unauthorised Arrivals by Sea and Air* (DIMA Fact Sheet 81). Canberra: DIMA.
———. (2000c). *Immigration Detention* (DIMA Fact Sheet 82). Canberra: DIMA.
Department of Immigration and Multicultural and Indigenous Affairs (DIMIA). (2001a). *Overstayers and People in Breach of Visa Conditions* (DIMIA Fact Sheet 80). Canberra: DIMIA.
———. (2001b). *Unauthorized Arrivals by Air and Sea* (Fact Sheet 74). Canberra: DIMIA.
———. (2002). *Overstayers and People in Breach of Visa Conditions* (DIMIA Fact Sheet 86). Canberra: DIMIA.

Flannery, T. (1994). *The Future Eaters*. Chatswood: Reeds Books.

Holton, R. (1994). Social Aspects of Immigration. In M. Wooden, R. Holton, G. Hugo, & J. Sloan (Eds.), *Australian Immigration: A Survey of the Issues* (pp. 158–217). Canberra: AGPS.

Hugo, G., Harris, K., & Rudd, D. (2001, February). *Emigration from Australia: Economic Implications* (Second Report on an ARC SPIRT Grant). Adelaide University: National Key Centre for Teaching and Research in Social Applications of Geographical Information Systems.

Hugo, G. J. (1986). *Australia's Changing Population: Trends and Implications*. Melbourne: Oxford University Press.

———. (1999a). A New Paradigm of International Migration in Australia. *New Zealand Population Review*, 25(1–2), 1–39.

———. (1999b). *Atlas of the Australian People 1996 Census: National Overview*. Canberra: DIMA.

Iredale, R. (1997). *Skills Transfer: International Migration and Accreditation Issues*. Wollongong, NSW: University of Wollongong Press.

Jones, G. (1998). "Australian Identity," Racism and Recent Responses to Asian Immigration to Australia. In E. Laquian, A. Laquian, & T. McGee (Eds.), *The Silent Debate: Asian Immigration and Racism in Canada* (pp. 249–266). Vancouver: University of British Columbia, Institute of Asian Research.

Jupp, J. (1993). Ethnic Concentrations: A Reply to Bob Birrell. *People and Place*, 1(4), 51–52.

Jupp, J., McRobbie, A., & York, B. (1990). *Metropolitan Ghettos and Ethnic Concentrations* (Vols. 1 and 2). Wollongong, NSW: Centre for Multicultural Studies.

Kippen, R., & McDonald, P. (2000). Australia's Population in 2000: The Way We Are and the Ways We Might Have Been. *People and Place*, 8(3), 10–17.

Kunz, E. F. (1988). *Displaced Persons: Calwell's New Australians*. Sydney: Australian National University Press.

Mares, P. (2001). *Borderline: Australia's Treatment of Refugees and Asylum Seekers*. Sydney: UNSW Press.

Martin, S., & Lowell, B. L. (2000, November 23–24). U.S. Immigration Policy, High Skilled Workers and the New Global Economy. In *Nation Skilling: Migration Labour and the Law: An International Symposium*, conducted at the University of Sydney.

McDonald, P., & Kippen, R. (1999, March 31). Population Futures for Australia: The Policy Alternative. Paper presented at the Vital Issues Seminar, Canberra.

Price, C. A. (1979). *Australian Immigration: A Bibliography and Digest* (No. 4). Canberra: Department of Demography, Australian National University.

Ruddock, P. (2001). *Background Paper on Unauthorised Arrivals Strategy*. Canberra: DIMIA.

Southern Cross. (2002). Estimates of Australian Citizens Living Overseas as at 31 December 2001. http://www.southern-cross-group.org/archives/Statistics/Numbers_of_Australians_Overseas_in_2001_by_Region_Feb_2002.pdf.

United Nations. (2000). *Replacement Migration: Is It a Solution to Declining and Aging Populations?* New York: United Nations.

Viviani, N., Coughlan, J., & Rowland, T. (1993). *Indo-Chinese in Australia: The Issues of Employment and Residential Concentration*. Canberra: AGPS.

Wooden, M. (1994). The Economic Impact of Immigration. In M. Wooden, R.

Holton, G. Hugo, & R. Sloan (Eds.), *Australian Immigration: A Survey of the Issues* (pp. 111–157). Canberra: AGPS.

Wooden, M., Holton, R., Hugo, G., & Sloan, R. (Eds.) (1994). *Australian Immigration: A Survey of the Issues*. Canberra: AGPS.

World Bank. (2000). *Entering the 21st Century: World Development Report 1999/2000*. New York: Oxford University Press.

2

BRAZIL

A Historical and Contemporary View of Brazilian Migration

Nobuko Adachi

INTRODUCTION

Profile of Brazil

Brazil is a large country, covering over 3 million square miles, about half of the South American continent. Some 171 million people live in Brazil today. Because of its huge landmass, internal geographical and social differences in Brazil are immense. Thus, addressing the totality of Brazil is very difficult, and the different regions are usually viewed independently, each with its own climate, physical features, socioeconomic history, culture, and views on race. Almost 60 percent of the people of Brazil are concentrated in the south—the major industrialized area of the country, which includes the states of São Paulo and Paraná. About 30 percent live in the northeast—home to the traditional agricultural areas like Perunambuco and Bahia. Less than 10 percent of the population lives in the Amazon River valley. There has been much migration to and from Brazil, and each geographical area has formed diverse cultures through different patterns of immigration at different times. According to the National Survey of 1998, 95.8 percent of children age seven or older enroll in primary school (although less than half of them were actually attending school). The rate of enrollment at secondary school is 30.7 percent (Europa World Yearbook, 2000).

Vignette

In 1908, 793 transnational migrants from Japan crossed the ocean for the first time for Brazil. When the immigrants were about to arrive in Brazil, they cried while looking at the stars of the Southern Cross, a constellation that appears only in the southern hemisphere, because they had never seen them before from the northern latitudes of Japan. They had mixed feelings of joy and anticipation on ending the long journey, which took two months by ship in those days. Soon they started to work in the coffee plantations, and they found many differences between their expectations and their experiences. On coffee plantations, the social status of the new immigrants was about the same as that of the former slaves. They worked side by side with former slaves and lived in quarters formerly used by slaves. These immigrants found themselves in near slavelike conditions, a proposition they had not bargained for.

Overview of Migration Issues

Since the mid-sixteenth century, when sugar cane was planted in the northeast region, a large number of slaves were imported to Brazil from Africa. African slaves provided the main source of manual labor for agricultural work in Brazil until the country began to feel strong outside abolitionist pressure in the mid-nineteenth century. Around the end of the nineteenth century when the abolitionist movement made plantation owners free their slaves, many Brazilian elites—who were of European descent and had largely received their higher education in Europe—welcomed European immigration, believing that European wage laborers would create a more suitable class of workers than one of "uncultured" Africans. However, after the price of coffee beans fell sharply on the world market around 1900, economic difficulties brought hard times for plantation owners and created tensions between owners and their European-immigrant labor force. Working conditions grew increasingly worse. After receiving a number of requests from European governments to improve living conditions for their nationals working in Brazil, Brazil finally decided to replace these farmhands with another kind of people: "Orientals." Arabs, Jews, and other Middle Easterners also migrated to Brazil at this time, but the vast majority of new agricultural workers were from Japan.

By the 1920s, many coffee planters could no longer see a future in growing coffee and sought their fortune in industrialization. As a result, coffee planters started selling off their lands in the interior at rock-bottom prices to obtain quick capital for expansion. They built factories like textile mills, clothing works, and food processing plants in the cities. Many Italian immigrants left the rural areas with plantation owners to be their workers in the new factories. Japanese immigrants, on the other hand, often grouped themselves together in collectives, pooling all their savings to rent or purchase small farm fields.

Before industrialization, Brazilian society was based on the *compadre* network system. The lower class people used this system to link themselves to individuals of the large and powerful elite families through relationships of godparenthood in order to gain socioeconomic security. Industrialization, however, brought a new type of social relationship to Brazilian society—one based on the new economic realities of modern wage-labor capitalism. This was especially true for the new workers in the factories in the cities. However, many of the smaller landowners (such as the Japanese immigrants) were self-sufficient enough to form the basis of what was to be a new middle class. The new members of this rising middle class used higher education as a means of social advancement, and they joined the ranks of the professionals.

By the 1960s, these new middle class professionals provided Brazil with another largely unanticipated advantage. Connections between immigrant members of the Brazilian middle class and their home country often allowed for the establishment of foreign investment in Brazil. Cultivating such relationships even became encouraged by the Brazilian government in the 1960s and 1970s. Immigrants became "intermediaries" between Brazil and their home countries. Regardless of these strong foreign connections, however, less than 1 percent of the real political elite were born abroad, and only 4 percent had one foreign parent (Love & Barickman, 1991, p. 9).

In the 1980s, the Brazilian economy began a long and hard inflationary period, lasting to some degree even until today. This inflation directly caused grave economic damage to the members of the middle class. Since the upper class Brazilians could place their assets in foreign (mainly Swiss and American) banks, their money was immune to the ravages of this inflation. However, the middle class people, who depended on their monthly wages and savings, were economically decimated. Seeking to restore their economic viability, some members of the new middle class—largely the children of the late-nineteenth- and early-twentieth-century immigrants—started to return to their ancestors' home countries to be returnee migrant workers. Because of the improvements in transportation, international travel has become quick and affordable. As a result, such returnee migrants travel between the two countries quite frequently, and in many ways have become almost "borderless" people.

HISTORY OF MIGRATION ISSUES

After the land known today as Brazil was "discovered" by the Portuguese in 1500, the area became a Portuguese colony until independence in 1822. During this period, the northeast was the center of social and economic life of the colony. There, sugar plantations formed the basis of a society of European aristocratic elites, backed by the labor of African slaves, who made their own cultural contributions to this emerging nation, especially in food, music, and religion. The first influx of new immigrants to Brazil after its colonization was the forced migration of Africans from Africa. It is commonly accepted that at least 3.6 million Africans were brought to Brazil during the slave trade period from 1502 to 1830. However, this is only the number of actual arrivals. Thousands more people, who were captured, branded, and placed in heavy iron manacles in Africa and shipped overseas, died on their way to Brazil. The voyage took as long as eight months. The human cargo hold on the slave ships was usually only two feet high and filled with some 20 slaves lying thirsty, hungry, and physically and psychologically in pain and fear (Benjamin & Mendonça, 1997, pp. 125–126). Although it has been suggested that the average mortality rate of the transport of slaves was 15 to 20 percent, data of five ships sailing in 1625 shows a much higher figure—an average of 47 percent (De Queirós Mattoso, 1996, p. 35).

After arriving in Brazil, ships sometimes remained undocked for several days as they waited to enter the harbor. During this time buyers went out to inspect their purchases and complete their transactions. Many slaves were sold by public auction as well as through private sales. Life on land was not much better for these African "immigrants" than their trials at sea. Work on the plantations was usually terrible and dangerous, particularly for women. Female slaves were often raped by their masters and gave birth to their children.

By the seventeenth century, around the same time gold was discovered in Minas Gerais in the east-central mountain region, the sugar plantations in the northeast were slowly in decline. The new gold mines, however, provided a new market for slaves. Some slaves were imported directly from Africa, while others were resold by northeastern sugar plantation owners. This gold mining in Minas Gerais even influenced the industrial revolution in England (Wagley, 1971, p. 26) as Brazil was a Portuguese colony, and Portugal had strong economic ties with England. After 1695, massive Portuguese immigration occurred. It has been estimated that at least 300,000—and as many as 500,000—Portuguese came to Brazil at this time (Wagley, 1971, p. 48). This immigration effectively doubled the number of Europeans in the total population in Brazil.

At the beginning of the nineteenth century, Portugal could conceivably have become a French colony, as Napoleon rapidly expanded his political power all over Europe. In 1808, fearing the worst, the royal family of Portugal moved its court to Rio de Janeiro, in Brazil. Right after Napoleon lost power, the Portuguese monarchy, however, went back to Lisbon in 1821. Although it lasted only a very short time, the Portuguese kingdom in Rio de Janeiro actually helped Brazil develop economically and fostered trade with European nations. Once again, a demand for plantation labor caused large numbers of African slaves to be imported from other Portuguese colonies, such as Angola and West Africa (which was geographically relatively close to Brazil). Returning to Lisbon, the Portuguese monarchy left the Crown Prince in Rio de Janeiro and let Brazil be governed independently under him. Although the country became self-governing when Prince Pedro

I declared its independence on September 7, 1822, there were few political and economic changes in Brazil, and the country still operated as a colony of the Portuguese kingdom.

During the period of colonial growth and independence, more European planters arrived in Brazil, and more African slaves were imported to be plantation laborers. The approximate number[1] of slaves imported in the sixteenth century was about 100,000 but grew in the seventeenth century to about 600,000. In the eighteenth century some 1.3 million slaves arrived in Brazil, and in the nineteenth century about 1.6 million. As a result, when the Rio-Portuguese kingdom moved to Brazil, the total population was 3.6 million, but over half of it (some 1.9 million) consisted of African slaves (Imin Hachijyû-nen-shi Hensan Iinkai, 1991, p. 17).

By the mid-nineteenth century, coffee had been planted in the south—the Paraíba River valley between Rio de Janeiro and São Paulo, both next to the state of Minas Gerais. The "coffee zone" rapidly moved farther south and west into the state of São Paulo. By the last quarter of the nineteenth century, the south had become the economic center of Brazil. Labor for coffee plantations was mostly provided by African slaves in the early period.

In 1850, under strong political pressure from the European abolitionist movement, the importation of slaves to Brazil was abolished. Although the law was enacted to avoid diplomatic problems with European nations, in practice, some slaves were still imported. In those days, due to the hard working conditions in the plantations, the life expectancy of the average Brazilian slave was only about 21 years (Bethell, 1993, p. 234).[2] Therefore, planters still needed to import slaves to replace their losses.

As the pressure from abolitionist movements from the West became stronger and stronger, in 1871 children born of slave mothers were freed; slaves over age sixty were freed in 1885. Slavery was finally banned in Brazil in 1888—the last nation in the Western Hemisphere to do so. Yet, while the government freed slaves politically, there was neither compensation nor any help for them at emancipation. Thus, the majority of these freed slaves were unable to free themselves from their former owners.

Because of the massive importation of slaves over the last three hundred years, the African population in Brazil is large. The Rio-Portuguese kingdom saw a need to encourage "white" population growth in the process of developing Brazil as a nation. The elite Brazilians, who were of European descent, believed the former African slaves to be lazy and unintelligent (Kinshichi, Sumida, Takahashi, & Tomino, 2000, p. 31) and attempted to transform Brazil from a "black" to a "white" society with the help of European immigration (Lesser, 1999, p. 82). Also, after the abolition of slavery, the country faced a shortage of cheap plantation labor. Thus, Brazil invited immigrants from Europe and allowed them to own land in Brazil; before this, only Portuguese citizens could own Brazilian lands (a law intended to prevent other European nations from influencing or taking over the colony).

Brazilian immigration policy brought in over 4 million Europeans from 1870–1963. The composition consisted of 1.6 million Portuguese, 1.5 million Italians, 700,000 Spanish, 200,000 Germans, and 110,000 Russians (Kinshichi et al., 2000, pp. 86–87). However, African and Asian immigrants were not welcome according to the immigration law of 1890 — at least not at first.

Brazil's immigration policy changed after 1896, when the price of coffee sharply fell on the world market, largely due to overproduction. Coffee supplied almost 70 percent of the national income, and both the Brazilian government and the coffee plantation owners tried to ride out this economic crisis by cutting costs as much as possible (Imin Hachijyû-nen-shi Hensan Iinkai, 1991, pp. 30–34). Yet, since the coffee tree requires constant care and must be picked annually throughout its 40-year lifespan, there was little they could do to cut labor costs. The working conditions of the immigrants became harder and harder, and plantation owners cut corners at every opportunity — usually at the expense of their farmhands.

As a result, the European contract coffee farmhands often turned to their consulates, asking to be taken back to their home countries even before their contracts ended. Over 65 percent of coffee plantation workers were immigrants, and a new source of labor was needed when European immigration became curtailed (Holloway, 1978, p. 188). Thus, the Brazilian government let the first Japanese immigrate in 1908, hoping that this new immigration policy would also result in new coffee markets and economic relationships with Japan (Imin Hachijyû-nen-shi Hensan Iinkai, 1991, p. 34). However, the Brazilian elites thought Asians were racially inferior. Manuel de Liveria Lima, who was Brazil's minister plenipotentiary in Tokyo in 1901, wrote to the Brazilian government on the suitability of bringing Japanese into Brazilian society, stating that it would be "dangerous to . . . mix inferior races in our populations" (Lesser, 1999, p. 84), and, in 1890, an immigration law was passed stating that "no Africans and Asians will be allowed to immigrate into Brazil."

Even knowing the potential hardships of immigrating to Brazil, many Japanese left — or were forced to leave — Japan. A severe economic depression and a revolution changed Japanese political power in the latter half of the nineteenth century. In 1868 the traditional Samurai-warrior government was replaced by a constitutional monarchy, but many average Japanese still suffered greatly. More than 640,000 Japanese crossed the Pacific from 1899-1937 (Ishikawa, 1975, p. 63). They first immigrated to Guam and Hawaii, geographically closer to Japan. After Hawaii became a possession of the United States, the number of Japanese emigrating to the mainland suddenly increased. Seeing this rapid increase in the number of Japanese coming to the shores of the west coast, many Americans began to fear the "yellow peril." In 1924, the Immigration and Exclusion Act was passed by the U.S. Congress, and later a very similar law was passed in Canada. These acts officially ended Japanese immigration to North America. After this, Japanese migration to Brazil rose significantly, from 2,673 in 1924 to 6,330 in 1925 (Ohara, 1972). Due to the rapid pace of Japanese immigration, institutional racial discrimination became strong in Brazil as well. Although not everyone was against Japanese immigration,[3] anti-Japanese feeling was sometimes very strong. This, of course, was often encouraged by the anti-Japanese sentiment in the United States (Lesser, 1999, pp. 116, 129).

Brazil requested that Japanese come with at least three family members (not counting children under the age of twelve, since small children could not do the work of an adult). This policy was institutionalized by formal agreements between Brazil and Japan. According to Handa (1970, 1987),[4] the reason for this family immigration policy was that if immigrants had their families with them they could not run away as easily under the cover of night. Thus, they would be stuck on the plantations for better or worse. Recalling the memory of his childhood, Handa reported that Japanese immigrants were not allowed to have visitors on the plantations, and their personal letters were checked by their supervisors, even though their supervisors could not read Japanese.

Japanese harbored strong desires to leave the coffee plantations as soon as possible and to stay with other Japanese, whom they trusted. Seeing their children playing with children of their neighbors, former slaves, and learning "undesirable" manners from their "uncultured" surroundings made the pressure to get out from these slavelike conditions urgent.

Because of a severe economic crisis in Brazil early in the twentieth century, the value of Brazilian currency fell compared to the Japanese currency, and it eventually became hardly worthwhile for Japanese workers to send their savings back to Japan. At the same time, because of the world depression of 1929, coffee markets crashed badly and planters found it more difficult to run their plantations than ever before. Thus, planters started selling off their land piece by piece. Since Japanese settlers migrated to Brazil with relatives and family members, it did not take them long to take advantage of these opportunities; plans changed, and many decided to stay on in Brazil longer than they had anticipated.

As soon as Japanese immigrants finished their contracts and paid off their debts to the planters, they left the coffee plantations to rent or purchase small farm fields that the owners were selling off. This usually required all their savings, so they often went into partnership with others, such as relatives, people from the same Japanese prefecture, or people who came over on the same ship. In 1932 in the state of São Paulo, 10,355 Japanese households were listed as landowners, owning a total of 370,000 hectares. The number of household landowners increased to nearly 15,000 by 1936, with aggregate holdings of 437,500 hectares. Japanese-owned land increased steadily throughout the 1930s. By 1940, 76.7 percent of Japanese immigrants owned their own farms. Only 7.5 percent were *colonos* (daily paid farmhands), while 15.9 percent cultivated rented farmlands (Smith, 1974, pp. 162–163).

Gathering in the same areas not only helped these immigrants physically and psychologically, but also economically. In 1927 Japanese in Cotia village started gathering potatoes from individual Japanese farmers and selling them together in city markets. Until then, small farmers were not able to sell their products in the markets, which was the planters' monopoly. The cooperative helped Japanese focus on cultivating without worrying about the sales of their products. The cooperative also researched and taught the farmers about the demand for farm products and better cultivation techniques for individual farm products. For instance, the Cotia cooperative introduced potato farmers to the systematic full-scale use of fertilizers on Brazilian soil, and they then devised improved means of soil preparation, spraying, seed selection, collective planting, cultivation, and irrigation. As a result, by 1939 almost 17 percent of state-wide agricultural crops were produced by the Japanese, who were only 5 percent of the population in the agricultural work force in São Paulo (Imin Hachijyû-nen-shi Hensan Iinkai, 1991, p. 109). Cooperatives like Cotia helped many Japanese-Brazilians establish themselves firmly in the middle class.

DIMENSIONS OF MIGRATION ISSUES

In 1930, after failing to be elected president of Brazil, Getúlio Vargas took over the government with the help of the military. This revolution was supported by young radical officers (*tenentes*) who were outcasts of the old political elite establishment. Before the Vargas regime (1930–1945), power in the Brazilian political economy had been held by the local elites. These elites had assured their continued incumbency through favors to real and fictive kinsmen—the traditional *parentela* system. Also, honorary military ranks had been given to many landowners to administer their regions in return for governmental favors, the so-called *coronelismo* or "colonel" system. Coming from outside the powerful *parentela* webs, Vargas was not able to win the election of 1930, despite his connections to the officers. After taking political power by force, Vargas then tried to destroy the *parentela*-based political system. The charismatic Vargas and his supporters attacked the *coronelismo* system, ostensibly offering liberal reforms that never actually materialized.

During the Vargas era, São Paulo, the center of Brazilian economics, also faced a dramatic shift from an agricultural economy to an industrialized one. This shift brought significant changes in the Brazilian social system. Seeing the success of the industrial economy in Europe—and the collapse of the coffee economy in Brazil—coffee planters switched from farms to factories. Immigrants who had been plantation laborers, especially Italians, came to work in the factories. The relationship between factory owners and workers was no longer one of almost master and slave as back on the farms; instead, it became one of modern wage-giving employer to wage-receiving employee. These new employees often organized labor unions to improve their work conditions. Soon, many of these workers entered the new fledging middle class—vis-à-vis the traditional Brazilian social hierarchy—as they and their children economically advanced.

While politics was centralizing under the Vargas regime and his Nationalization project, the foundation of the modern Brazilian economic system was formed by foreign ideas and immigrant labor. This contradiction of mixed social structures, conflicting goals of nationalization and globalization, and economics is still often seen in today's Brazil. In the 1960s, Brazil invited foreign investment to strengthen its industrial infrastructure. Immigrants again played a significant role by encouraging investments and enterprises from their home countries. As a result, the 1970s saw something of an economic miracle for Brazil. Because of such foreign investments from their home nations, immigrant settlers and their descendants have strengthened their political, social, and economic position in Brazilian society today.

In the 1980s the Brazilian economy started to suffer a number of setbacks, and the monthly wage workers suffered the most. Wage workers, most of whom were immigrants and their descendants, started to return to their ancestors' homelands to make ends meet. Many nations have provided special permits, or have not required permits at all, to allow descendants of immigrants to return. In the new globalized world, the ethnic identities of these new middle class people are dynamic and changing; sometimes such people are called "borderless" people. The question is, do they really identify themselves as borderless people, or rather as multinational citizens of the world? Ethnic identity, as well as the local and global movements of people as a modern social phenomenon, will now be considered, using the case of the Japanese-Brazilians to explore these issues in the following sections on political, social, and economic dimensions of migration in Brazil.

Political Dimensions

After Getúlio Vargas took over political power in Brazil in the 1930s, he put pressures and restrictions on immigration and immigrant rights. This political restriction is commonly recognized as a part of his Nationalization project, and has been described as a "state-driven homogenization program [with the intention of] preserving Brazilian identity from the encroachment of ethnicity by eliminating distinctive elements of immigrants' culture" (Lesser, 1999, p. 130). Saito (1976, p. 75) explains the reason for the Nationalization project using some specifics. For one, Brazil, as a former colony, looked to Europe for cultural and educational values. Brazilians judged intelligence and breeding by things like a knowledge of French or schooling on the Continent.

Thus, after the institution of immigration quotas in 1935, the number of new migrants was limited to two percent of the total number of settlers who had already immigrated in the last 50 years. Since the history of Arab, Jewish, and Japanese immigration to Brazil was very short compared to that of western Europeans, these laws affected these newcomers the most (Kinshichi et al., 2000, p. 140; Lesser, 1999, p. 130). Thus, nationalization in effect was direct discrimination against Japanese, Arabs, Jews, and "nonwhite" undesirables. Just as in the United States, Brazilian political elites tried to eliminate nonwhite immigration. (Lesser, 1995).

The constitution of 1937, called the Estado Novo, was especially designed to restrict immigration. The Estado Novo supported Vargas' xenophobic policies throughout World War II. Though legislation restricted the freedoms of all immigrants from axis nations, Japanese-Brazilians were particularly singled out. In 1942, Vargas ordered Japanese-Brazilians to move from the Japantown areas in the city of São Paulo to the interior within ten days. In 1943 Japanese-Brazilians along the coast were ordered to move to the interior within 24 hours. Moreover, Japanese had to apply for special permits to travel, even inside Brazil, and they were prohibited from buying and selling any real property. In effect, most of their property was seized. Japanese immigrants were subjected to legal domiciliary searches under the excuse that they might have a radio to listen to Japanese news broadcasts, or that they were hiding arms and secret information from the Brazilian army. In 1944 many Japanese were arrested under the suspicion of being spies.

Although they were deprived of many political rights, most Japanese-Brazilians were reluctant to view this policy as xenophobia or racial discrimination. Japanese settlers believed their contribution to Brazilian society was substantial and that the government really favored Japanese settlers. Also, they believed the Vargas government could not afford to destroy the Japanese interior farming communities, which provided much sustenance for the nation. Unlike North America, there was little competition between Japanese settlers and other ethnic groups in Brazil. If the Japanese had not farmed, the state of São Paulo would have lost almost one-fifth of its agricultural production, and in the case of cotton and potatoes it would have lost more than half. Some of these contributions are seen in Table 2.1 (Makabe, 1999, p. 707).

Until 1960, Japanese-Brazilians had kept to themselves and preferred not to live in urban areas. In such isolated farming communities, these Japanese transnational migrants ran their lives much as if they were back in Japan. They built Japanese schools, pharmacies, rice-cleaning mills, lumber mills, oil refineries, ice plants, and silk factories to send silk to Japan (Imin Hachijyû-nen-shi Hensan Iinkai, 1991, pp. 96–98). And they spoke only Japanese both day and night.

Although Japanese-Brazilians did not really participate in the traditional *parentela* system of the local elites, Japanese settlers united themselves

Table 2.1
Agricultural Products of Brazil

Crop	Total Output (in 1939 US$)	Japanese Output (in 1939 US$)	Percentage of Total Crops Produced
Potatoes	2,280,000	1,282,500	56.5
Cotton	55,511,302	24,015,193	43.3
Rice	122,265,000	1,330,000	10.9
Corn	131,670,000	665,000	5.1
Coffee	54,647,895	2,660,000	4.9
Others	20,745,198	1,527,838	9.8

Source: Makabe (1999), p. 707.

through agricultural cooperatives and their own "*parentela*" system based on ethnicity and geography. In their communities, Japanese-Brazilians controlled even their own local politics and elected their own mayors from among their own in-groups. In mainstream Brazil the *coronelimo* politics gave way to the populism movement as a way to place values ahead of connections in politics. Joining the populism movements, Japanese-Brazilians started to enter Brazilian politics outside their villages. In 1968, there were 6 Japanese-Brazilian mayors, 3 vice-mayors, and 19 city councilmen. In the following election year, 1972, this increased to 13 mayors, 14 vice-mayors, and 137 city councilmen.

Social Dimensions

Some descendants of immigrants who arrived around the turn of the twentieth century as plantation laborers are now well established in the middle class. Some of these new middle class members have "married up" and entered the upper classes (Wagley, 1971, pp. 117–121). Being in both the middle class and upper class, these new upper class people enjoy the benefits of both the old *coronelimo* system and the more egalitarian *populismo* movement. For instance, three descendants of immigrants have been President of Brazil: (1) Juscelino Kubitschek, the grandson of a Czechoslovakian immigrant, in 1956; (2) Emílio Médici, a descendant of Italian immigrants, in 1971; and (3) Ernest Geisel, a descendant of German immigrants, in 1974. It is important to note, however, that regardless of the sociopolitical mobility of the descendants of European immigrants, Japanese-Brazilians have not been able to marry up, join the high society of Brazilian elites, or hold national political leadership. This is all the more remarkable considering that Brazil is thought by some to be a society free of racial discrimination.[5]

By the 1970s Japanese-Brazilians had improved their socioeconomic conditions remarkably, and some left their communities to receive a higher education in mainstream Brazilian society. In 1982 about 13 percent of students at the Universidade de São Paulo, one of the most prestigious universities in Brazil, were Japanese-Brazilians (Imin Hachijyû-nen-shi Hensan Iinkai, 1991, p. 265), and by 1988 it became 16 percent (Page, 1995, p. 105). In the 1960s many Japanese-Brazilians majored in the subjects that would prepare them for occupations that elites had traditionally taken themselves, such as medicine, pharmacy, and accounting. However, by the 1970s Japanese-Brazilians started to choose less immediately practical subjects, such as astronomy, anthropology, biochemistry, and meteorology (Imin Hiachijyû-nen-shi Hensan Iinkai, 1991, p. 265).

Around this period, foreign enterprises started investing in Brazil, and well-paying, white-collar positions opened up to educated people. Investments by Japan's corporations were some of the largest in Brazil (along with those of the United States and West Germany). For instance, the number of Japanese foreign enterprises in Brazil was 41 in the 1950s, 50 in the 1960s, and 362 in the 1970s (Kinshichi et al., 2000, p. 234). The annual Japanese investment was $1.2 billion in 1971, $1.6 billion in 1972, and $4.35 billion in 1973. Investments dropped in 1974 to $2.5 billion (Kinshichi et al., 2000, p. 234) due in part to the world oil crisis in 1973 and 1974, which hurt Japanese foreign investment and affected Brazil deeply.

Many Japanese corporations hired Japanese-Brazilians in order to form links to Brazil. However, working with Japanese in Japan made Brazilian-educated, urban Japanese-Brazilians aware of the large gap between themselves and the Japanese from Japan, making Japanese-Brazilians feel like mere *nikkeijin* (people overseas who's ancestors originally came from Japan) rather than *nihonjin* (literally, Japanese persons). Technology has contributed to this new ethnic identity; airplanes have shortened the two months it used to take by ship to about a day. The fares are now substantially less. Cheap transportation costs have also flooded Brazilian markets with many Japanese goods, no doubt eliminating Japanese-Brazilian feelings of loss for items from their home country or parents' country.

Economic Dimensions

Since the mid-1980s Japanese-Brazilians, in contrast to Japanese nationals, have returned to Japan because of Brazilian economic problems. Brazil has been suffering high inflation and a number of economic setbacks for the last twenty years. For instance, in 1987 Brazilian inflation stood at 366 percent, in 1988 at 933.6 percent, and in 1989 it reached a disastrous 1,764.9 percent (Komai, 1995, p. 201). This was all while Japan's economy was in full swing—the height of the so-called Japanese miracle. The average monthly salary in Japan was five to ten times the best Brazilian wages, even for an

Table 2.2
Number of Japanese Immigrants to Brazil, 1988–1996

1988	1989	1990	1991	1992	1993	1994	1995	1996
4,159	14,528	56,429	119,333	147,803	154,650	159,619	176,000	201,795

Source: Tsuda (1999), p. 690.

unskilled factory worker. The average returnee Japanese-Brazilian worker can save an average of about $20,000 per year in Japan, which is approximately four to five times the average yearly income in Brazil (Tsuda, 1999, p. 693).

At first, Japanese-Brazilians worked in Japan hoping to make enough money to expand their farm fields or rebuild their houses for their children in Brazil. Many Brazilian nationals, including urban professional Japanese-Brazilians who barely understood the Japanese language, followed their parents and grandparents to Japan. These urban professionals had even better reasons for wanting to go to Japan than their older relatives. Urban Brazilians felt more of the economic burden than farming people, since inflation more directly affects people who depend on monthly salaries than those who depend on trade or home-grown everyday farm products. These temporal workers are called *dekasegi* in Japan and *dekassegui* in Brazil. Table 2.2 shows the increasing numbers of migration of Japanese-Brazilians to Japan from 1988 to 1996.

Consideration of the Dekasegi/Dekassegui Phenomenon. This transnational migration of *dekasegi/dekassegui* workers is creating several sociopolitical issues at the local and global levels. First, their *dekasegi/dekassegui* experiences have made many Japanese-Brazilians better appreciate Brazilian culture and society. Japanese-Brazilians, especially those who remained in the farming areas, believed themselves to be very "Japanese," largely keeping their ancestors' culture, including the Japanese language. Urban Japanese-Brazilians, who are highly educated and have achieved a high degree of socioeconomic status in Brazil, have obtained a large measure of professional and social respectability in their home country. The Japanese in Japan, however, see these Japanese-Brazilians as poorly educated foreigners from some underprivileged country. Their lack of linguistic ability or different speech styles make them appear childlike in the eyes of the elite-minded and status conscious Japanese (Nakane, 1970), who only see a Japanese face speaking a poor approximation of a mutual language. Also, institutions in Japan usually do not accept educational credits or diplomas from schools in what they consider to be developing countries.

Feeling discriminated against by the Japanese in Japan, these *dekasegi/dekassegui* Japanese-Brazilian workers feel a great social distance while working in the country (Adachi, 1999). For instance, neither group of people (Japanese-Japanese or Japanese-Brazilian) go out drinking together after work, a common custom for coworkers in Japan. In Japan, after-work drinking entertainment is seen as an important social activity—a time to get to know one another away from the stress and hierarchy of the office or the factory floor, or a time to negotiate business or work issues in a relaxed atmosphere. However, being in a "foreign" country to save money, Japanese-Brazilians do not prefer to spend their savings on socializing with people who look down on them anyway. Instead, they work overtime to earn extra money. This "work ethic" reinforces the social distance with the Japanese. As a result, Japanese-Brazilians identify themselves in Japan not as *nihonjin* (as they do in Brazil), or *nikkeijin* (as they are labeled in Japan), but as "Brazilian."

Unfortunately, the *dekasegi/dekassegui* experience does not always accomplish what is intended. Returning to Brazil after their work permits have expired (usually after two years), *dekasegi/dekassegui* workers often stay in urban areas instead of returning to the farm, even if they were farmers in the first place. Urban Japanese-Brazilians also do not return to the original jobs they had before they went to Japan. Moreover, many of these people do not get jobs at all upon their return to Brazil, but instead live on their savings made in Japan. After they use their savings up, they might go back to Japan to work for another two years. Some Japanese-Brazilians who were interviewed in Brazil in 1993 felt it was silly to work in Brazil for a month just to receive one day's salary in Japan. They said they would rather take a rest in Brazil and go back to work in Japan (author's notes, 1993). As a result, some firms whose managing positions used to be occupied by Japanese-Brazilians have filled these positions with non-Japanese-Brazilians. The *dekasegi/dekassegui* workers have even spread out to the United States. Seeing and hearing about problems in Japan, some Japanese-Brazilians have become disenchanted with Japan and instead have turned to the United States, a nation with a strong economy and a population consisting largely of immigrants.

THE FUTURE

The international immigrants of the nineteenth and twentieth centuries have played important roles in reforming modern Brazilian society. However, because of a long series of economic setbacks and one of the worst inflation rates in history, the most dynamic social class in Brazil—the middle class—has been losing its most vigorous people, educated Japanese-Brazilian professionals. These people are often found wandering the world.

Social discrimination toward an unfamiliar people by locals is a common practice everywhere. Because the world is now a smaller place, transmigration is easy, and Japanese-Brazilians are forming different ethnic relationships and creating new self-identities.

NOTES

1. In 1890, after abolition was completed in Brazil, the governments burned all written documents on slavery. Thus, today it is very hard to find out exactly how many slaves were actually imported from Africa to Brazil.

2. The average life expectancy of male slaves was even lower, about 18 years (Kinshichi et al., 2000, p. 84).

3. Among Rio de Janeiro and São Paulo newspapers in 1934 and 1935, 13 newspapers were in favor of Japanese entry, 7 were actively opposed, and 6 took no discernible position (Lesser, 1999).

4. Handa was one of these people, having immigrated to a coffee plantation in São Paulo with his parents when he was 11 years old.

5. It has been said by influential scholars, including prominent anthropologists like Marvin Harris and Kottak and Hiroshi Saito (a Japanese-Brazilian), that Brazil has no racial discrimination. However, recently many scholars, such as Thomas Skidmore (1992), Pierre-Michel Fontaine (1981), and France Twine (1998), are challenging the theory of racial democracy in Brazil.

BIBLIOGRAPHY

Adachi, N. (1999). Japanese Voices in the Brazilian Forest: Cultural Maintenance and Reformed Ethnic Identity in a Transplanted Community. *World Communication, 28*(2), 68–82.

Benjamin, M., & Mendonça, M. (1997). *Benedita da Silva: An Afro-Brazilian Woman's Story of Politics and Love*. Oakland, CA: Food First Books.

Bethell, L. (Ed.). (1993). *Brazil: Empire and Republic, 1822–1930*. New York: Cambridge University Press.

De Queirós Mattoso, K. M. (1996). *To Be a Slave in Brazil 1550–1888*. New Brunswick, NJ: Rutgers University Press.

Europa World Yearbook. (2000). *The Europa World Yearbook 2000*. Vol. 1. London: Europa Publications.

Fontaine, P. (1981). Transnational Relations and Racial Mobilization: Emerging Black Movements in Brazil. In J. F. Stack, Jr. (Ed.), *Ethnic Identity in a Transnational World* (pp. 141–162). Westport, CT: Greenwood Press.

Handa, T. (1970). *Imin no Seikatsu to Rekishi: Burajiru Nikkei-jin no Ayunda Michi*. São Paulo: Centro de Estudos Nipo-Brasileiros.

———. (1987). *Imigrante Japones: Historia de sua vida no Brasil*. São Paulo: Centro de Estudos Nipo-Brasileiros.

Harris, M. (1964). *Patterns of Race in the Americas*. New York: W.W. Norton & Company.

Harris, M., & Kottak, C. (1963). The Structural Significance of Brazilian Racial Categories. *Sociologia, 25*, 203–209.

Holloway, T. H. (1978). Creating the Reserve Army? The Immigration Program of São Paulo, 1886–1930. *International Migration Review, 12*(2), 187–209.

Imin Hachijyû-nen-shi Hensan Iinkai. (1991). *Burajilu Nihon Imin-shi 80-nen-shi* [The History of 80 Years of Japanese Immigration in Brazil]. São Paulo: Burajiru Nippon Bunka Kyôkai.

Ishikawa Tomonori. (1975). Setonai Chiiki kara no (Shutsu) Imin. [Emigration from the Setonai Region]. *Shigaku Kenkyu*, *126*, 54–71.

Kinshichi, N., Sumida, Ikuo, Takahashi, Kunihiko, & Tomino, Mikio. (2000). *Burajiru Kenkyû Nyûmon: Shirarezaru Taikoku 500-nen no Kisek i* [Introduction to Brazilian Studies: 500 Years of Paths to an Unknown Huge Nation]. Tokyo: Shôyô-Shobô.

Komai, H. (1995). *Migrant Workers in Japan* (J. Wilkinson, Trans). London and New York: Kegan Paul International.

Lesser, J. (1995). *Welcoming the Undesirables: Brazil and the Jewish Question*. Berkeley, Los Angeles, and London: University of California Press.

———. (1999). *Negotiating National Identity: Immigrants, Minorities, and the Struggle for Ethnicity in Brazil*. Durham, NC and London: Duke University Press.

Love, J. J., & Barickman, B. J. (1991). Regional Elites. In M. L. Conniff & F. D. McCann (Eds.), *Modern Brazil: Elites and Masses in Historical Perspective* (pp. 3–22). Lincoln and London: University of Nebraska Press.

Makabe, T. (1999). Ethnic Hegemony: The Japanese Brazilians in Agriculture, 1908–1996. *Ethnic and Racial Studies*, *22*(4), 702–723.

Nakane, C. (1970). *Japanese Society*. Berkeley, Los Angeles, and London: University of California Press.

Ohara, Y. (1972). *Burajiru Keizai to Tôshi-Kankyô* [The Brazilian Economy and Its Investment Environment]. Tokyo: Ajia Keizai Kenkyûjo.

Page, J. (1995). *The Brazilians*. Reading, MA: Addison-Wesley Publishing Company.

Saito, H. (1976). *Burajiru no Seiji* [Brazilian Politics]. Tokyo: The Simul Press.

Skidmore, T. (1992). *Fact and Myth: Discovering a Racial Problem in Brazil* (Working Paper No. 173). The Helen Kellogg Institute for International Studies. Notre Dame, IN: University of Notre Dame.

Smith, L. (1974). The Assimilation and Acculturation of Japanese Immigrants. In T. Lynn Smith (Ed.), *Brazilian Society* (pp. 153–179). New York: Scott, Foresman.

Tsuda, T. (1999). The Permanence of "Temporary" Migration: The "Structural Embeddedness" of Japanese-Brazilian Immigrant Workers in Japan. *The Journal of Asian Studies*, *58*(3), 687–722.

Twine, F. W. (1998). *Racism in a Racial Democracy: The Maintenance of White Supremacy in Brazil*. New Brunswick, NJ, and London: Rutgers University Press.

Wagley, C. (1971). *An Introduction to Brazil* (2nd ed.). New York: Columbia University Press.

3

CHINA

Chinese Immigrants in the Global Economy

Yu Zhou

INTRODUCTION

Profile of China

China is the world's largest country with 1.3 billion people, one-fifth of the world's population. It is also one of the oldest civilizations. Since ancient times, China has been regarded as a predominantly agrarian society. Its marked traditions are often associated with land-bound agrarian values, stressing the importance of family and loyalty to villages and homeland. According to Confucianism this has been China's guiding philosophy for some 2,000 years—a person should not travel very far from home when his or her parents are still alive so that he or she is ready to serve them in their old age. Westerners since Marco Polo's time saw China as a rich but isolated oriental empire, unlike European kingdoms that were busy in adventure, exploration, and overseas trade.

Despite the perception of China as internal-oriented, China, as one of the world's largest economic centers, was not only a key player in overseas commerce prior to Europeans in the age of discovery, but it has also had a long tradition of overseas emigration. The emigration trend has accelerated since the fifteenth century, in part because of increasing international commercial trade at the time, but also because of western colonization, which brought Chinese as indentured labor to southeast Asia, Pacific islands (Hawaii included), and Central and South Americas. Many Chinese also went on their own to North America and Europe. Chinese arrived in the continental United States as early as the 1850s. Most of them came from the southeast coast of China, today's Guangdong and Fujian provinces. One can track the prevailing languages spoken in the older overseas Chinese communities all over the world back to a handful of local dialects spoken in these two provinces. Cantonese, the main language spoken in North America Chinatowns, for example, is the major language spoken in Guangdong province and Hong Kong.

Today, approximately 50 million Chinese and their descendents live outside mainland China (Redding, 1990; Yeung, 2000). About 80 percent live in Southeast Asia, including 22 million in Taiwan and 6 million in Hong Kong. Chinese are a significant minority population in Malaysia, Indonesia, Thailand, and Vietnam, and they are the majority in Singapore. In addition, in many of the world's largest cities you can find old or contemporary Chinese settlements, including ones in faraway places such as Johannesburg, South Africa; Havana, Cuba; and Sydney, Australia.

China today is the world's largest developing country. The average income of Chinese is very low by the American standard—US$840 GNP per capita in 2000 (World Bank, 2002). After adjusting to price differences, however, the real GNP per capita of China measured by purchasing power parity is $3,600. The Chinese population is among the better educated in the developing world, with an 80 percent literacy rate. China has also been the fastest growing country in the world during the last twenty years; its total output has quadrupled since 1978 (*CIA World Factbook: China*, 2002). As a result of the economic growth in the last two decades, many of China's coastal urban areas have become relatively wealthy with a rapidly growing middle-class population, although the country's vast central western interior remains very poor. Rising global awareness and income growth have provided both the incentives and resources for many Chinese to desire a better life abroad, leading to a sharp increase in emigration. Yet, language and other cultural barriers present major challenges for the new Chinese immigrants, underlying many of the difficulties they experience in the United States and elsewhere in the world.

Vignettes

Ms. Zhang came to the United States in the early 1990s from a rural area in Fujian province, southeastern China, which since the late 1980s has seen the most active human smuggling operations in China, if not the world. She and her husband both came to the United States illegally and therefore had to pay back a considerable debt. Neither of them had a good education in China or spoke much English. They worked long hours for little pay in separate Chinese restaurants in the area. When she had her first child, Ms. Zhang did not have the option to stop working because her husband's income could not support the entire family, not to mention paying back debts. Just as many other poor Chinese immigrant mothers in the same situation as her, she decided to send her two-month-old baby away to China to be raised by her family. She expected her child to come back when he was old enough to enter public school; meanwhile she and her husband would work hard to accumulate enough money for her son's return.

In contrast to Ms. Zhang, there are other better-educated Chinese professionals or entrepreneurs who have become very successful and integrated into the social fabric of middle class or even wealthy America. Some have made major contributions to the social and economic life of America. Ang Lee, the famous Chinese American film director, is a good example.

Ang Lee directed several Oscar-winning films, including wildly successful ones like *Crouching Tiger, Hidden Dragon* and *Sense and Sensibility*. He was born in Taiwan in 1954 and came to the United States in the middle 1970s after he finished his college education. He was among a large number of Chinese students from Taiwan in the 1970s who pursued an advanced education in the United States. Even larger numbers of students have come from mainland China since 1980. Ang Lee received his master's degree in film from New York University in 1983. Lee's early films gained success in Taiwan at first but won critical international fame as Oscar-nominated foreign language films, and he was later recruited to direct a film version of Jane Austen's novel *Sense and Sensibility*, which won several prestigious Oscar awards. The film *Crouching Tiger, Hidden Dragon* not only won the Oscar in 2001 for best foreign language film, but it also set the box office record for a foreign language film in the U.S. market. One cannot help but note that the success of Ang Lee's career owes as much to Hollywood as to his connection with his homeland. With his fame in the high-profile film industry, Ang Lee is, perhaps, the most well-known Chinese American, but there are many Chinese American professionals like him who have had major achievements in their professional careers in the United States. These include top executives, doctors, researchers, and engineers. Some of them have thrived upon the multiple linkages they have cultivated between the United States and China.

Overview of Migration Issues

It is impossible to detail Chinese migration all over the world during the last 500 years; instead, the experiences of contemporary Chinese immigrants to the United States will be the focus. Chinese immigration to the United States has a long history. A large number of Chinese first arrived in the United States around the 1850s and peaked around 1880. However, their numbers were sharply limited and reduced by the Chinese Exclusion Act passed by the U.S. Congress in 1882, the first U.S. federal immigrant law excluding a population solely because of race. In 1965 immigration reform in the United States changed racially biased quota systems, and the Chinese population in the United States has increased rapidly since then, first with immigrants from Hong Kong and Taiwan. In 1978, the Chinese government adopted an open-door policy, allowing its citizens to travel abroad for study, family, and business purposes, and now a growing share of Chinese immigrants comes from mainland China.

The chapter will launch from two contrasting immigrant stories. As shown in the stories above, contemporary Chinese immigrants to the United States are polarized between low-skilled, little-educated immigrants who work in the lowest wage jobs in inner city areas and highly educated professionals or entrepreneurs in the prestigious institutions and corporations of America. The demographics of contemporary Chinese immigrants will be examined. An overview of the prominent historical and current issues Chinese immigrants face in the political, social, and economic dimensions of the United States will be provided. In particular, the impact of globalization on diverse Chinese populations will be highlighted through a close look at two cases: Chinese involvement in the garment industry in New York City and Chinese transnational migrants in high-tech sectors of Los Angeles.

According to the U.S. population census of 2000, there are 2,432,585 Chinese in the United States, a 47 percent increase from 1990. If we take into account that some ethnic Chinese identify themselves as Taiwanese or Vietnamese, it will be likely that the Chinese comprise just about 1 percent of the entire U.S. population. Chinese population concentrates on the coastal areas; 40 percent make California their home. Some major Chinese settlements in the United States are over 100 years old, such as the Chinatowns in New York and San Francisco, but others are brand new, having emerged since the 1980s, such as Monterey Park in Los Angeles, San Jose in northern California, and Flushing in Queens, New York.

Post-1965 Chinese immigrants to the United States differ significantly from their earlier counterparts in both their places of origin and their social characteristics. The first wave of immigrants was a homogenous group of male laborers with little or no education who came from rural regions in Guangdong province and spoke Cantonese. They viewed America as a temporary residence to make money so that they could eventually go back to China. Contemporary Chinese immigrants are far more heterogeneous. Take the Los Angeles metropolitan area, for example, which hosts one of the largest Chinese communities in the United States: the Chinese population is predominantly foreign born, with immigrants making up over three-quarters of the population by 1990 (Zhou, 1998). Among the immigrants, people originating from China, Taiwan, and Hong Kong together accounted for 70.7 percent of the total foreign-born in 1990. Chinese from Vietnam accounted for another 11.7 percent (U.S. Census Bureau, public use micro-data sample, 1990). Although linguistically diverse, this group is far more likely than the first wave of Chinese immigrants to speak Mandarin (the official language for both China and Taiwan) as well as local dialects. They tend to settle permanently in the United States and have usually brought their families with them.

It would be tempting to find among these newcomers the classic American tales of immigrants struggling to attain their American dream through hard work. These stories are indeed playing out on a daily basis in immigrant communities by people such as Ms. Zhang, mentioned earlier. But one also has to recognize that today's immigrants are living in a very different world from the European immigrants who came to the United States in the eighteenth or nineteenth century. Most profoundly, globalization has led to major changes in urban economies across America. New immigrants who do the labor work now have to compete with low-wage labor in third world countries from which the immigrants often came. The competition generates great pressure for even lower wages and poorer working conditions compared to what immigrants experienced at the turn of the twentieth century.

On the other hand, globalization has brought an increasing share of Chinese immigrants to the United States from better-educated and sometimes wealthy backgrounds. These immigrants become professionals and entrepreneurs in their adopted country and settle in prosperous suburbs without first stopping at inner city ethnic enclaves. Largely facilitated by communication and transportation technology, these middle class immigrants thrive on the multiple linkages they have maintained or cultivated with both home and host countries.

HISTORY OF MIGRATION ISSUES

Chinese Americans have a long history in the United States—a history characterized by discrimination, exclusion, violence, and isolation in the early period. The earliest wave of Chinese immigrants to California was comprised of gold miners and railway construction workers, lured by the promise of gold fortunes and the labor shortages in America and pushed by the poverty of rural southern China. Unlike other immigrant groups from Europe, the earlier Chinese migrants were largely male sojourners hoping to make enough money to eventually return home to marry and have children. In the late nineteenth century, Chinese immigrants comprised about 10 percent of the entire California population (Chinese comprised 2.9% of the population in California in 2000) (U.S. Census Bureau, 2000). The flow of Chinese immigrants to the United States was reduced to a trickle, however, after the Chinese Exclusion Act passed in the U.S. Congress in 1882. This act limited new Chinese immigration to students and merchants and severely restricted Chinese women from coming. As a result, Chinese population in the United States remained small and predominately male until the 1960s. To escape violence, discrimination, and hardship, many Chinese returned to China. The Chinese population in the United States decreased from 105,465 in 1880 to 85,202 in 1920. The remaining Chinese population redistributed itself, consolidating the originally scattered settlements into a few concentrated enclaves in San Francisco, New York, and Los Angeles. During these

years of exclusion, many cities in California also banned Chinese from land
ownership, public education, and professional occupations. Chinatowns became the sole living places for the Chinese and the only safe havens for them
to escape from the larger society. Chinese mostly found jobs or set up businesses that whites disdained, in restaurants, laundries, and domestic services.
It was during this period that Chinatowns gradually assumed their distinct
cultural profile: closely knit bachelor societies governed by traditional Chinese hierarchical systems and secret organizations, and completely alienated
from American society. This separate social structure reinforced the isolation
of the Chinese communities (Tsai, 1986; Yuan, 1988; Zhou, 1992).

The situation did not change much until World War II, when China and
the United States became allies to fight Japanese aggression. This led to the
repeal of the Chinese Exclusion Act in 1942. Despite the repeal, the Chinese
community in the United States remained small because immigration from
China was subjected to a biased quota that allowed in only 104 Chinese
immigrants annually. The second wave of Chinese immigrants reached the
shores of the United States after World War II. In 1949, the defeat of the
American-supported nationalist government by the Communist Party in
mainland China prompted a large number of Chinese to flee to the United
States. About 30,000 students and merchants were trapped in the United
States because of the changing governments and they were subsequently
allowed to adjust to permanent residency (Tsai, 1986). Much of the nationalist elite also escaped from China to the United States.

The real turning point for Chinese immigration came in 1965 when the
U.S. Congress abolished the national origin immigration quota that had
favored European countries. Since then, the number of immigrants from
Asia has grown sharply. During the 1960s, 102,649 Chinese immigrants
were admitted to the United States. This number increased to 261,151 in
the 1970s and 444,962 in the 1980s (U.S. Department of Justice, 1991,
1996). Unlike the first immigration waves, the new immigrants tended to
be permanent residents and brought their families with them. Since 1970,
the long-skewed gender ratio in Chinese communities of the United States
has become almost balanced (Tsai, 1986; Zhou, 1992).

It can be seen that historically the main problems Chinese suffered had to
do with the restriction of U.S. immigration policies and their consequent
isolation from the mainstream society. Chinese immigrants were welcome at
one time as needed labor but not accepted as full-fledged citizens with rights
of participation in mainstream society. Various social ills, such as gangs and
prostitution, associated with old Chinatowns are symptoms of such exclusion. With the rise of a more professional Chinese population and the coming of age of American-born Chinese, politically conscious activism and
participation have grown in Chinese communities. With the Civil Rights
movement in the 1960s, once-isolated Chinatowns and new Chinese com-

munities became increasingly integrated within the larger society (Kwong, 1996).

DIMENSIONS OF MIGRATION ISSUES

Political Dimensions

If historically the racist politics directed against Chinese were blatant, the political reality today is very different. The outright racial discrimination has largely been reduced, and Chinese Americans have become an integral part of many dimensions of American life. Yet, the sense that Asians are "inassimilable others" or "permanent aliens" lingers in America, shown by such examples of Japanese internment during World War II (Okihiro, 1994) and recent allegations of Chinese espionage. For Chinese Americans, their heritage and continued ties with the homeland often become the subject of suspicion. From time to time, xenophobic attitudes and the paranoia of some politicians can lead to periodical assaults on Chinese Americans.

The best examples occurred in the late 1990s, when several political scandals broke out involving unfounded allegations of Chinese Americans being spies for China. Both allegations were sensationalized by the national mass media and cast a long, suspicious shadow over many Chinese Americans. Yet, both cases were not substantiated and were eventually thrown out of the courts. One case involved John Huang, a Los Angeles Chinese American banker who also worked for the Clinton administration. He was identified along with a few other Chinese Americans as a central figure in a financial scandal of illegal political contributions from abroad during the Clinton-Gore 1996 presidential campaign. Despite a lack of evidence, mainstream media freely speculated about them as agents for the Chinese government aimed at influencing American policies (Foer, 2001; Lawler, 2000; Wang, 1998). Similarly, in 1999 Taiwan-born nuclear physicist Wen Ho Lee was named as the chief suspect in an investigation of a potential leak of nuclear secrets from the U.S. weapons program at Los Alamos National Laboratory. In both cases, the suspects were not born in China, nor did they ever live for a period in China. Yet zealous politicians and mass media had no trouble labeling them as Chinese agents based on their overseas Chinese heritage and past trips to Southeast Asia and China. After prolonged investigations, however, both cases evaporated into highly embarrassing outcomes for the government. The careless racial profiling and rising hostilities during this time alerted Chinese Americans of the potential impact of racism in America. An article in the *New Republic* illustrated a new sense of urgency for political activism in Chinese American communities: "The Committee of 100, a prestigious Chinese-American fraternal club that had never expressed much interest in domestic politics, suddenly sounded like the campus radicals. Henry S. Tang, the group's chairman, told the *Los Angeles Times*: 'No matter how accomplished, no matter how educated, no matter how wealthy, no matter how loyal, [an Asian American] could still become suspected of activities counter to the interests of this country' " (Foer, 2001, pp. 16–17).

These events became the rallying point for the larger Chinese American population to become more active in political participation, both in terms of voting and in seeking political representation. With more and more second-generation Asian Americans coming of age, one can expect that Asian Americans will become increasingly active in the American political scene (Foer, 2001; Marshall, 2000).

Social Dimensions

The social dimension of Chinese immigrant experiences is a complex subject, primarily because of the diversity of the population. Despite the two contrasting narratives of Ms. Zhang and Ang Lee, which mark the two extremes on the wide spectrum of Chinese immigrants, Chinese population tends to be homogenized in the mind of mainstream America. Chinese Americans, as part of Asian Americans, are often labeled the "model minority" by mainstream America because they have shown in several consecutive census since 1970 to have the highest median family income among five racial groups[1] in America. In addition, their education achievements are well known; a much higher proportion of Asian American youth go to college than non-Hispanic whites. In 1997, 42 percent of Asian Americans ages 25 or older had a college or professional degree, compared with 26 percent of non-Hispanic whites, 13 percent of blacks, and 10 percent of Hispanics ages 25 or older (Lee, 1998). In the nation's most prestigious colleges and universities, Asians are highly visible. The social, economic, and educational achievements of Asian Americans are certainly commendable, but one has to be rather careful not to draw sweeping generalizations based on these statistics.

There are several reasons why Asian Americans have a slightly higher median family income. First of all, their family sizes are larger than non-Hispanic white families because Asians are more likely to have several generations living in the same household, and there is less prevalence of single-parent households. As a result, although Asian Americans have a higher household income than non-Hispanic whites, their per capita income is lower than comparably educated whites, indicating that they continue to suffer from disadvantages and discrimination (Lee, 1998). The second reason for a higher household income is that Asians tend to live disproportionately in larger cities in the coastal areas. These tend to be locales with higher costs of living and salaries than smaller cities, rural areas, and places in the midwest.

In educational attainment, Chinese have benefited from the selected immigration process, Chinese cultural heritage, and a strong motivation for success typical of immigrant families. American immigration policies provide preference for those with higher education and desirable job skills, leading to a better-educated foreign-born population to begin with (Lee, 1998). In addition, Chinese culture has historically attached high value to academic education. In China, since the Tang dynasty (A.D. 618–907), education and passing imperial administrated exams were the only ways for boys from ordinary or poor families to move up the social ladder. Many Chinese immigrants internalized these values to pursue a better education for their children. Lastly, most Chinese immigrants, suffering from their own limitations due to language barriers, place their best hope of upward mobility on the education of their children. Parents thus impose greater pressures for school performance. At the same time, however, many Chinese American children also suffer from language problems and a lack of parental guidance because their parents do not speak English or they are too busy to help with school work. As a result, despite stereotypes, Chinese Americans still experience educational failure (Lee, 1998). Overall, one needs to realize that the Chinese population, as other Asian populations, is a very diverse group. While some members enjoy a high level of success, there are many others who continue to be plagued by poverty, social isolation, and powerlessness. "Model minority" as a label, on the one hand, is based on undeniable achievements by Asian Americans, yet on the other hand, it obscures the polarized reality within and among many different Asian groups and it disguises the discrimination this population continues to suffer.

In the following section, the diversity among the Chinese population will be examined in greater detail by moving through two case studies conducted in the 1990s in the two largest U.S. metropolitan areas. The first case study focuses on working class Chinese in the garment industry of New York City. The second one emphasizes the transnational practices of middle class Chinese Americans in Los Angeles. The discussion will be limited mostly to the economic dimension, but it also has great social implications.

Economic Dimensions

Case One: Garment Industry in New York. New York City, the fashion center of North America, hosts a large concentration of immigrant entrepreneurs and workers in the garment industry. The birth, growth, and decline of New York's garment industry are intimately intertwined with the fortune and miseries of immigrants. It was Eastern European Jews and Italian immigrants who created the ready-made garment industry in New York at the turn of the twentieth century. Since the 1960s, newer immigrant groups, particularly Chinese and Hispanics, have again changed the face of the industry (Green, 1997).

The structure of New York's garment industry over the past 150 years has evolved into a sophisticated network of specialization characterized by a two-tiered system. The upper tier, represented mostly by manufacturers, jobbers, and retailers,[2] requires high education; financing capacity; design, marketing, and management skills; and extensive industrial connections. It is dominated by established native-born capitalists, many of whom are descendants of Jewish and Italian immigrants. Newer immigrants, by contrast, are severely limited by their poor English skills and educational background to contend for activities in the upper tier. Instead, they tend to be concentrated in the lower tier, represented by contractors, subcontractors, and small manufacturers of various sorts. If trendy designs, professional management, and lucrative pay characterize the upper tier, fierce price competition, acute time pressure, and sweatshop conditions characterize the lower tier (Zhou, 2001).

Immigrants move into the garment industry for good reasons. The sewing jobs require little language proficiency. The skill is something many immigrant women already have from their home countries or can learn rather quickly through on-the-job experience. The work also offers flexible, although long, hours that are desirable for women with young children. Working in garment factories gives immigrants the experience and inside knowledge of the sector. Some of the more successful ones later become entrepreneurs in this sector. Becoming contractors involves low entry costs. Once some immigrants get started in this industry, others are introduced into the trade through informal ethnic networks (Bailey & Waldinger, 1991).

Since the 1960s, Chinese involvement in the garment industry has grown at a rapid pace. In the 1960s the previous generation of Jewish contractors either died out or moved to different industries, leaving enough vacancies to be taken over by new immigrants, of which the Chinese were the most visible group. The influx of unskilled immigrants from mainland China since the late 1970s filled the industry with inexpensive and disciplined labor. Many immigrants, after working in the industry for some time, used their savings to become self-employed, which turned Chinatown into the largest concentration of garment shops in New York City. Many shops owned by the Chinese also sprang up in midtown Manhattan, Queens, and Brooklyn.

However, Chinese immigrants joined New York's garment industry at a time of intensifying international competition. Offshore producers, with labor costs that are a fraction of American labor, are increasingly capable of producing sophisticated fashion-oriented clothing in a shorter time and at a lower cost. The direct competition with low wage countries in the third world has forced New York garment makers to focus even more on the higher-value-added products, striving for shorter lead time, more styles, higher quality, and better services in an environment of the accelerated life cycle of fashion products.

These changes translate into the growing power of the upper tier, particularly that of retailers and manufacturers. They are able to exert downward price pressure and to increasingly shorten time to immigrant-owned contractors and subcontractors (Appelbaum & Gereffi, 1994). This happens at the same time more and more immigrants crowd into this industry. An oversupply of contractors inevitably intensifies the competition and generates a downward price spiral. Pitting one contractor against the other, the retailers, manufacturers, and jobbers depress the piece rate and reduce their responsibilities, but they ensure a bigger labor pool and lower risk. This competition has been seen as the primary cause of poor working conditions and the rising rate of sweatshop conditions in garment factories (Bonacich, 1994; Buford, 1999; Zhou, 2001). The razor-thin profit also causes high failure rates among immigrant-run garment factories, which discourages capital investments for technology and personnel training, and thus generates a vicious cycle that prevents contractors from advancing their businesses and reforming sweatshop conditions.

According to the estimate of the director of the Chinese Contractors Association, 30 to 40 percent of Chinese-owned firms cannot survive the first year of operation. Up until the mid-1990s, a vast majority of Chinese garment factories were unionized, but as intensified competition made conditions worse, more and more nonunionized shops opened in New York's outer boroughs, and unionized firms become a minority among Chinese-owned factories.

The downward price pressure on the contractors is inevitably transferred to garment workers who already have meager wages. Even more problematic is that in order to meet more stringent deadlines, more work is subcontracted down the chain, so the payment delay is extended to the workers at the bottom of the chain, leading to serious back wage problems (Buford, 1999; Zhou, 2001). According to the U.S. Department of Labor, which conducted 262 labor investigations in 1998, 111 violations of the Fair Labor Standards Act were found, a total of $800,000 in back wages were collected, and $124,715 in civil fines were issued in New York City alone. A U.S. Labor Department report issued on October 1999 showed that only 35 percent of New York garment shops surveyed were in compliance with federal minimum wage and overtime laws (Bowles, 2000).

The sweatshop phenomenon is also perpetuated by the influx of illegal immigrants. The surge of illegal Chinese immigrants from Fujian province since the late 1980s as part of human smuggling operations has brought a large number of Fujianese into New York City's Chinatown. Desperate for jobs to pay off the debt they incurred in the journey, the illegal Fujianese have greatly depressed the wages of garment workers in Chinatown (Kwong, 1996, 1997).

Most Chinese workers in the garment industry are women. The garment worker's union, Union of Needletrades, Industrial and Textile Employees (UNITE), has over 20,000 Chinese women members. There are also many Chinese workers in nonunionized factories. The large concentration of garment employment translates into a low income level for Chinese men and women, with women's income being lower than men's. In the five-county area of New York, Chinese women's personal median earnings are only $8,000 per year, which is two-thirds of Chinese men's earnings, and 40 percent of the median earning of white women in the same location. In low-income areas like Chinatown and Brooklyn, where employment options have largely been limited to garment shops, women's median earnings are around $7,000 annually (Zhou, 2000b).

In addition to low wages, working conditions in the garment industry are notorious for long hours and poor physical conditions. Many of the factories operate in basements to save rent and have insufficient light and ventilation. In the busy seasons, garment workers routinely work six or even seven days a week, 12 to 14 hours per day. In the low season, however, they are periodically laid off. Yet, for unskilled Chinese women, harsh conditions and low wages are no deterrent. Whatever income they earn in garment factories or restaurants is essential for their families' survival. In the metropolitan area as a whole, Chinese women contribute one-third of household income for households with at least one male member. In Chinatown, women's income makes up about half of the household income and is critical for lifting families out of poverty (Zhou, 2000b).

Despite poverty, grim working conditions, and long hours, poor Chinese immigrants are nevertheless striving for the American dream. A decent education and a future for their children—one in which they will eventually have the opportunity to launch successful careers in the professional world of America—is the objective of these immigrants' hard work and modest lifestyles. Chinatown and other inner-city Chinese settlements are poor, but they provide a foothold for newcomers to survive, find a job, raise a family, and perhaps eventually own a small business (Zhou, 1992). In this sense, New York City is still seen as the Promised Land (Waldinger, 1996).

Case Two: Transnational Immigrant—Making It With Pacific Rim Ties. In contrast to New York, Los Angeles hosts a similarly sized but more well-off Chinese population. Emerging from restructuring since the 1970s and 1980s, Los Angeles has become a post-modern capital of North America and a Pacific–Asian trade and financial center. Along with Los Angeles' increasing Asian linkages is the growing Asian population, in which the Chinese is one of the largest groups. From 1970 to 2000, the Chinese population in Los Angeles County grew eight times (U.S. Census Bureau, 1970, 2000). The new Chinese immigrant population consists of an increasing proportion of people with professional skills and financial capital (Ong et al., 1994). While the old pattern of unskilled labor migration has not entirely disappeared, a substantial number of new immigrants are from urban, educated, middle class backgrounds and come to the United States as professionals, managers, and entrepreneurs (Tseng 1994a, 1994b).

We can identify three clusters within the Chinese population. The first is unskilled immigrant laborers. According to the 1990 census, 29.3 percent of Chinese employed in Los Angeles County engaged in unskilled, non-agricultural occupations. This is much lower than the same statistic in New York, in which 44.7 percent engaged in unskilled jobs in 1990 (Zhou, 1998). As with the garment workers in New York, these are the most disadvantaged group among the Chinese, often confined to low-paying jobs within the Chinese community. However, the portion of Chinese engaged in unskilled labor is, in fact, lower than the Los Angeles County average.

The most significant Chinese population in Los Angeles is the Chinese professionals; managerial, professional, and specialty occupations accounted for 33.1 percent of the employed Chinese population in Los Angeles in 1990. Another 37 percent of Chinese were engaged in white-collar jobs, such as technicians or clerks; both were overrepresented compared with the county average. These were people like Ang Lee who usually had a good education from their home country, received advanced degrees in the United States, and finally obtained professional jobs. Some of them also started their own businesses.

Since the 1980s, there have also been a large number of wealthy Chinese immigrants moving to major cities on the American west coast and Canada. These people tend to be entrepreneurs or business people from Taiwan and Hong Kong, and later from mainland China. They migrated primarily as a result of political concerns, fearing the instability in East Asia. Many of these business people have bought property, invested in business ventures in the United States and Canada, and were the engine behind the rise of wealthy suburban Chinatowns in San Gabriel Valley in Los Angeles, San Jose, Flushing in New York City, and Vancouver. Many of these people lead a spatially split lifestyle, often leaving part of the family in Asia while the other half is in North America. They are called "astronauts" because they shuttle between the two sides of the Pacific to attend to their businesses and families.

The largely middle class background of this migration influx leads to several unique developments in Los Angeles. First, during the 1980s, Los Angeles became the single largest Chinese business center in the United States (U.S Census Bureau, 1992). With a population size virtually identical to the Chinese population in New York City in 1990, the Chinese population in Los Angeles in 1992 had 32 percent more Chinese-owned firms, hired three times as many paid employees, and generated more than three times as much in revenue (Zhou, 1998). Second, the Chinese economic structure has become increasingly diversified and sophisticated. Prominent Chinese self-employment sectors in Los Angeles today include not only the ethnic staples such as groceries, restaurants, and gift shops, but also skill-intensive professional services such as banks and high-tech firms, and the hotel and motel sector (Tseng 1994a, 1994b).

Third, the structural change of Chinese businesses in Los Angeles has been accompanied by spatial change during the last two decades (Fong, 1994; Li, 1998a, 1998b; Tseng, 1994a, 1994b; Zhou, 1998). The rapid increase in

Chinese population since the 1970s has largely been a suburban phenomenon. Although downtown Chinatown expanded in the absolute number of people, particularly with the heavy influx of Southeast Asian refugees, the bulk of Chinese immigrants and newly developed Chinese businesses located themselves in the suburban community of Monterey Park, about 8 miles east of Chinatown and immediately adjacent to the city of Los Angeles (Zhou, 1998). Although Monterey Park was proclaimed "America's first suburban Chinatown" by the Los Angeles Times (Arax, 1987; Fong, 1994), it has never become an exclusive ethnic enclave, growing to less than 40 percent in its Chinese population.

At the heart of the growth of the Chinese community in Los Angeles is the role of transnational linkages. It would be difficult to find a major Chinese business sector in Los Angeles that is not involved one way or another with overseas capital, market, information, or labor forces. For example, as of 1999 there were 23 Chinese American owned banks, the largest minority owned banking sector in the country. Among them, nine are owned by foreign banks, corporations, and businesses. Others also have strong international connections (Li et al., 2001). It can be argued that the Chinese business community in Los Angeles is not an isolated ethnic enclave, nor is it simply a vibrant outpost of Chinese business people. Rather, it has become a transnational anchor point in a vast global web of ethnic Chinese in such diverse cities as Vancouver, Sydney, Singapore, Kuala Lumpur, Bangkok, and Manila (Zhou & Tseng, 2001). The Chinese community in Los Angeles exemplifies a new type of ethnic economy within which financial, labor, information, and commodity flows are international in scope, yet deeply intertwined and embedded within a local milieu of intense ethnic networking and entrepreneurship (Zhou, 2000a; Zhou & Tseng, 2001). The following example of Mr. B., who owns a computer accessory firm in the Los Angeles metropolitan area, illustrates how the transnational ties work in the high-tech sector:

I studied for an MBA after I came from Taiwan. My family has factories in Taiwan, but they did not do computer-related products. After I graduated, I sent them some product samples of computer accessories, asking them to produce them. They manufactured the products and I sold them here. Now, most of my manufacturing facilities are in mainland China. I got to set up these factories to further lower down my costs. (Interview by the author, 1992)

This shows one way a Chinese businessperson is able to weave his network through a number of locations on the Pacific Rim—spanning Los Angeles, Taiwan, and mainland China. He is one among many Chinese entrepreneurs well represented in the dynamic high-tech computer and aircraft industries of southern California (Zhou & Tseng, 2001).

Another type of Chinese high-technology entrepreneur is comprised of scientists and engineers who obtained postgraduate degrees in the United States, some after working for large American companies. They often decided to pursue self-employment partially due to the glass ceiling effect they experienced at large companies. Capital from Asia often supports the entrepreneurial ventures of Chinese American engineers and scientists. Southern California has attracted foreign capital to its thriving high technology, capital-intensive industries. Due to the presence of a large number of Chinese scientists and engineers in California, Chinese source countries interested in high-technology ventures have invested capital in this area (Liu, 1991). In 1990, California absorbed 45 percent of all high-technology venture capital collected in Taiwan, and almost all the capital was invested in Chinese-owned ventures (Liu, 1991). Information, electronics, and biotechnology were the three most favored industries (Zhou & Tseng, 2001).

Chinese high-tech firms are only one example of how Chinese businesspeople employ transnational resources to foster their business success. Unlike immigrants who left Europe for America at the turn of the century, and for whom the Old World represented treasured yet fading memories, this case study shows a new type of immigrant entrepreneur whose well-being in the New World depends heavily on connections to the Old World.

THE FUTURE

This chapter offers an overview of the diversity among Chinese immigrants in the United States in a globalized age. China has long been an important center of emigration to other parts of the world. Chinese Americans have also been part of American history since the 1850s. Earlier Chinese immigrants were mostly male laborers, yet today the most distinguished feature of Chinese immigration is its diversity. The two case studies of Chinese immigrants in New York and Los Angeles show the diverse trajectories of contemporary Chinese immigrants—a picture far more complex than the "model minority" label. Globalization has influenced Chinese immigrants in different ways. For the low-wage workers, they have to face the pressure of even steeper wage reductions. For professionals and entrepreneurs, however, it has opened new opportunities and possibilities of cross-cultural information, capital, and commodity flows. As the economy of East Asia becomes increasingly more integrated with the U.S. economy, we expect the roles of "transmigrates" to become more prominent.

The future of Chinese Americans is manifold, therefore. Immigration will continue and continue to draw a polarized population. As a result, the Chinese community needs on the one hand to provide support and financial relief for its most exploited members. On the other hand, it needs to improve mainstream society's understanding of the transnational practices and networks of Chinese immigrants. Greater participation in politics and other aspects of society in the United States is no doubt the necessary step for Chinese Americans to take.

NOTES

1. These groups are defined by the U.S. Census as Whites, African Americans or Blacks, Asian and Pacific Islanders, Hispanics, and American Indians.

2. Manufacturers purchase material, design, cut, assemble, finish the final product, and market it for retailers. Jobbers are outsourcing manufacturers who do everything manufacturers do except garment assembly and finishing. This part is contracted out to contractors who cut, make, trim, and do finishing tasks.

BIBLIOGRAPHY

Appelbaum, R. P., & Gereffi, G. (1994). Power and Profits in the Apparel Commodity Chain. In E. Bonacich, L. Cheng, N. Chinchilla, N. Hamilton, & P. Ong (Eds.), *Global Production: The Apparel Industry in the Pacific Rim* (pp. 42–62). Philadelphia: Temple University Press.

Arax, M. (1987, April 6). Nation's 1st Suburban Chinatown. *Los Angeles Times*, p. A1.

Bailey, T., & Waldinger, R. (1991). Primary, Secondary, and Enclave Labor Markets: A Training Systems Approach. *American Sociological Review, 56*(4), 432–445.

Bonacich, E. (1994). Asians in the Los Angeles Garment Industry. In P. Ong, E. Bonacich, & L. Cheng (Eds.), *The New Asian Immigration in Los Angeles and Global Restructuring* (pp. 137–163). Philadelphia: Temple University Press.

Bowles, J. (2000, February). *The Empire Has No Clothes: Raising Real Estate Prices and Declining City Support Threatens the Future of New York's Apparel Industry.* Retrieved from the Center for an Urban Future, http://www.nycfuture.org/econdev/clothes.htm.

Buford, B. (1999, April 26). Sweat is Good. *The New Yorker, 75*(9), 130–139.

CIA World Factbook: China. (2002). http://www.cia.gov/cia/publications/factbook/geos/ch.html.

Foer, F. (2001, July 2). Reorientation—Asian America Discovers Identity Politics. *The New Republic*, pp. 15–18.

Fong, T. P. (1994). *The First Suburban Chinatown.* Philadelphia: Temple University Press.

Garment Industry Development Corporation. (1995). *New York City Fashion Industry Statistics* [Brochure].

Green, N. L. (1997). Ready-to-Wear and Ready-to-Work: A Century of Industry and Immigrants in Paris and New York. In A. Gordon, D. James, & A. Keyssar (Series Eds.), *Comparative and International Working-Class History.* Durham, NC and London: Duke University Press.

Kwong, P. (1996). *The New Chinatown.* New York: Hill and Wang.

———. (1997). *Forbidden Workers: Illegal Chinese Immigrants and American Labor.* New York: New Press.

Lawler, A. (2000, November 10). Silent No Longer: "Model Minority" Mobilizes:

Asian Americans Protest Discrimination in Scientific Community. *Science*, *290*(5494), 1072.

Lee, S. M. (1998). *Asian Americans: Diverse and Growing* (Population bulletin). Washington, DC: Population Reference Bureau.

Li, W. (1998a). Anatomy of a New Ethnic Settlement: The Chinese *Ethnoburb* in Los Angeles. *Urban Studies, 35*(3), 479–501.

———. (1998b). Ethnoburb Versus Chinatown: Two Types of Urban Ethnic Communities in Los Angeles. *Cybergeo, 10*, 1–12.

Li, W., Zhou, Y., Dymski, G., & Chee, M. (2001). Banking on Social Capital in the Era of Globalization: Chinese Ethnobanks in Los Angeles. *Environment and Planning A, 33*, 1923–1948.

Liu, C. (1991, January). *The Growth Patterns of Venture Capital in Taiwan*. Paper presented at the Conference of Asian Venture Capital, Taipei.

Lughod, J. A. (1989). *Before European Hegemony: The World System A.D. 1250–1350*. New York: Oxford University Press.

Marshall, J. M. (2000, October 23). Year of the Scapegoat. *The American Prospect, 11*(22), 12.

Okihiro, G. (1994). *Margins and Mainstream*. Seattle: University of Washington Press.

Ong, P., Bonacich, E., & Cheng, L. (1994). *The New Asian Immigration in Los Angeles and Global Restructuring*. Philadelphia: Temple University Press.

Redding, G. S. (1990). *The Spirit of Chinese Capitalism*. New York: Walter De Gruyter.

Sengupta, S. (1999, September 14). Squeezed by Debt and Time, Mothers Ship Babies to China. *New York Times*, p. 1.

Tsai, S. H. (1986). *The Chinese Experience in America*. Bloomington: Indiana University Press.

Tseng, Y. (1994a). Chinese Ethnic Economy: San Gabriel Valley, Los Angeles County. *Journal of Urban Affairs, 16*(2), 169–189.

———. (1994b). *Suburban Ethnic Economy: Chinese Business Communities in Los Angeles*. Unpublished doctoral dissertation, University of California, Los Angeles.

U.S. Census Bureau. (1972). *Survey of Minority Owned Business*. Washington, DC: U.S. Government Printing Office.

———. (1977). *Survey of Minority Owned Business*. Washington, DC: U.S. Government Printing Office.

———. (1982). *Survey of Minority Owned Business*. Washington, DC: U.S. Government Printing Office.

———. (1987). *Survey of Minority Owned Business*. Washington, DC: U.S. Government Printing Office.

———. (1990). *Census of Population*. Washington, DC: U.S. Government Printing Office.

———. (1992). *Survey of Minority Owned Business*. Washington, DC: U.S. Government Printing Office.

———. (2001). *Census of Population*. Washington, DC: U.S. Government Printing Office.

U.S. Department of Justice. (1991). *Statistical Yearbook of the Immigration and Naturalization Service*. Washington, DC: U.S. Government Printing Office.

———. (1996). *Statistical Yearbook of the Immigration and Naturalization Service*. Washington, DC: U.S. Government Printing Office.

U.S. Department of Labor. (1998). Garment Enforcement Quarterly Report. Retrieved from http://www.dol.gov/cgi-bin/consolid.pl?media+report.

Waldinger, R. D. (1996). *Still the Promised City? African-Americans and New Immigrants in Postindustrial New York*. Cambridge, MA: Harvard University Press.

Wang, L. L. (1998). Race, Class, Citizenship and Extraterritoriality: Asian Americans and the 1996 Campaign Finance Scandal. *Amerasia Journal, 24*(1), 1–21.

World Bank. (2002). *World Development Indicators Database: China*. Retrieved from http://www.worldbank.org/data/countrydata/countrydata.html.

Yeung, H. W. (2000). The Dynamics of the Globalization of Chinese Business Firms. In H. W. Yeung & K. Olds (Eds.), *Globalization of Chinese Business Firms* (pp. 75–104). New York: St. Martin's Press.

Yuan, D. Y. (1988). *Chinese American Population*. Hong Kong: UEA Press.

Zhou, M. (1992). *Chinatown: The Socioeconomic Potential of an Urban Enclave*. Philadelphia: Temple University Press.

———. (1998). How Do Places Matter? A Comparative Study of Chinese Ethnic Economies in Los Angeles and New York. *Urban Geography, 11*(6), 531–553.

———. (2000a). Bridging the Continents: The Roles of Los Angeles Chinese Producer Services in the Globalization of Chinese Business. In H. W. Yeung & K. Olds (Eds.), *The Globalization of Chinese Business Firms* (pp. 167–194). London: Macmillan.

———. (2000b). The Fall of "The Other Half of the Sky?"—Contemporary Experiences of Mainland Chinese Immigrant Women in New York City. *Women's Studies International Forum, 23*(4), 445–459.

———. (2001). New York: Caught Under the Fashion Run-Way—Immigrant Enterprises in the Garment Industry of New York. In Institute for Migration and Ethnic Studies (IMES) (Ed.), *Unravelling the Rag Trade—Immigrant Entrepreneurship in Seven World Cities* (pp. 113–134). Oxford: Berg Publishers.

Zhou, Y., & Tseng, Y. (2001). Regrounding the "Ungrounded Empires"—Localization as the Geographical Catalyst for Transnationalism. *Global Network, 1*(2), 131–154.

4

CUBA

Colonizers, Slaves, Exiles, and Refugees in Cuban History

Felix Masud-Piloto

INTRODUCTION

Profile of Cuba

Cuba is the largest island in the Caribbean in both territory (42,804 square miles) and population (11.1 million). A colony of Spain since 1492, it gained independence in 1898 after 406 years of colonial domination. A republican government was in place from 1902 to 1958, and the revolution of 1959 officially established the current socialist state in 1976. Catholicism has been the dominant religion since the colonial era, but Cubans practice a wide variety of other religions, including African religions that are practiced by the majority of the population, including Catholics. The population of Cuba is racially mixed: 51 percent mulatto, 37 percent white, 11 percent black, and 1 percent Chinese. Social reforms brought about by the revolution have placed Cubans among the most literate and healthiest people in Latin America. The literacy rate is 98 percent, life expectancy is 76 years, the infant mortality rate is 7.5 per 1,000 live births, and the doctor–patient ratio is 1/200. Education and medical care are free and available to everyone.

Vignette

Overcoming an Unfair Stigma. Roberto Martínez Padrón was 25 years old when he arrived in Key West, Florida as part of the Mariel boatlift (also known as the Freedom Flotilla) during the summer of 1980. Upon arrival, he, like the other 125,000 Cubans who arrived in the United States during the five months the boatlift lasted, was placed in a special immigration category: "entrant, status pending." In addition, due to the fact that several thousand "entrants" had criminal records in Cuba, the Cuban and U.S. media stereotyped all Mariel entrants under the label of *Marielito*, which in the public mind and opinion implied that they were all criminals, dishonest, lazy, and social deviants of various sorts. Thus they were deemed unfit for U.S. society, or at best, inferior to the 1 million Cubans who had arrived in the United States from 1959 to 1980. This was particularly painful for Martínez Padrón because he was quite the opposite of the stereotype pinned on him. He was honest, hardworking, and educated—a graduate in mathematical sciences from the University of Havana.

The early years in the United States were very difficult for Martínez Padrón. He was first detained in Fort Chaffee in Arkansas for eleven months until a cousin sponsored him out of detention and took him to Miami. In Miami, he struggled for a while until he was able to find a job washing dishes at a restaurant. A few months later he took a second part-time time job and began attending school at night to learn English. After five years of menial jobs, but with a good command of the English language, Martínez Padrón was able to continue the career he had started in Cuba when he was hired to teach mathematics at Miami-Dade Community College. He also continued going to school to work on his master's degree, which he obtained in 1990. He currently is a tenured professor at Miami-Dade Community College.

Unfortunately, Roberto Martínez Padrón's story is not unique. On the contrary, it is just one among millions of other stories of stereotyping, criminalizing, and negative labeling of immigrants and refugees. Sadly, despite the fact that the overwhelming majority of Mariel entrants resembled Roberto Martínez Padrón more than the dreaded *Marielito* created by the media, the group is still stigmatized by the media and the general public.

Overview of Migration Issues

Cuba's colonial legacy, coupled with the reality that it is a small, natural resource-poor, undeveloped country, has made emigration, for economic and social reasons, one of the dominant factors in Cuban society. In addition, Cuba's long-term dependent relationship with the United States and the two nations' geographic proximity have made the United States the most obvious and convenient place for emigration. Those conditions have made Cuba, from the creation of the Cuban republic 100 years ago to the present, an emigration "sending" country. Emigration has had and continues to have a deep impact on both Cuban society and the main receiving society, which since the late nineteenth-century has been the United States (Olson & Olson, 1995).

Cubans have been migrating to the United States for more than 170 years, and although the causes for the migrations have varied from economic to political, the main cause for every Cuban migration has, in some way, always been motivated or set off by political events in Cuba. The current migration that began in 1959 as a result of the revolution is no different. In fact, due to the United States' deep political disagreements with the revolution and the tensions between the two nations, it is considered to be the most political of all Cuban migrations to the United States and clearly the largest (1.3 million) and longest lasting (43 years).

Both the size and longevity of the migration can be attributed to several key factors that set the revolution of 1959 and the migration it has generated apart from all others: (1) the Cuban Revolution proved to be more radical and politically stronger than any previous government or movement in Cuban history, and (2) the United States, in its efforts to overthrow the revolutionary government and cope with a fast-growing number of refugees, adopted an open-door immigration policy for Cubans disaffected with the revolution.

The Cuba policy was loosely based on the United States' Hungarian Refugee Program (1957) and developed within the context of the Cold War. It was designed as a short-term emergency operation; none of its architects believe it would be in effect as it has been for more than four decades. Today, more than a decade after the end of the Cold War and despite some revisions to the open-door policy, Cuban migrants are still viewed by the United States as refugees from communism and given preferential treatment unlike any other immigrants from the Americas and most of the world (Masud-Piloto, 1996).

HISTORY OF MIGRATION ISSUES

Migration has been an important and constant factor in Cuban history, from the arrival of the island's first known settlers, Ciboney Indians in 1000 B.C., to the revolution of 1959 that triggered the largest emigration in the nation's history. For more than five centuries, migrations from Europe, Africa, and Asia converged on the island to forge the Cuban people out of a rich mixture of races and cultures.

The Spanish conquest that began in 1492 triggered the first large-scale migration to the island, which would continue through the 406 years of Spanish colonial rule. During that period, more than 1 million African slaves were brought in to replace Indian labor, which had been exterminated through warfare, disease, and forced labor throughout the first 50 years of conquest. Similarly, from the late 1840s to the early 1870s, 125,000 Chinese contract laborers were imported to work under indenture. In addition, a massive migration of more than 2 million Spanish soldiers, bureaucrats, business people, and fortune seekers also took place during the same period, making European and African the most common and largest racial groups in Cuba.

When Cuba gained its independence from Spain in 1898, it remained militarily occupied by the United States until 1902, when the Cuban Republic was created. By that time, however, Cuba had become economically and politically dependent on the United States, a state of affairs that lasted throughout the republican period (1902–1958). The dependent relationship made the United States the first choice for emigration in times of economic and/or political crisis on the island. Thus, during the 1950s more than 60,000 Cubans emigrated to the United States for periods ranging from a few months to years, depending on the severity of the crisis. The current migration, triggered by the Cuban Revolution in 1959, continues going strong after more than four decades (Pérez, 1995; Thomas, 1971).

DIMENSIONS OF MIGRATION ISSUES

Political Dimensions

The first significant Cuban exile community was established in Key West, Florida in the 1830s. The pioneers of that community were cigar manufacturers who went to Key West mainly to avoid the excessively high tariffs the United States government imposed on their products. The cigar factory owners and their workers also engaged in political activities and conspiracies aimed at ending Spain's imperial control over Cuba.

The relocation of an important sector of the cigar industry from Havana to Key West, and later (1869) to Tampa also, was both an economic and political act that triggered a migration of several thousand skilled workers and their families. As the Cuban population in Key West and Tampa grew, so did the political organizations advocating Cuban independence. José Martí, the political, organizational, and inspirational leader of Cuba's final and decisive offensive against Spain in the 1890s and the founder of the Cuban Revolutionary Party in New York, considered Key West and Tampa two of the revolution's most important strongholds.

By the time Cuba finally won its independence from Spain in 1898, after a long and bloody thirty-year war, the Cuban population in the United States had grown to well over 100,000. With independence, many Cubans returned home to play important roles in the nation's government and society, or simply to help with the mammoth reconstruction efforts of a country devastated by war. Most, however, remained in the United States and today both Key West and Tampa still preserve the flavor of the Cuban communities that once flourished there during much of the nineteenth century.

During the first five decades of the twentieth century, smaller groups of Cubans emigrated to the United States to escape political instability and/or repression in Cuba. In the late 1920s and early 1930s, a small group of political activists opposed to dictator Gerardo Machado found refuge in Miami and New York City. After Machado's overthrow, most of them returned to Cuba and were replaced in exile by Machado loyalists and the former president himself, who would later die and be buried in Miami. The same cycle was repeated, almost without variance, during the presidencies of Fulgencio Batista (1940–1944), Ramon Grau San Martín (1944–1948), Carlos Prio Socarrás (1948–1952), and Fulgencio Batista (1952–1958). It must be noted, however, that the United States government was usually reluctant to grant political asylum to Cuban political leaders and activists (Smith, 1966). It did so assuming that their stay in the country would be, as it usually was, short term.

When the rebel movement led by Castro defeated Fulgencio Batista's U.S.-trained army on January 1, 1959, Cuba entered a very different political era that quickly transformed its society in a most radical way and strained relations with the United States like never before. These two factors set the tone and the stage for the new Cuban migration to the United States. Once again, the United States, and especially Miami, Florida, became the choice place of asylum for those who fell out of grace or became disaffected with the new government. As was often the case before, among the first to go into exile were a few hundred close collaborators of the deposed government. By the end of 1959, more than 25,000 Cubans had requested and received political asylum in the United States.

The competing political objectives of both governments were played out in April 1961, when a force of 1,500 Cuban exiles, armed and trained by the United States government, invaded Cuba at the Bay of Pigs. The invasion, which was easily defeated in 72 hours, had profound repercussions for all parties involved. For the Cuban government, the victory over the exiled army concluded the consolidation process. For the Untied States, the defeat meant not only an embarrassment for the Kennedy administration, but also the loss of momentum and confidence in a military option. For the 135,000 Cubans living in the United States since 1959, the Bay of Pigs fiasco brought the painful realization that their exile would be prolonged for a longer period than most were ready to accept.

Responding to the "loss" of Cuba to Castro and the failure of the Bay of Pigs, Cuban exile politics, especially in Miami, became increasingly violent, passionate, and single-issue oriented. However, because the revolution endured beyond all expectations, Cuban exiles began getting more involved in local, state, and national politics during the 1970s. By the mid-1980s and early 1990s, Cubans controlled the City Council of Miami and the Florida legislature, and they elected three representatives to the U.S. Congress: Ileana Ros-Lehtinen (R., Florida), Lincoln Díaz-Balart (R., Florida), and Bob Menéndez (D., New Jersey). The election of most Cuban politicians was and continues to be supported and financed by the Cuban-American National Foundation (CANF), a powerful political lobby and interest group founded in 1990. CANF has a record of supporting politicians from both parties, as long as they have a clear and strong anti-Castro position.

Social Dimensions

The Cuban Revolution, and the migration it generated, affected every aspect of Cuban society. Its egalitarian social agenda called for and enacted a series of profound reforms: public health care and education, agrarian reform, the nationalization of foreign corporations, and the eradication of hunger and discrimination. As a response to Cuba's social reforms that negatively affected American social, economic, and political interests on the island, the United States broke diplomatic relations with Cuba on January 3, 1961.

Fearing the consequences of a war with the United States, as well as a loss of social status in the new revolutionary society, more Cubans opted for emigration. Ironically, both the Cuban and United States governments saw the diplomatic confrontation as an opportunity. The Cuban government believed that the departure of disaffected citizens, especially the members of the upper class, would allow a faster and smoother consolidation of the revolution. The United States government felt that welcoming refugees from Cuba, especially the professional class, would accelerate the revolution's demise. At a minimum, the departure of thousands would embarrass the revolution at home and abroad. Ideally, the "brain drain" caused by the exodus would strangle the Cuban economy, and the massive departure of Cuba's best trained professionals would make it more difficult, if not impossible, for Castro to deliver the revolution's promised social reforms.

To cope with the increase in the number of Cubans pouring into Miami (49,000 in 1961), the Kennedy administration moved to create the Cuban Refugee Program to provide financial, medical, and employment assistance for the newcomers. The program, which remained in operation for 15 years, helped over 700,000 Cubans at a cost of more than $1 billion (Garcia, 1996). The administration also provided funds to establish an airlift from Havana to Miami for those who were able to get the Cuban government's permission to travel or to emigrate permanently. The Cuban Refugee Program was the longest running and most expensive aid program for refugees from Latin America ever established by the United States.

The arrival in Miami of tens of thousands of professionals from the upper echelons of Cuban society led to the creation of a very successful social and economic enclave in that city. Calle 8 (8th Street) became the center of Cuban Miami, as small shops, professional offices, schools, churches, radio stations, and social clubs began to spring up to provide services to the growing community. Business, social events, and church masses were conducted in Spanish (Portes & Bach, 1985). The reconstruction of prerevolutionary Cuba in the United States is probably the most remarkable feat of the exile community. In Cuba, the departure of the upper class during the first years of the revolution allowed the government to accelerate the construction of a classless society through a more egalitarian distribution of resources and services. On the other hand, the "brain drain" had an almost devastating

effect on the revolution's social agenda, as more than 50 percent of all doctors left the country from 1959 to 1962. Likewise, the emigration of most
U.S.-trained technicians caused serious disruptions and breakdowns in key
industries.

The most profound, difficult, and damaging social effect of the Cuban
migration since 1959 has been and continues to be the division of the Cuban
family. With more than 1.5 million Cubans living abroad and strict travel
regulations imposed by the U.S. and Cuban governments, reconciliation has
proven elusive.

Economic Dimensions

In September 1965, the Cuban migration took an unexpected and unprecedented turn. The Cuban government, forced by the effects of a sharp
economic decline and public pressures for migration venues, decided to open
the port in the fishing town of Camarioca to exiles willing to transport their
relatives to the United States. Castro announced his unilateral decision directly to the Cuban people during a speech, and within a few days hundreds
of boats from Miami arrived in Camarioca to transport the refugees. Since
the United States and Cuba did not have diplomatic relations, the United
States was faced with a difficult dilemma: It could exercise its sovereignty
by refusing to accept the unauthorized migration, but that would mean closing the doors to refugees from a communist country. The Cuban government, on the other hand, correctly assumed that since the United States had
served as a haven for all Cubans disaffected with and who had defected from
the revolution, it could not refuse those who decided to accept Castro's offer.
As it turned out, due to seasonal bad weather, the boatlift lasted only six
weeks, but it paved the way for a bilateral agreement between Cuba and the
United States to create the Cuban Airlift, popularly know as the "Freedom
Flights." The flights, sponsored by the United States government, operated
for seven years and transported more than 260,000 Cubans to exile in the
United States. The flights remain the longest and largest refugee operation
in U.S. history (Philipson & Llerena, 1980).

What set the Camarioca boatlift and airlift migrants apart from their pred-
ecessors was that by the mid-1960s the main motivation for Cuban emigration had shifted from political to economic. By that time the revolutionary
government had consolidated its political power, but it was having great
difficulty keeping the economy afloat as it tried to survive the economic
embargo imposed by the United States and the restructuring of the economy
from free market capitalism to state-managed socialism. The Camarioca boatlift and the Cuban Airlift led to the passing of the Cuban Adjustment Act
by the United States Congress in 1966. That act placed Cubans in a privileged and prioritized position over all other immigrant groups. Under the
act, any Cuban who arrives in the United States, legally or illegally, can

qualify for permanent residency after living in the United States for only one year and one day. The average wait for all other immigrants is five years.

The Cuban Airlift marked the beginning of Cuban Miami's economic boom. From the mid-1970s to the late 1980s, Cubans opened and owned more than 25,000 businesses and 40 banks and employed more than 250,000 workers (Grenier & Stepick, 1992). Economically, Miami was changed from a quaint, quiet retirement haven to a world-class city with a bustling international business center. The city became the United States' gateway to Latin American trade. Despite the strong entrenchment of the Cuban economic enclave in Miami, or perhaps because of it, a bigger and more dramatic boatlift from Cuba took place in 1980.

The Mariel boatlift was caused by a dispute over the custody of asylum seekers who had invaded the Peruvian embassy in Havana. When the Peruvian government refused to surrender the asylum seekers, the Cuban government responded by withdrawing its guards from the embassy compound and publicly "inviting" anyone who wanted to leave the country to go to the Peruvian embassy to receive exit visas. As more than 10,000 would-be refugees jammed the embassy compound in 48 hours, Cuban officials unilaterally announced the opening of the port in the city of Mariel for another Camarioca-style boatlift. Like 15 years earlier, Cubans in Miami responded eagerly to Castro's offer. This time, however, the boatlift went on for five months and the strictly maritime operation brought 125,000 Cubans to the United States.

Throughout the duration of the frantic boatlift, exaggerated and often false stories about Castro's attempts to pack the boats with the worst criminal and "undesirable" elements of Cuban society appeared often in the United States media. In reality, less than 5 percent of the new arrivals had criminal records or mental illnesses. Nonetheless, the bad press resulted in the stigmatization of everyone who arrived in the boatlift. *Marielito*, the label applied arbitrarily to all the boatlift entrants, implied that they were all social deviants, criminals, or dishonest (see the case of Roberto Martínez Padrón above). The false and unfair label tarnished the image and reputation of the new refugees and of the Cuban community in general.

Despite two boatlifts and an expensive airlift, the U.S. government continued viewing the Cuban migration as a temporary affair, so it did not make any attempts to normalize immigration from Cuba. On the contrary, after 1980, Cubans wishing to emigrate to the United States were left with few options: (1) going through the long, complicated, and expensive process of acquiring exit visas, (2) risking their lives at sea, (3) seeking asylum in foreign embassies, or (4) defecting while traveling abroad on official business.

The Mariel boatlift was extremely expensive for the United States. In addition to more than $100 million in detention and relocation costs during the five months of the boatlift, the federal government had to continue spending tens of millions a year for the detention and processing of the

2,800 Mariel entrants considered "excludables" by the Immigration and Naturalization Service (INS) due to their criminal records in Cuba. The high costs and the lack of control over immigration made the United Sates realize that in the absence of full diplomatic relations with Cuba, it would be greatly beneficial and much more economical to normalize, or at least regulate, the migratory flow from Cuba.

In December 1984, after a series of secret negotiations, the United States and Cuba signed an immigration agreement that would, among other things, result in the repatriation of all "excludables" and the issuance of 20,000 U.S. visas per year to Cubans who qualified for permanent residence in the United States. The accords were welcome by both governments, but as had often been the case since 1959, politics got in the way. In May 1985, the Reagan administration approved funds for and created "Radio Marti," a radio frequency used to broadcast to the Cuban people the "truth" according to Washington and "enemy propaganda" according to Havana. To protest the broadcasts, the Cuban government cancelled the immigration agreements of 1984. The cancellation effectively closed the doors to the United States for Cubans hoping to emigrate for family reunification, economic, or political reasons. Expectedly, the closing of the only legal channel for emigration led to an increase in the number of Cubans attempting to reach the United States in rafts or in hijacked commercial planes and ships. The number of those who died trying also increased (Grenier & Stepick, 1992).

Increased public pressure to return the more than 2,500 Mariel "excludables" to Cuba and to open safe channels for migration drew the United States and Cuba back to the negotiation table in 1987. The two nations agreed to renegotiate and eventually reactivate the 1984 accords.

During the 1990s Cuba experienced the worse economic crisis in its history. Brought about by a series of long-term domestic problems, the crisis was accelerated and deepened by the political crises that led to the collapse of all socialist governments in eastern Europe and the disintegration of the Soviet Union. Within a few months, Cuba lost 75 percent of its general trade and its capacity to import was reduced by 80 percent. As a result, the already troubled Cuban economy went into an uncontrollable downward spin. As the economic crisis deepened, the number of Cubans leaving the country illegally by sea increased dramatically from 567 in 1990 to 3,656 in 1993 (Torres, 1999).

The depth of the Cuban economic crisis, coupled with the worldwide crisis of socialism, seemed to set the perfect stage for the end of the Cuban Revolution and Castro's government. Hoping to speed up that process, in 1992 the U.S. Congress, responding to the strong antirevolutionary lobby of Cuban Miami and U.S. interests in a post-Castro Cuba, passed the Cuban Democracy Act (CDA). The CDA was designed to tighten the U.S. economic embargo against Cuba and to strengthen the prospects for democracy on the island. Among other things, the bill prohibited trade with Cuba by U.S.

subsidiaries in third countries and blocked access to U.S. ports to ships that had recently visited Cuban ports. The Cuban Democracy Act hurt the Cuban economy, but not enough to achieve its main objective of toppling Castro's government. On the contrary, it led to a government crackdown on the internal opposition movement that was accused of being influenced and financed by the United States. More than anything else, the CDA made life even more difficult for the Cuban people.

During the summer of 1994, more than 30,000 Cubans arrived in the United States aboard or hanging on to extremely dangerous and precarious homemade floating devices, generously described as "rafts." The causes for the uncontrolled migration were many, but chief among them were the economic hardships brought on by the collapse of socialism in Eastern Europe and stronger U.S. economic pressures, as well as the increase in political repression applied by the Cuban government against its internal opposition. Those harsh realities led many to head north on anything that floated.

With the number of rafters increasing daily, on August 5, 1994, Fidel Castro addressed the Cuban people to explain the causes for a small riot in Havana earlier that day and to discuss his concerns over a series of embassy invasions and ship hijackings by Cubans seeking to emigrate to the United States. He angrily accused the United Sates of not complying with the 1984/1987 immigration accords by failing to issue the 20,000 visas per year that the two counties had agreed to, and he pointed to the fact that from 1985 to 1995 the United States issued 11,222 visas, only 7.1 percent of the 160,000 allotted for that period of time. Castro finished the speech by declaring that due to the long history of U.S. encouragement for Cubans to leave the country illegally, and in light of the events he had outlined earlier, his government would stop putting obstacles in the way of people wishing to leave the country (Rodríguez Chávez, 1999).

Castro was true to his word and Cubans interpreted them accurately as a green light to head north in whatever way they could. From August 13 to 25, the U.S. Coast Guard rescued 13,084 rafters. On August 23, a record 2,886 Cubans were rescued in the Florida Straits, and the total for the month of August alone was 21,300. The high and fast rate of arrivals in this new unsolicited migration alarmed the Clinton administration into action. On August 19, the president ordered the Coast Guard to continue rescuing Cuban rafters, but that instead of transporting them to the United States for processing, as it had done in the previous 25 years, to take them to the U.S. Naval Base at Guantanamo Bay, Cuba, where they would be detained indefinately.

President Clinton's order to stop the Cuban rafters and detain them off U.S. shores represented a complete reversal of a 35-year-old immigration policy designed to welcome, as political refugees, almost any Cuban claiming to be "escaping" Fidel Castro's repression. Cubans, who had had the doors to the United States opened to them since 1959, were suddenly not only denied entry, but were also being taken to what they came to call "concentration camps." Once there, they were technically in safe haven and out of danger, but they were without the right to claim political asylum in the United States. Despite its harshness, Clinton's action failed to discourage people and the migration continued unabated.

The rafters' crisis officially ended in May 1995, after a long series of talks between the United States and Cuba resulted in what may be the most important immigration agreement between the two countries since 1959. Under the new accords, the United States agreed to return to Cuba all Cuban migrants rescued by its Coast Guard at sea and to help them apply for legal immigration to the United States. The accords kept the number of visas for Cubans at 20,000 per year and created a visa lottery for people who did not have relatives in the United States, but who desired to emigrate anyway. Cuba agreed to peacefully discourage would-be illegal migrants, not to arrest those who were sent back, and to encourage them to apply for legal emigration to the United States through the new channels established under the 1995 immigration accords.

The 1995 immigration accords were historical on several counts: (1) It was the first time since 1959 that the United States and Cuba agreed to collaborate on a long-term basis to regulate Cuban migration to the United States; (2) For the first time since World War II, the U.S. government agreed to return refugees to Cuba, signaling the end of Cuban refugee exclusivity; and (3) Cuba decriminalized emigration to the United States and the desire to emigrate.

THE FUTURE

Both the United States and Cuba hoped that the rafters' crisis of 1994 was the last time they would have to cope with an uncontrolled migration. They also hoped that the immigration agreement of 1995 would work and lead to a more normal migratory process. Unfortunately, politics got in the way once again. In February 1996, the U.S. Congress approved the Cuban Liberty and Democratic Solidarity Act (also known as the Helms-Burton law). In addition to further tightening the U.S. economic embargo against Cuba, it threatened to retaliate against foreign businesses investing in Cuba, and it gave Cuban nationals residing in the United States the right to sue the Cuban government in U.S. courts to recover lost property in Cuba.

The Helms-Burton law increased the hostile environment between Cuba and the United States. It was a clear reminder that the cold war between the two nations was far from over, and as long as that environment existed, it would be extremely difficult, if not impossible, to have a normal migratory flow between Havana and Miami. In fact, even before the enactment of the Helms-Burton law, a new unwritten immigration policy affecting only Cubans had come into being: the wet feet vs. dry feet policy. That is, any Cuban rescued or stopped by the U.S. Coast Guard before reaching U.S. soil—wet feet—would be immediately returned to Cuba in accordance with the 1995 immigration agreements. Any Cuban who arrived undetected by the U.S. immigration authorities—dry feet—would almost automatically gain the right to apply for political asylum (González-Pando, 1998).

The wet/dry feet policy has developed into an extremely dangerous and often fatal cat and mouse game between the U.S. Coast Guard and private *lancheros* (high-speed boat operators) in the Florida Straits. According to Coast Guard estimates, from October 1998 to April 1999, more than 1,000 Cuban migrants arrived illegally in Florida aboard high-speed boats. Passengers paid at least $2,000 and up to $10,000 to improve their chances of arriving in the United States with dry feet. In accordance with U.S. immigration regulations affecting only Cubans and in a clear contradiction with the U.S. Refugee Act of 1980, all arrivals are rewarded with political asylum, regardless of whether they have a "well founded fear" of political persecution at home or not. In addition, because the Cuban Adjustment Act of 1966 is still in effect, those who make it can apply for permanent resident status one year and one day after their arrival. The Cuban Adjustment Act and the wet/dry feet policy continue to keep Cuban migration to the United States in a peculiar, yet privileged situation vis-à-vis migrants from the rest of the world. The United States and Cuba are very far from having a normal migratory process. In the meantime, rafters continue risking their lives in hopes of arriving in the United States with dry feet in order to "benefit" from the United States' peculiar Cuban immigration policy.

BIBLIOGRAPHY

Bender, L. (1975). *The Politics of Hostility: Castro's Revolution and United States Policy*. Hato Rey, Puerto Rico: Inter-American University Press.

García, M. C. (1996). *Havana USA: Cuban Exiles and Cuban Americans in South Florida, 1959–1994*. Berkeley: University of California Press.

González-Pando, M. (1998). *The Cuban Americans*. Westport, CT: Greewood Press.

Grenier, G. J., & Stepick, A. III (Eds.). (1992). *Miami Now: Immigration, Ethnicity, and Social Change*. Gainesville: University Press of Florida.

Masud-Piloto, F. (1996). *From Welcomed Exiles to Illegal Immigrants: Cuban Migration to the U.S., 1959–1995*. Lanham, MD: Rowman & Littlefield.

Olson, J. S., & Olson, J. E. (1995). *Cuban Americans: From Trauma to Triumph*. New York: Twayne Publishers.

Pérez, L. A. (1995). *Cuba: Between Reform and Revolution*. New York: Oxford University Press.

Philipson, L., & Llerena, R. (1980). *Freedom Flights: Cuban Refugees Talk About Life Under Castro and How They Fled His Regime*. New York: Random House.

Portes, A., & Bach, R. (1985). *Latin Journey: Cuban and Mexican Immigration in the United States*. Berkeley: University of California Press.

Rodríguez Chávez, E. (1999). *Cuban Migration Today*. Havana: Editorial José Martí.

Smith, R. F. (1966). *Background to Revolution: The Development of Modern Cuba*. New York: Knopf.

Thomas, H. (1971). *Cuba: The Pursuit of Freedom*. New York: Harper & Row.

Torres, M. (1999). *In the Land of Mirrors: Cuban Exile Politics in the United States*. Ann Arbor: University of Michigan Press.

5

FRANCE

The Melting Pot of Europe

Jeremy Hein

INTRODUCTION

Profile of France

France has a population of about 60 million people, of which about 1.6 million live in four overseas departments. Paris is the capital of France. Over one-third of all immigrants in France live in the Paris region, compared to only about 15 percent of the native population. Life expectancy for males is 75 years (the same as the Western European average) and for women 83 years (two years higher than the average). Its rate of natural increase is .4, which is substantially higher than for Western Europe (.1). France is also slightly less urban than the average country in Western Europe (74% compared to 79%). The Gross National Income in France is $23,020 per capita, about $600 less than the average for Western Europe, but about $8,000 greater than the average for all of Europe. Although more than 80 percent of the French identify as Catholics, societal norms are very secular, and there is a strong separation of church and state.

Vignettes

The experiences of a kinship network of Cambodian refugees living in the suburbs of Paris exemplify many of the issues faced by immigrants in France (Hein, 1993c). This Cambodian kinship network consists of 7 families totaling 26 individuals, of which 15 are adults and 11 are children. The core of this kin group is four families consisting of two sisters and their spouses and the sisters' two male cousins, who in the context of Cambodian kinship are considered brothers. In addition there are two families composed of an uncle by blood and a "fictive kin" uncle (a man not related by marriage or ancestry but treated as a close relative). Another family consists of a brother-in-law. All of these adults lived through the four-year period in the 1970s when the Khmer Rouge (Cambodian communist) revolution destroyed Cambodia and left about 2 million Cambodians dead.

The adult males and most of the adult females in this kinship network attended high school or university in Cambodia and could speak some French before they arrived in France. Indeed, French immigration officials selected these families for resettlement in part because of their proficiency in the French language. Ability to speak French is by far the most important trait on which immigrants in France are judged.

The first family member to arrive in France was the uncle. He fled from Cambodia to Thailand after only a few months under the Khmer Rouge. Like most refugees, he wanted to resettle in the United States but he also applied for resettlement with the French embassy and was accepted by France first. He arrived in France in 1976 and stayed in a government-funded refugee center for two months. The existence of these centers and other forms of public housing and social services for immigrants indicates how the French government plays a very strong role in shaping the adaptation of immigrants.

The family of the brother-in-law did not pass through a refugee center. Instead, he and his wife and young daughter were sponsored by a French reception group composed of residents of a Parisian suburb who responded to the mayor's appeal that groups be formed to assist refugees from the former French colony of Indochina. Mayors in France have considerable formal and informal power to regulate immigrants in their city. In this case the mayor was supportive and was able to muster local support and resources to help refugees from Southeast Asia. Conversely, some French mayors seek to limit the arrival of immigrants in their city and minimize assistance to those who live there.

Members of this Cambodian kinship network maintain close ties that are a great resource to them. Kinship is a very important social bond that enables immigrants to help each other migrate to a new society and adjust to conditions there. Thus the first way these Cambodians assisted each other was for those already in France to sponsor relatives still in Southeast Asia. As noted above, the first member of this extended family arrived in France in 1976. Upon leaving the refugee center he immediately set about sponsoring another family, which arrived in 1980. Other families arrived in Thailand, contacted members already in France, and were eventually admitted to France on the basis of having close relatives there. By 1983 all seven families in this kin group were living in France within close proximity of each other.

The second way kinship assists immigrants is through ties that support their socioeconomic adaptation. Once residing in the suburbs of Paris, these

Cambodian families began to reconstitute their economic ties. All the adult women in this family own sewing machines and produce finished articles of clothing on a piece-rate system from precut pieces of fabric distributed to them by other refugees. One woman estimated that approximately 50 percent of the Cambodian women she knows produce clothing at home. The clothing is usually for children and the ratio of the piece-rate price to the retail price is approximately 1:50. Work in this so-called underground or informal economy is common among immigrants in France.

The women in this Cambodian kinship network work for two Chinese-Cambodian middlemen who distribute the fabric, pick up the finished garments, and then bring them to clothing stores. Chinese immigrants from Cambodia, Vietnam, and other countries in Asia are particularly active in entrepreneurship. Indeed, the Thirteenth Arrondissement of Paris was transformed into a Chinatown during the last two decades of the twentieth century and now contains numerous shops and restaurants operated by Chinese immigrants. Although not reaching the level of ethnic Chinese, North Africans and Portuguese have also started many small businesses, particularly groceries, cafés, and restaurants.

One of the Chinese-Cambodian middlemen knew members of this kinship network from having lived near one family in a Thai refugee camp. After being resettled in France it was expected that the Chinese Cambodian would recruit workers from among people he already new and trusted. The second Chinese-Cambodian middleman obtained five or six female workers from the other one (about half of the latter's work force) after marrying his sister, again indicating how kinship among immigrants promotes their economic adaptation. With this group of workers the new in-law was able to go into business for himself. As he reports, "I saw a sign for an entrepreneur with ten to eighteen machine operators to make clothes. It was in a Jewish store. Many Jews in Paris work with clothes. I have only eight operators and that's not a lot. Some entrepreneurs have twenty" (Hein, 1993c, p. 153).

Another significant economic tie among members of this kinship network is their practice of pooling money. They term this practice, whereby each household takes turns acquiring the whole sum, a "tontine." A similar tontine or "hui" system has been documented among Chinese Cambodians in Paris (Hassoun & Tan, 1986). The basic principle of the tontine saving system is that each member regularly contributes a predetermined sum of money. Each member can collect the sum of all money contributed when it is his or her turn. Those members who forfeit their turn and allow another member to take the sum are paid interest by the member who claimed the sum in their place.

Six of the seven families in this Cambodian kin group participate in the tontine. They each paid 1,000 French francs a month, or about US$300. One of the sisters reported that she and her relatives had practiced (she used the French verb *jouer*, to play) the *tontine* in Cambodia for as long as she could remember, and that up to 30 people had taken part. In her opinion:

The *tontine* is better than a bank because there is no fixed interest and you can get the money when you need it. I don't take my share very often. I save it for an emergency, maybe one of my children will get sick or my husband will lose his job. Other people use the money to buy a car or a television. My husband doesn't play because he has a regular job, but I only sew at home so I play. (Hein, 1993c, p. 155)

Although well adjusted by many measures, some members of this kinship network occasionally experience incidents with French natives that remind them of their status as foreigners. One such incident occurred when one family was out shopping and their toilet sprung a leak. The water came through the ceiling of the Algerian neighbors below who then called the fire department. The firemen broke in through a window and turned the water off. They then cleaned up the water using a pile of what appeared to be rags near a sewing machine. These were precut pieces of cloth that were delivered by a middleman to the wife in the family to be sewed as piecework. Three police officers came by about a half hour after the family returned home and asked for their identification papers and proof that they were legal residents, which they were. The family and their relatives agreed afterwards that the police had not come to help them but to check up on a disturbance involving foreigners.

The Cambodians in this vignette are unique from other immigrants in France in some ways, particularly in the fact that they arrived as political rather than economic migrants. But in other ways they exemplify themes that cut across immigrant groups in France. Like other immigrants, they are from a former French colony and reside in the Paris region. They used their kinship network to organize their migration to France, and they rely on close kin for assistance and support during the adaptation process.

Overview of Migration Issues

It is well known that the single most symbolic icon of American immigration history—the Statue of Liberty—was given to the United States by France. Less well known is the fact that a small replica of the statue sits on an island in the Seine River, which runs through Paris. In 1987 refugees from Vietnam, Laos, and Cambodia, dressed in ethnic clothing, were towed up the Seine aboard a boat that had actually been used by refugees to escape from Vietnam to Thailand. The refugees were met by French government officials and dignitaries who gave speeches about the right of asylum being part of the constitution since the revolution in 1789. They also noted the increasing ethnic pluralism in France that was resulting from international migration. This highly revealing event symbolizes an important feature of international migration to France. Although France is not a settler society of immigrants like the United States, Canada, or Australia, it has the most developed national model of a melting pot among all countries in Europe. In fact, France has the longest modern history of immigration in Europe. About one in five inhabitants of France has an immigrant parent or grand-parent.

Unlike the United States where the term immigrant means foreign rather than native born, official statistics on immigrants in France only include those who are not yet citizens and exclude immigrants who have become French nationals. In France, statistics on immigrants use the term foreigners (*étrangers*) to mean only those foreign-born residents who retain the citizen-ship of their homeland. Thus, from the perspective of American social sci-ence, statistics on "immigrants" in France underestimate the total number of foreign-born people since once an immigrant becomes a French citizen they are no longer deemed to be "foreigners."

The proportion of foreigners in France (5.6%) is slightly higher than the European average (4.5%). About 17 percent of children born in France during the late 1990s have at least one foreign-born parent, indicating that immigrants are contributing to population growth. Ever since its population was decimated by casualities in World War I, France has viewed an increas-ing population to be in the country's political and economic interests. In fact, the population in Europe as a whole is declining (the rate of natural increase of −.1), a social problem that is particularly serious in Germany and Russia. Because fertility is insufficient to replace the population in Eu-rope, the region needs immigrants to maintain its labor force and generate the taxes that support an ever increasing number of senior citizens. France, for example, actually would need to add 100,000 more immigrants each year from 2000 to 2050 simply to maintain its working age population.

The largest foreign nationality group is the Portuguese, who constitute 17 percent of all foreigners. Yet because of their similar ethnic and historical backgrounds, immigrants from North Africa are frequently considered by social scientists, the media, and the public in France to form a single pop-ulation. North Africans are comprised Moroccans (44%), Algerians (42%), and Tunisians (14%), and together constitute 35 percent of all foreigners in France. Other significant immigrant populations include those from South-east Asia (primarily Vietnam and Cambodia), sub-Saharan Africa (primarily Senegal), the Middle East (primarily Turkey), and Europe (primarily Italy and more recently the former Yugoslavia). Since 1992, citizens of the 15 countries forming the European Union have had the freedom to migrate and settle in any other member country. This political arrangement creates a unique form of international migration to France and other European Union members. Immigrants from European Union countries constitute 37 percent of all foreigners in France, with those from Portugal, the United Kingdom, Italy, Germany, and Spain being the largest groups (respectively).

France can expect an increase in this source of immigrants because many countries in Eastern Europe will join the European Union in the near future, as may Turkey at some point.

HISTORY OF MIGRATION ISSUES

France has the longest modern history of immigration in Europe. More than 2 million immigrants came to France between the 1880s and the 1930s. Most were from Belgium, Italy, and Poland. Spaniards fleeing the civil war in Spain during the 1930s added another important group.

Post–World War II immigration to France typifies immigration to Western Europe as a whole in several respects. Like the United Kingdom and Portugal, France receives immigrants from former colonies in Asia and Africa. Vietnam, Laos, and Cambodia formed the French colony of Indochina from the 1880s to the 1950s, and refugees from this region arrived in France during the 1970s and 1980s. Yet there were already about 100,000 Southeast Asians living in France when the first refugees from this region arrived in 1975. Immigrants from Algeria, Tunisia, and Morocco—French colonies in North Africa since the 1830s—have a long history of immigration to France. Migration accelerated after these countries gained independence from France in the 1950s and 1960s. Immigrants from Senegal, Mali, Togo, and other former French colonies in West Africa are a third stream of migration.

Like Belgium and Germany, France recruited large numbers of Muslim immigrant workers during the post–World War II economic expansion. Most of these workers were from North Africa and the French government halted the recruitment of all foreign workers when the economy began a long-run decline in the mid-1970s. Although government policy assumed that these workers would return home when no longer needed, instead they began bringing their wives and children from their homeland to France. This important shift from labor to family migration during the 1970s marked a decisive change in contemporary international migration to France and also challenged public policy and public opinion to think about immigrants in a new way. Rather than a temporary economic commodity, from the mid-1970s onward immigrants increasingly had to be thought of as communities and future citizens. During the late 1990s more than 130,000 immigrants arrived in France to join family members, constituting about two-thirds of all immigrants. Only 10 percent of all immigrants arrived because they were granted work permits.

As in Sweden and Norway, a large proportion of immigrants who arrive in France are refugees and asylum seekers from throughout the world (about 25 percent of all immigrants in 1999). The right to political asylum has been guaranteed in the French constitution since the Revolution of 1789. All subsequent constitutions have included the sentence: "All men persecuted for their actions in favor of liberty have the right to asylum in territories of the Republic." Yet France received few displaced persons following World War II and even fewer refugees fleeing new communist regimes in Eastern Europe. Instead, the flow of political migrants to France during the 1950s and 1960s was dominated by decolonization and the arrival of nearly 1.5 million repatriating French citizens. More than two-thirds of these repatriates were the *pieds noirs* from Algeria. Since the 1980s, however, comparatively large numbers of asylum seekers have arrived in France, claiming official protection as refugees. During the late 1990s nearly 17,000 refugees arrived (who had permission to remain in France) along with almost 100,000 asylum seekers (who faced an 80 percent rejection rate). Most refugees and asylums seekers are from Asia and Africa.

DIMENSIONS OF MIGRATION ISSUES

Political Dimensions

France has a long history of political conflict involving immigrants. North African political activism in France started with the decolonization movement in the 1920s and continued until Morocco and Tunisia achieved independence in 1954 and Algeria in 1962. The workplace became the focus of North African activism in the 1960s and 1970s. But in 1983 a remarkable protest ushered in a new phase of North African collective action. Forty North African youths marched the 750 miles from Marseilles to Paris to protest a rise in racist killings. Initially these *beurs* (a slang term for second-generation North Africans) drew little media attention and public support. But when the marchers reached Paris 45 days later, they led a column numbering 100,000. Two years later, a crowd of 275,000 attended an antiracism protest sponsored by a new multiethnic youth organization called SOS-Racisme. By the late 1980s, one study (Muxel, 1988) estimated that 14 percent of Muslim immigrant youths were members of antiracism associations, compared to 8 percent of Catholic immigrant youths, and 3 percent of French youths. But the greatest sign of the new political mobilization among immigrants was the formation of *France Plus*. North African youths formed this organization to register voters and nominate candidates, which broke the French taboo on the use of ethnicity in the political arena.

Although Islam is central to politics in the Middle East and North Africa, and thus to French foreign policy, it has been conspicuously absent from French domestic politics. Nonetheless, there is an unavoidable connection between developments in the Islamic world and those immigrants of the Muslim faith in France. In 1973, OPEC (Organization of Petroleum Exporting Countries) dramatically raised oil prices, enabling Saudi Arabia and other oil-rich nations to fund Islamic religious organizations in France and other countries in Western Europe. There has been extraordinary growth in the number of Islamic associations and mosques since then. The rise of Islamic fundamentalism following the Iranian revolution in 1979 was viewed with concern by many French politicians. But Islam was conspicuously absent from North African activism during the 1980s. The Grand Mosque of Paris, constructed for a colonial fair in 1926, remained distant from the political turmoil during the decade. Pakistanis, not North Africans, conducted the single protest in Paris supporting the Iranian death sentence for the author Salman Rushdie. In 1989, the expulsion of three North African girls from high school for wearing Islamic scarves did not produce a protest wave among North Africans. The much-feared North African immigrant backlash against France's participation in the 1991 Persian Gulf War never materialized. The most visible political manifestations of Islam have been protests by North Africans denouncing Israeli policies toward Palestinians, but this activism is only indirectly linked to religion.

Rather than Islam being a source of political instability in France, a much more serious problem has been anti-immigrant sentiments among natives. Nativism existed in France long before the arrival of contemporary immigrants. In 1893 near Marseilles, a French mob numbering more than 500 killed 7 Italian immigrants and wounded 40 others following the hiring of immigrants at lower wages than natives. Yet apart from native attacks on Algerians in France during the Algerian independence movement (1954–1962), nativism lacked a political foundation until the early 1980s.

In 1972, Jean-Marie Le Pen and others created the National Front (*Front National* or FN) to unify a number of extreme-right hate groups. The FN labored in obscurity for the remainder of the decade, but in 1983 it scored 17 percent in a municipal election followed by 11 percent of the national vote in the 1984 election for the European Parliament. In 1988, Le Pen received 14 percent of the first-round vote in the presidential election. Support for the National Front has remained at about 15 percent nationally although it is considerably higher in some regions of the countries, such as the southern departments. In the 2002 presidential election, Le Pen beat the Socialist prime minister in the first round of voting (where there are multiple candidates) and scored nearly 20 percent of the national vote in the final round (when there are just two) against the incumbent president.

The rise of the FN resulted from the political skill of Le Pen and others in making immigrants a political issue at a time when other traditional political divisions in France were waning. Around the FN there coalesced negative reactions to pro-immigrant social policies, the new mobilization among second-generation immigrants, and media-saturated events about immigrants like the controversy over the wearing of Muslim head scarves in French schools. The end result was a new electorate that, in contrast to other voters, overwhelmingly prioritizes immigration as a political problem. Yet the rise of the FN is not the result of a sudden surge in anti-immigrant sentiment among the French. Instead, the FN has effectively persuaded a portion of the French electorate that some social problems are caused by immigrants. For example, a high unemployment rate in a department translates into a large proportion of votes for the FN only when the department also has a large proportion of immigrants in its population.

Although France has one of the strongest anti-immigrant political parties in Western Europe, the country also has a strong antiracist tradition that is firmly embedded in the legal system, such as the regulation of hate speech. Racist slander and publicly provoking racist hate can result in a fine of $50,000 and a prison term of one year. Even insults based on race, ethnicity, nationality, or religion are punishable, with maximum penalties of $25,000 and six months in prison. A 1990 law made contesting the existence of crimes against humanity—a reference to the Holocaust—an offense. The leading civil rights organizations in France devote comparatively little of their resources to legal actions against discrimination in employment, education, housing, and government services. Instead they focus on verbal, written, and pictorial racism. For example, a typical case would involve charging a man with expressing racism for publicly distributing a tract that stated, "There are too many immigrants in the public housing project."

The most important feature of the French political system with respect to immigrants is its liberal procedures for gaining citizenship. Children born in France to immigrant parents who have not naturalized do retain their parent's citizenship. By contrast, any person born in the United States is a citizen at birth regardless of their parents' nationality. Yet in France the children of foreign parents automatically become French citizens when they reach the age of 18. Conversely, other countries in Europe have much more restrictive citizenship policies. In Germany becoming a citizen is a complex process that largely ignores length of residence or place of birth. Instead, citizenship is primarily determined by being born to someone of German ancestry. Thus Germany has granted citizenship to over 1 million ethnic Germans who left Eastern Europe and the former Soviet Union but severely restricts access to citizenship for children born in Germany to Turkish parents. The more liberal French policy is swiftly incorporating the children of immigrants who initially arrived as workers or refugees. In fact, naturalization among their parents increased during the 1990s, with Moroccans (28%) and Algerians (12%) constituting the largest groups of new citizens.

Social Dimensions

Culture, geography, and history are the primary determinants of social relations in France as they affect immigrants. Unlike the United States, culture is more important than race for social relations. Surveys of public opinion have consistently documented that the French have far more antipathy toward North Africans than black Africans. Among people of African ancestry in France, those from the overseas departments of Guadeloupe, Martinique, and Reunion are perceived as more socially acceptable than those from countries in Africa. The importance of culture for social relations in France was poignantly revealed in 1989. That year a school administrator asked three Muslim teenage girls not to wear head scarves in school on the grounds that the garments displayed religion too overtly and thus violated the French constitution's separation of church and state. The girls' parents refused, causing a national debate over religious tolerance and the function of French schools as an institution that promotes cultural integration. The vast majority of the French public disapproved of the Minister of Education's decision to allow the girls to wear the head scarves in school.

The French public is particularly sensitive to the geographic concentration of ethnic groups. Drugs and delinquency are seen as the most serious problems caused by immigrants, but of almost equal importance is their geographic settlement pattern. Whether it concerns a building, a city block, a neighborhood, or an urban district, the French public and government become extremely concerned whenever there is evidence of an "ethnic ghetto," or what in the United States would be called an ethnic community. More evenly distributing immigrants geographically and rehabilitating rundown neighborhoods are among the most popular proposals to promote immigrant integration into French society.

Added to this sensitivity to immigrants' religion and residential concentration is their link to colonial history. About one-half of the foreign population in France are first- and second-generation immigrants from former colonies in Asia and Africa. Violent decolonization in North Africa, but bloodless French departure below the Sahara, in part explains the different tolerance levels for North versus West Africans. Jean-Marie Le Pen, the leader of the far right National Front, is a former paratrooper who served in Algeria, and many of his supporters are the *pieds noirs*. Hate groups in France still invoke the name of the French king who defeated an army of invading Moors in 732.

While immigrant social relations in France are at times characterized by conflict, there is also considerable evidence of accommodation and integration. Intermarriage between immigrants and natives is increasing and now constitutes about 10 percent of all marriages (with French women slightly more likely to marry an immigrant than French men) (Hargreaves, 1995). Very few immigrant youth decline French citizenship when they become eligible upon turning 18 years old. Among North African youths, Islam is viewed more as an identity to be respected because of its importance to their parents rather than a religion that defines morality and conduct. Indeed, North African parents usually choose to have their children learn English as a second language in school rather than Arabic.

The complexity of these patterns in immigrant social relations has led to a number of different interpretations by French social scientists. Silverman (1992, p. 15) summarizes the debate: "Immigration can represent both the liberal republic and the threat to the liberal republic; it is the embodiment of France's capacity for assimilation and proof of a break-down in assimilation." The French historian Gérard Noiriel (1996) advocates the first position. He argues that "the French melting-pot" has historically absorbed immigrants and is doing the same for contemporary international migrants despite the shift in national origins from eastern and southern Europe in the early 1900s to North and sub-Saharan Africa after World War II. For every contemporary issue concerning immigrants, such as their supposed reluctance to assimilate, it is easy to find a similar, if not the same, concern about immigrants in the late nineteenth century and early twentieth century. According to Noiriel, contemporary fears about immigrants are the result of historical amnesia and the exclusion of immigrants from the French national myth, such as their contribution as workers to economic industrialization.

Conversely, the French historian Fernand Braudel (1990) advocates the second position described by Silverman. He argues that the culture and history of Muslim immigrants are fundamentally distinct from that of France. Braudel cites as the leading differences Islam's fusion of religion and politics, as well as patriarchal norms about marriage, family, and gender roles. Taken together, distinctive Islamic values and norms create a "major obstacle confronting immigrants from North Africa: a clash of civilizations" (Braudel, 1990, p. 215). Although not specifically cited by Braudel, his interest in the history of the Mediterranean region suggests that he views the south of France and North Africa as constituting an irreconcilable cultural fault line.

A third view of immigrants and social relations in France is offered by Dominique Schnapper (1991). She believes that French society has changed since the 1960s and is now less capable of absorbing immigrants than in the past. According to Schnapper, the voluntary migration of immigrants to France shows that they wish to participate in a modern economy and lifestyle, which inevitably requires adjustment and adaptation to French society and culture. But the national trend toward individualism and a weakening of collective norms and values since the 1960s means that French culture lacks the assimilationist power that it once had even if immigrants wish to assimilate. Schnapper believes that core French institutions such as the church, army, unions, and schools served to integrate immigrants in the past. These institutions, however, no longer have this power because French society has become fractured and less structurally cohesive. There clearly is evidence for Schnapper's perspective of immigrant social relations, as well as that of Braudel and Noiriel.

Economic Dimensions

Immigrant workers made an extraordinary contribution to France's post–World War II economic development. One estimate suggests that they built 70 percent of the roads, 40 percent of the buildings, and 25 percent of the cars in the country during the 1950s and 1960s. Immigrants' proportion of the labor force contracted sharply when this economic expansion ended. Yet "the utility of foreign labor for many firms did not cease even after the recession of the 1970s" (Hollifield, 1992, p. 95).

Immigrants remain concentrated in vital industrial sectors. Foreign workers account for about 17 percent of all workers in the French construction and public works sector. This level exceeds the highest concentration of foreigners in Belgium (11%), Germany (13%), the Netherlands (6%), and the United Kingdom (6%) in any economic sector. Clearly, foreign labor is still very important to the French economy. North African immigrants in particular are greatly over represented in certain sectors of the economy compared to native workers, particularly in the realms of manufacturing cars and other forms of transportation, foundries and other metal work, and especially construction and public works.

Even the French public recognizes the importance of immigrant labor. In 1966, 76 percent of the public agreed that foreign workers took jobs the French did not want to do (Dupin, 1990), as did similar proportions during the 1970s (Girard, Charbit, & Lamy, 1974). In 1982, eight years after the state ended labor migration and during a severe recession, only 38 percent of the public believed that French citizens would take the jobs vacated if immigrants left the country; 52 percent believed they would not (Hastings & Hastings, 1984).

While immigrants play a central role in the French economy, one consequence of their concentration in certain economic sectors is a high level of class inequality. Immigrants are twice as likely as the French to be blue-collar workers and much less likely to be service workers or professionals. North African and sub-Saharan Africans in particular have a much lower socioeconomic status than the French, while Portuguese and Spanish immigrants are somewhat better off. Among the most critical measures of economic well-being is the unemployment rate, which is more than double for foreigners compared to French nationals. Discrimination against immigrants is certainly one cause of their lower socioeconomic status. But many French social scientists think that the shift from an industrial economy to one based on service and information jobs is the primary reason why there is such pronounced stratification between immigrants and natives in France. If this view is correct, then the economic progress of immigrants in France will lag behind that of natives for a considerable period of time.

THE FUTURE

International migration to France will continue for economic, political, and social reasons. The aging of the French population means a lower ratio of younger workers to retired persons and thus the need to recruit labor from outside of France. The immigrant communities already there maintain close ties to family and kin in their homelands and seek to assist some of them in migrating to France. Modern means of communication and travel greatly facilitate the maintenance of these connections between homeland and host society. Political crises in countries both near and far from France will translate into new waves of asylum seekers in search of safety. Even illegal immigration will be difficult to regulate because of the highly profitable and well-organized international human smuggling networks. Conflict over immigrants and ethnic issues will thus certainly continue to be a central feature of social relations and the political process in France.

Yet France is well equipped to cope with the challenge of international migration. Its long immigration history has given the country one model of how a society can become a melting pot of different cultures. France's strong civil rights laws and tradition of liberal citizenship requirements also provide a framework for integrating existing and new populations. Finally, there is considerable evidence that contemporary immigrants from Asia, North Africa, and sub-Saharan Africa are assimilating in a way that is much more similar than different to that of earlier immigrants from Europe.

BIBLIOGRAPHY

Braudel, F. (1990). *The Identity of France, Volume Two: People and Production*. New York: HarperCollins.
Brubaker, R. (1992). *Citizenship and Nationhood in France and Germany*. Cambridge, MA: Harvard University Press.
Dupin, E. (1990). *Oui, non, sans opinion: 50 ans de sondages IFOP*. Paris: Inter Editions.
Feldblum, M. (1999). *Reconstructing Citizenship: The Politics of Nationality Reform and Immigration in Contemporary France*. Albany: State University of New York Press.
Girard, A., Charbit, Y., & Lamy, M-L. (1974). Attitudes des Français à l'egard de l'immigration étrangère: Nouvelle enquête d'opinion. *Population*, 6, 1015–1069.
Gran, B., & Hein, J. (1997). International Migration, Ethno-Politics, and the French Nation-State: Explaining Natives' Views of Immigrant Assimilation. *Social Science Quarterly*, 78, 369–384.
Hargreaves, A. G. (1995). *Immigration, "Race" and Ethnicity in Contemporary France*. New York: Routledge.
Hassoun, J., & Tan, Y. P. (1986). Les Chinois de Paris: Minorité culturelle ou constellation ethnique? *Terrain*, 7, 34–44.
Hastings, E. H., & Hastings, P. K. (Eds.). (1984). *Index to International Public Opinion, 1982–1983*. Westport, CT: Greenwood Press.
Hein, J. (1993a). *Cross-National Variation in Civil Rights Eras: The United States and France*. Paper presented at the annual meeting of the American Sociological Association, Miami.
———. (1993b). Rights, Resources, and Membership: Civil Rights Models in France

and the United States. *The Annals of the American Academy of Political and Social Science*, 530, 97–108.

———. (1993c). *States and International Migrants: The Incorporation of Indochinese Refugees in France and the United States*. Boulder, CO: Westview Press.

Hollifield, J. F. (1992). *Immigrants, Markets, and States: The Political Economy of Postwar Europe*. Cambridge, MA: Harvard University Press.

Ireland, P. (1994). *The Policy Challenge of Ethnic Diversity: Immigrant Politics in France and Switzerland*. Cambridge, MA: Harvard University Press.

Jazouli, A. (1986). *L'action collective des jeunes Maghrébins de France*. Paris: CIEMI and Harmattan.

———. (1992). *Les années banlieues*. Paris: Seuil.

Kepel, G. (1991). *Les banlieues de l'Islam: Naissance d'une religion en France*. Paris: Seuil.

Martin, P. & Widgren, J. (2002). International Migration: Facing the Challenge. *Population Bulletin*, 57, 1. Washington, DC: Population Reference Bureau.

Muxel, A. (1988). Les attitudes socio-politiques des juenes issus de l'immigration Maghrébine en région Parisienne. *Revue Française de Science Politique*, 38, 925–940.

Noiriel, G. (1996). *The French Melting Pot: Immigration, Citizenship, and National Identity*. Minneapolis: University of Minnesota Press.

Organization for Economic Cooperation and Development. (2001). *Trends in International Migration*. Paris: Organization for Economic Cooperation and Development.

Population Reference Bureau. Retrieved from http://www.prb.org.

Schnapper, D. (1991). *La France de l'intégration: Sociologie de la nation en 1990*. Paris: Gallimard.

Silverman, M. (1992). *Deconstructing the Nation: Immigration, Racism, and Citizenship in Modern France*. New York: Routledge.

Simmons, H. G. (1996). *The French National Front: The Extremist Challenge to Democracy*. Boulder, CO: Westview Press.

6

GHANA

Internal, International, and Transnational Migration

Joseph R. Oppong

INTRODUCTION

Profile of Ghana

At independence in 1957, Ghana had the highest GNP on the African continent, a sound infrastructure, and to most observers, a bright future (World Bank, 2002). During the next 25 years, the government changed hands nine times in almost revolving–door military coups. This produced political instability and severe economic problems in the 1970s. Inflation, averaging 60 percent yearly, compounded the situation further, as did the regular budget deficits, the seriously overvalued currency, and a flourishing black market.

The economic stagnation that began in the 1970s produced falling wages and an overall decline in social and economic living standards. Per capita income fell drastically, and inflation exceeded 100 percent in the 1980s (World Bank, 2002). The 1983 return of more than 1 million Ghanaians (about 10% of Ghana's total domestic population then) who had been working illegally in Nigeria, and the subsequent intensified competition for an already limited food supply, brought the economy under considerable strain (Chazan, 1991; Rimmer, 1992). Widespread drought that year led to the outbreak of extensive forest fires that produced even greater shortages of food, leading to outbreaks of famine-related diseases and increased mortality. Increasing deterioration of the economy left the government with few resources for maintaining the existing infrastructure. Consequently, it began an aggressive program of structural adjustment in 1983 that entailed severe cutbacks of health care and other social services and the laying off of government workers. These stringent measures exacerbated the deterioration of an already crippled economy (Kraus, 1991; Weissman, 1990). Cutbacks in health expenditure, for example, resulted in large layoffs, significant reductions in real income (due to inflation), and the closure of many health facilities. Many physicians left the country in search of better economic livelihoods in Europe and North America (Vogel, 1998).

Amid this economic crisis, political instability and conflict plagued Ghana. In the 1980s under the ruling military regime of Flight Lieutenant Jerry John Rawlings, who later became President Rawlings, human rights abuses, repression of political opinions, seizures of property, false imprisonment, and wanton murders and harassment were rampant (Opoku-Dapaah, 1993; Oquaye, 1995). The declining employment opportunities and the volatile political situation provided the impetus for the flight of many Ghanaians to other countries—most pursuing economic prosperity, others seeking political freedom.

Today, Ghana's economy remains dependent on rural agriculture and the export of raw materials. The major sources of foreign exchange include timber, pineapples, and gold. Cassava, fruits, and cocoa are also being processed. In 1999, with falling prices for the leading exports, cocoa and gold, and rising prices for petroleum products, a major import, Ghana's economy suffered a severe jolt. Inflation increased significantly and the value of the cedi, the national currency, fell dramatically. This continued through 2000. Timely intervention by the government, through raising taxes and postponing some public expenditure, has reduced inflation and produced some economic stability.

The political situation has also stabilized. In the first democratic transfer of power since 1981, John Kufour became president in January 2001 after his New Patriotic Party (NPP) beat the former ruling party, National Democratic Congress (NDC), in both the presidential and parliamentary elections. Following this peaceful transition, the economy is beginning to rebound, thanks to IMF and World Bank support. Despite more recent economic and political instability, Ghanaians of all backgrounds, skilled and unskilled, left the country throughout most of the 1970s, 1980s, and 1990s in unprecedented numbers to countries that were thriving, like Nigeria and the Ivory Coast.

Excessively high unemployment at home and the associated difficulties of making ends meet only served to enhance the visible benefits of emigration and created a culture of dependence and emigration. Children would excitedly discuss their intentions to "get out" when they grew up. Because the poor wages provided no incentive to work hard at home in Ghana, emigration was highly coveted and honored. Former international migrants, "Been tos," especially those who were relatively rich, were revered (Graham, 1998). Regardless of what career they pursued—musician, athlete, commercial sex worker, manual laborer, doctor, or lawyer—the Ghanaian living and working overseas who returned home flamboyantly dressed with pockets bulging with foreign exchange was a celebrity (Graham, 1998). Today, the ever present milling crowds of relatives and friends at the Kotoka International Airport testify to the widespread and lingering effect of Ghana's infatuation with international migration. The narratives of Victoria and Joseph probably capture the most common experiences of Ghana's international migrants.

Vignettes

Victoria. Victoria is the fifth of nine children from a poor family in rural Ghana. Her parents divorced when she was 10 years old, and her mother died shortly thereafter. Life then became unbearably difficult. Her oldest sister, who lived in the city, took care of Victoria and the other children. While good in school, academic success remained a dream for Victoria due to lack of financial support. She met a man who, after several months of providing material support for her in exchange for sex, took her to Germany. Victoria did not know any German and spoke little English. On arriving in Germany, the man abandoned her and returned to his wife. Because she did not want to go back to Ghana, she applied for asylum as a "political refugee." During the two and a half years it took to decide on her application, she was not allowed to work or travel outside the area where she lived. During regular, surprise visits by the authorities, her visitors would be "kicked out." She was virtually held like a prisoner. Nevertheless, she was given money for food and clothing, out of which she remitted a portion to her family back home. She also secretly earned additional income by plaiting hair for West African women.

Two and a half years later, Victoria was refused political asylum in Germany. Sensing trouble, she fled to Holland before she could be repatriated. Initially life in Holland was tough. Victoria had no job; she survived on the meager proceeds she garnered from braiding hair. The anxiety of living as an illegal in a foreign land was just overwhelming. Finally she met a Ghanaian man, a legal resident, who fell in love with her and married her. Now she has a Dutch passport. She has visited her family in Ghana once but does not think she will return to Ghana permanently for a very long time. She wants to stay in Holland so that she can support her family back in Ghana. She has no child of her own yet, but she hopes that God will give her children of her own someday.

Joseph. Joseph was a teacher in an elementary school in Ghana before he received admission to the University of Ghana. After completing a bachelor's degree, he worked for two years as a teaching/research assistant in the university during the mandatory two-year national service. His meager allowance was inadequate, and the tough economic conditions were very oppressive; he did not even have a decent pair of shoes. In 1983, under the Rawlings regime, life became quite unbearable. The biggest problem was providing food and sustenance for his wife who lived about 200 miles away from the university where he worked.

Graduate studies overseas seemed to be the only solution, and he pursued it aggressively. In 1984, he gained admission to study in Canada with a relatively generous teaching assistantship. A Ghana government scholarship paid for his travel to Canada where he supported himself on the teaching assistantship. Within a year, he had saved enough money to pay for his wife to join him in Canada. After completing master's and doctorate degrees, Joseph found a job in the United States where he has settled permanently with his wife and four children. Joseph goes to Ghana every other year, while his wife goes when there are funerals and other emergencies. They used to send remittances home frequently, but lately this happens only when there is a demonstrated emergency. The financial constraint of raising teen-age children makes extended family support extremely difficult.

Joseph has also been struggling with an ever growing pressure to build a "nice house at home." His aging mother is the chief proponent. So far he has successfully resisted the pressure. "I don't need a vacation home that I visit every other year for less than a week," he argues, but the pressure is taking its toll. There has also been considerable pressure from other family members, including his mother-in-law, to come and take some family members to the United States. Here again, Joseph has resisted the pressure, but he will probably have to cave in soon. He cannot afford to be too unpopular at home.

Victoria and Joseph represent the two most common categories of Ghana's international migrants—the unskilled and the skilled. Motivated by economic opportunity, both proceeded in a stepwise fashion. The challenges they face—loneliness, demands for money from Ghana, financial pressure, uncertainty, and hope—while living within two cultures simultaneously are ubiquitous to Ghana's emigrants.

Overview of Migration Issues

Rural-to-urban migration is perhaps the most well-documented spatial phenomenon in the history of West Africa. The promise of better livelihoods in colonial towns and cities, typically located in the coastal regions, usually drew many young people away while the harsh realities of daily survival and limited opportunities in the villages and farming districts pushed them out. Migrants would go back to rural areas frequently, particularly during holidays, taking gifts to extended family members. Remittances from these urban migrants provided a major source of sustenance for aging parents and other family members.

In recent times, however, deteriorating national socioeconomic and political conditions have made living conditions in African towns and cities as unstable as those in the village. Migrants have needed to find new "urban" centers. At the same time, globalization has brought the world closer. In fact, globalization has changed the scale of traditional migration: Ghana has become the village while the developed world—the United States, England, Germany, and others—has become the colonial city or urban area. Thus, while the spatial scale and volume of migration from Ghana has changed, the underlying principles have not. The universal desire of people to make better lives for themselves and their extended families fuels the escalating international migration among Ghanaians. It appears that for most Ghanaian migrants, a series of stepwise moves, which may have started in their home-towns or villages, to the national capital via regional cities and across the borders to a number of countries before arriving at a final destination is the norm (Konadu-Agyeman, 1999).

Ghana has become one of the major countries of emigration in West Africa since the late 1960s, but determining the exact number of Ghanaian emi-grants is difficult. In the 1990s an estimated 10–20 percent of all Ghanaian citizens were living abroad, which would correspond to between 2–4 million people based on the current population. Over 22,000 people with Ghanaian passports reside legally in Germany alone, which means that they form the largest group originating from sub-Saharan Africa among German immi-grants (Nieswand, 2001). In Europe, Germany is second only to Great Brit-ain in its number of Ghanaians. Italy had an estimated 14,000 Ghanaians in 1999 and Ghanaians claimed almost 2 percent of the total residence permits issued by 2000 (SOPEMI, 2000).

North America appears to be the primary destination of choice for Ghan-aian migrants. Between 1991–1998, Ghana was the third leading source of African immigration to the United States (Parillo, 2000). Considering that Nigeria's population is almost six times Ghana's, the 27,580 immigrants from Ghana (52,684 for Nigeria) is truly remarkable. According to the 1996 Canadian census, 14,935 Ghanaian immigrants (by ethnic origin) were in Canada, and 10,025 (67 percent) were in the Toronto Census Metropolitan Area (CMA) (Statistics Canada, 2000).

The demographics of Ghana's migrants are intriguing. Whereas most in-ternational migrants from Morocco, Egypt, and Senegal are men who mi-grate in their twenties, the proportion for Ghanaian females is very high (EUROSTAT, 2001). A massive study commissioned by the European Un-ion and conducted by EUROSTAT and the Netherlands Interdisciplinary Demographic Institute (NIDI) reported that while female migrants are more likely to be married at the time of migration than men, migrating as a single female is quite common among Ghanaians. Moreover, while most female migrants leave for family-related motives, economic motives appear to be more important for Ghanaian women (Van Hear, 2000).

These observations hold true for the few areas with good studies or data, such as Canada. Demographically, the majority of Ghanaian immigrants in Canada are men, with women constituting about 30 percent (Owusu, 1994).

Ghanaian emigrants are socially and ethnically heterogeneous and primarily from the larger cities and surrounding towns in the southern half of Ghana.

HISTORY OF MIGRATION ISSUES

Beginning in about 1970, there has been a large exodus of Ghanaians from their homeland, largely as a result of serious socioeconomic difficulties at home. Initially, two neighboring countries, Nigeria and the Ivory Coast, whose economies were relatively strong and stable, were the preferred destinations for the mostly male migrants (Stock, 1995). Nigeria's booming oil economy attracted most of the skilled workers—schoolteachers, university professors, nurses, engineers, and some traders. Most unskilled men who went to the Ivory Coast became farm laborers on the cocoa farms.

Increasingly unable to meet their obligations to children and other dependents (Manuh, 1994), Ghanaian women also migrated in large numbers, particularly to neighboring West African (Oppong, 1998) and European countries. Unskilled females preferred the Ivory Coast. Risky sexual behavior, including commercial sex work, became increasingly necessary and viable among these economic refugees, frequently for economic survival. Such commercial sex work by Ghanaian women in the Ivory Coast, the country with the highest HIV/AIDS prevalence in West Africa, has been blamed for Ghana's HIV/AIDS problem (Decosas, 1995; Oppong, 1998). In fact, the "spread of HIV to and within Ghana" has been attributed to returning Ghanaian female commercial sex workers (Hotard et al., 1998).

In the 1980s, when these neighboring economies began to experience some downturn—and especially after the repatriation of some 1 million Ghanaians who had been working in Nigeria—emigration did not cease, but the destinations became much more diverse. With the savings accumulated in Nigeria, these returning (and new) migrants began to target Europe, North America, and the oil-rich Persian Gulf countries, particularly Libya. Emigration continued even when economic, social, and political conditions began to improve at home. Today, a large Ghanaian diaspora is spread all over the globe. Many Ghanaians aspire to migrate, and many others depend heavily on money sent by their relatives abroad.

The initial wave of migration directed to Europe, North America, and the Persian Gulf was heavily male dominated, but more women today migrate over longer distances and for longer periods (Adepoju, 1991, 1995; Findley & Williams, 1990). This pattern of preferred destinations is not surprising. Historical and cultural ties traditionally influence the destination of international migration flows. Due to linguistic, administrative, and political links, former colonial powers receive a disproportionate majority of migrants from their former colonies. Because English is Ghana's official language, migration to the United Kingdom and the United States was to be expected. Since French is taught in secondary schools in Ghana, and the Ivory Coast,

a French-speaking country, was an initial principal destination, the extension
to France makes sense. Why and how so many Ghanaians prefer Germany,
a non-English-speaking country with weak colonial ties to Ghana, is a perplexing question. Equally perplexing are the large numbers of Ghanaians in
such climatically hostile countries as Norway and Finland.

The contemporary causes of emigration in Ghana center on economics.
They include overall deteriorating socioeconomic conditions, declining standards of living, and spreading poverty. Increasing unemployment resulting
from economic reforms and structural adjustment programs is an important
determinant of emigration (Adepoju, 1995). Faced with a continually declining purchasing power, skilled Ghanaians have simply left to obtain better
livelihoods for themselves and their families, and this has produced great
losses of highly skilled professionals (Zachariah & Conde, 1981). The emigration pattern of Ghanaians is quite mixed, but the United States, Germany,
Italy, and Nigeria are the top four preferred destinations (EUROSTAT,
2001).

Beginning in the late 1980s, Toronto became a major hub for Ghanaians
who left Ghana to escape economic and social crisis (Peil, 1995). An estimated 20,000 Ghanaians live in the greater Toronto metropolitan area, although official census figures are lower (Manuh, 1998). Because the military
regime in Ghana (1982–1992) suspended the constitution and abrogated
many civil liberties, many Ghanaians claimed (and were granted) refugee
status on arrival in Canada. In addition to the influx of immigrants during
the 1980s, other Ghanaians have lived in Canada since the mid-1970s, many
of whom have become citizens of Canada and call themselves Ghanaian Canadians. In fact, the Ghanaian Canadian community provides very good
insights into the livelihoods of the Ghanaian international migrants.

Ghanaian migrants in Toronto include members of nearly all social classes
and ethnic groups in Ghana, although northern Ghanaians tend to be in the
minority. Most Ghanaian migrants to Canada are highly educated and fluent
in English and French, Canada's two official languages, while others can
barely communicate except in Ghanaian languages (England & Stiell, 1997).
Migrants include individuals who were formerly petty traders, artisans,
schoolteachers, and junior civil servants. Women migrated both autono-
mously and as wives. Few Ghanaians in Toronto are homeowners; many
live in cramped conditions while pursuing home ownership in Ghana.

Ghanaian migrants maintain close ties with one another through living
arrangements, work situations, family or hometown relationships, churches,
and other associational ties. Important rites of passage such as births and
deaths provide opportunities to express solidarity and give presents according to traditional Ghanaian cultural norms. Canada's emphasis on multiculturalism has encouraged the proliferation of Ghanaian migrant organizations
(Manuh, 1998).

Some migrants expect their stay to be temporary, but many have been forced to remain in the destination country much longer. Conditions in Canada and in Ghana have made it impossible to accumulate sufficient capital to enable migrants and their families to return to Ghana and live comfortably. Moreover, social expectations of what migrants should bring home with them—cars, television sets, and lately, computers—and the expectation that the migrant will build or buy a nice home, preferably in the large city, keeps many people away.

Due to the difficulty of obtaining visas for legal entry within Ghana, some Ghanaian leave for intermediate countries and use them as stepping stones to more desirable destinations. Another reason is the total cost of travel. Many migrants move to an intermediate country where, after working for a while, they save enough money for the trip to the desired destination. This is particularly common among the unskilled. In the narratives, both Victoria and Joseph followed this stepwise pattern.

Preferred choice for intermediate countries has changed over the years. In the early 1980s, when the Nigerian economy was booming, Nigeria was a favorite intermediate destination. During the early stages of the Rawlings regime, when very strong ties existed between Libya and Ghana, Libya became another favorite. Recent favorites have included Liberia and Zimbabwe. Currently, South Africa is the most favored intermediate country, particularly for those seeking to move to Canada or the United States.

DIMENSIONS OF MIGRATION ISSUES

Political Dimensions

To be able to take advantage of opportunities that exist both in Ghana and abroad, Ghanaian migrants have sought foreign citizenship. Beginning in the mid-1990s, Ghanaians living overseas, particularly in the United Kingdom and Canada, began a struggle for the recognition of dual citizenship in Ghana. Citing their increasing contributions to the Ghanaian economy, they sent memoranda and delegations to Ghana to lobby politicians. In 1996 the Ghanaian Parliament adopted a constitutional amendment that recognized dual citizenship but excluded dual citizens from holding elective office or participating in public life. These exclusions, which are perceived to be politically motivated, have bred discontent (Manuh, 1998).

Dual-citizen Ghanaians regard their foreign citizenship as instrumental for economic health and livelihood and Ghanaian citizenship as an attribute of birth that can never be taken away. Moreover, they expect Ghana to be the beneficiary of the skills they have acquired during the time of their migration. Although it may be difficult for the state or anyone else to know which Ghanaians living in Ghana are dual citizens, migrants want restrictions on their political participation to be removed so that they are treated as Ghanaians in the land of their birth. Although migrants formulated their demands for dual citizenship in economic terms, they regard it as a remuneration and recognition for their efforts (remittances) that should entitle them to the full range of participation in Ghanaian society and economy, including the political institutions of the state. Having been abroad for years, migrants see themselves as innovators regarding rights and entitlements for all Ghanaian citizens. In their view, governments are obligated to provide certain services for their citizens to ensure their livelihoods and to foster development. During a visit to France in early 2002, Ghana's President John Agyekum Kufuor announced that his government would soon pass a law providing for dual citizenship. The decision was partly due to the fact that in 2001, Ghana received $400 million in remittances, indicating the extent to which the country owed a debt to Ghanaians overseas (http://www.transcomm.ox.ac.uk/traces/iss16pg2.htm).

In fact, the political clout of these migrants is beginning to be felt in Ghanaian politics. The leading political parties have branches in the leading European and North American countries with sizable Ghanaian populations. The migrants are courted for their expertise and money, and as candidates for political office. Ghanaian politicians regularly make the rounds to court their favors and investment. In fact, during the 2000 election, a completely new political party targeted at them emerged. It was called EGLE—the acronym for Every Ghanaian Living Everywhere.

Social Dimensions

The decision to migrate is rarely made by individuals acting alone. Rather, migration decision making often involves entire families as well as wider social structures and networks. In West Africa, migration has been seen to result from a complex series of implicit and explicit "negotiations" occurring within the household (Cordell, Gregory, & Piche, 1996, p. 15). Migration is thus a matter of household strategy, particularly for coping during times of adversity such as what Ghana faced in the recent past. When and how to move, who should go, how to raise the resources to travel, how to use any proceeds from migration, and other decisions are commonly matters for the whole household rather than the individual migrant (Findley & Sow, 1998). Households normally select and invest in the migrant who has the greatest potential for supporting the entire household in terms of remittances. This is the norm in Ghana's migration.

Migrant families and relations pool resources to cover part or all of the costs of migration. In return they expect migrants to send home remittances and gifts, to visit regularly, to remain in contact by mail or phone, and, as quickly as feasible, to sponsor other family members to emigrate. Migrants may also be encouraged to marry locally to guarantee that eventually they will return home. Thus, migration does not only concern those who go, but also those who stay. Strong social ties bind emigrants and their families and relations back home together.

Like other household strategies, migration involves outlays or investment, and there is an expectation of return from that investment. One of the principal outlays in recent years has been for the services of agents, "Visa Contractors," to arrange travel and required documentation. As passage to the affluent countries in particular has become increasingly difficult and elusive, the agents' charges have become inflated, and the resources that must be raised have increased. Thus remittances are not a simple one-way transfer from those abroad to those at home, but rather a kind of exchange between those who go and those who stay (Ammassari & Black, 2001). Migration of Ghanaians for education or professional advancement is long established but depends on resources and connections and is largely the preserve of the more prosperous or those fortunate enough to earn academic scholarships. The less well off pursue a number of different strategies; asylum migration is one among several in the repertoire, which also includes marriage, stowing away on ships, and other forms of illegal migration.

Economic Dimensions

Remittances from Ghanaians abroad contribute an ever increasing share of Ghana's foreign exchange earnings. In fact, they are becoming a major factor in Ghana's economic recovery. Private transfers, comprised mainly of remittances, now compare favorably to the value of official transfers (Manuh, 1998). In 1983, for example, private transfers were only $16.6 million, while official transfers totaled $72.4 million. Since 1991, private transfers have equaled or surpassed official transfers. In 1995, private transfers totaled $263 million but official transfers only came to $260 million. Other remittances that are paid to recipients in Ghanaian currency, usually through Western Union in Ghana, have also increased significantly (Manuh, 1998). Beginning at $3 million in 1994, it rose to $24 million in 1996 and was expected to reach $48 million by the end of 1997. In 2000, official money transfers from Ghana's international migrants exceeded US$400 million; remittance was the third largest foreign exchange earner, after gold and cocoa. In fact, the estimated total remittance figure for 2000 was more than $1 billion (Ramsey, 2001).

These remittances do not reflect other contributions that Ghana's international migrants make to their extended families, relatives, friends, schools, and communities. Besides sending home durable consumer goods such as automobiles, refrigerators, television sets, textiles, and clothing, they also build houses or acquire plots of land to do so. Through ethnic and school associations, migrants donate money and equipment for hospitals and schools and respond generously to specific requests for assistance following natural disasters or other emergencies. For example, they have outfitted hospitals, provided books and computers to local schools, and donated electricity plants and water pumps to communities. Due to such contributions, beneficiaries have been able to maintain an unprecedented level of well-being beyond what they can afford.

Thus, the mass exodus precipitated by the socioeconomic crisis has provided part of the means, through remittances, for Ghana's economic recovery. In fact, remittances from, and trade relations with, Ghana's international migrants have become more and more important for economic growth and the well-being of many families. One concern is that Ghanaian households may become dependent on foreign earnings that are nonetheless uncertain and vulnerable due to changes in migration policies and economic or political crisis (Appleyard, 1989). As opportunities to migrate—particularly seeking asylum—continue to shrink and more migrants get deported, international remittances may contract and produce instability.

It is arguable whether money transferred has been deployed productively, but remittances appear to have helped the survival of many thousands of Ghanaian households by giving them the breathing space or resources needed to claw back and reconstruct. There appears to have been substantial investment in housing and in schooling of family members, and considerable investment in businesses. Those leaving in the later 1980s seem to have been notably more successful in terms of accumulating funds from abroad and investing them at home than those who left in the 1990s (Ammassari & Black, 2001).

At the same time, remittances have arguably had corrosive effects. Socioeconomic differentiation has been accentuated, especially between those households with migrant members abroad and those without. Differences also exist between those households with successful migrants and those with migrant failures. Furthermore, relations between migrants and those at home may be tense, not least over the deployment of remittances (Van Hear, 2000). There are often bitter disputes within extended families about the ownership or disposal of property and common housing financed from abroad. Conversely, those at home often complain about the lack of reciprocity from migrants for the help they may have been given.

One negative side effect of the Ghanaian international migration is the loss of skilled labor, what has been dubbed the "brain drain." Skilled workers such as teachers, engineers, nurses, and doctors have left the country, negatively influencing economic and other developments. The health care system, which is losing not just physicians but also pharmacists and nurses, is probably the worst affected. Out of an estimated 2,458 physicians produced by Ghana's medical schools, only 1,669 remain in the country. The physician population ratio was estimated as 1:16,000, while for nurses it was 1:3,500 (Ghana Home Page, General News, May 19, 2002). Fifty pharmacists left the country between 1997 and 2000, but between January and March of 2001, 24 pharmacists had already emigrated (Ghana Home Page, General

News, September 10, 2001). Ghana's health minister has equated the seriousness of the brain drain in the health sector to the threat of HIV/AIDS.

The problem is compounded by the fact that relatively more affluent countries such as the United States, the United Kingdom, and Saudi Arabia are aggressively recruiting Ghanaian health professionals directly in Ghana. The salary difference is surely a big draw—a U.K. nurse receives an average monthly salary of £2,000 whereas a senior counterpart in Ghana receives some 600,000 cedis (less than US$100). Similarly, a doctor in the United Kingdom earns at least £60,000 per annum and has numerous opportunities for postgraduate work and for specialization.

THE FUTURE

Due to the culture of emigration that has developed in Ghana, the future of international migration is expected to stay strong. In the NIDI study referred to earlier, the proportion of Ghanaians who intend to migrate was much higher than in Turkey, Morocco, Egypt, or Senegal (Schoorl et al., 2000). This suggests that the future of emigration continues to be bright, and the desire to migrate remains strong.

Every day, milling crowds of relatives and friends at the Kotoka International Airport testify to the widespread expectations from international migration. This is not going to change very quickly. The emergent international migration culture promises to withstand sporadic improvements in Ghana's economic conditions. In fact, the ongoing deterioration of Ghana's major universities is likely to produce an escalated emigration of education emigrants to continue the cycle. As Ghana's government makes efforts to protect and enhance this major source of foreign exchange through effective implementation of its dual-citizenship act, emigration can be expected to increase.

Migration has a long history in Ghana. In colonial times, it was from the village to the colonial city and aimed at obtaining better living conditions for the migrant and supporting social group. Due primarily to difficult economic conditions, Ghanaians, both males and females, have migrated in large numbers to relatively affluent countries for similar reasons. While Ghana's emigrants have been a major source of blessing to the country (huge remittances of precious foreign exchange), they have also been the source of a major scourge (e.g., emigrants have contributed to the spread of HIV/AIDS). Socially and culturally, emigration is here to stay. Increasing dependence on remittances from these migrants guarantees that government policies are going to favor emigration. Moreover, the emerging political clout of this group, expressed in dual-citizenship legislation and political party recruitments, assures this support. At the same time, the country continues to struggle under the crushing weight of a devastating brain drain, particularly in the health sector. Ghana has no easy options. In an increasingly small global village, the highest bidder gets the most skilled workers.

Until Ghana and other countries are able to pay their skilled nationals livable wages, the emigration drum will continue to beat; the appeal to patriotic nationalism and self-sacrifice may go unheard, and more likely, unheeded. Like Victoria and Joseph, personal hunger and pain will drown the call of the motherland.

BIBLIOGRAPHY

Adepoju, A. (1991). South–North Migration: The African Experience. *International Migration, 29*(2), 205–223.

———. (1995). Emigration Dynamics in Sub-Saharan Africa. *International Migration, 33*(3/4), 315–391.

Ammassari, S., & Black, R. (2001). *Harnessing the Potential of Migration and Return to Promote Development: Applying Concepts to West Africa.* Sussex Migration Working Papers. Sussex, UK: Sussex Center for Migration Research.

Anarfi, J. K., Awusabo Asare, K., & Nsowah Nuamah, N.N.N. (2000, March). Push and Pull Factors of International Migration: Country Report. Ghana. Accra. In *EUROSTAT Working Papers*, no. 10. Luxembourg: EUROSTAT.

Appleyard, R. T. (1988). *International Migration: Challenge for the Nineties.* Geneva: International Organization for Migration.

———. (1989). Migration and Development: Myths and Reality. *International Migration Review, 23*(3), 486–505.

——— (Ed.). (1998). *Emigration Dynamics in Developing Countries, Volume I: Sub-Saharan Africa.* Aldershot, UK: Ashgate.

Bank of Ghana Research Department. (1997). Unpublished statistics, 1997.

Basch, L., Schiller, N. G., & Blance, C. S. (1994). *Nations Unbound: Transnational Projects, Postcolonial Predicaments and Deterritorialized Nation-States.* Langhorn, PA: Gordon and Breach.

Birchard, K. (2001). Academics' Emigration Said to Hurt Africa. *Chronicle of Higher Education, 48*(10), A63, 3, 4.

Chazan, N. (1991). The Political Transformation of Ghana Under the PNDC. In D. Rothchild (Ed.), *Ghana: The Political Economy of Recovery.* Boulder, CO: Lynne Rienner.

Cordell, D. D., Gregory, J. W., & Piche, V. (1996). *Hoe and Wage: A Social History of a Circular Migration System in West Africa.* Boulder, CO: Westview Press.

Decosas, J. (1995). Epidemic in Ghana: A Very Distinct Profile. *AIDS Analysis Africa, 5*(3), 12.

Decosas, J., Kane, F., Anarfi, J. K., Sodji, K.D.R., & Wagner, H. U. (1995). Migration and AIDS. *The Lancet, 346*, 826–828.

England, K., & Stiell, B. (1997). "They Think You're As Stupid As Your English Is": Constructing Foreign Domestic Workers in Toronto. *Environment and Planning A, 29*, 195–215.

EUROSTAT. (2001). Why Do People Migrate? Statistics in Focus: Population and Social Conditions (Theme 3-1).

Findley, S. E., & Sow, S. (1998). From Season to Season: Agriculture, Poverty and Migration in the Senegal River Valley. In R. Appleyard (Ed.), *Emigration*

Dynamics in Developing Coutries, Volume 1: Sub-Saharan Africa (pp. 69–144). Aldershot, U.K.: Ashgate.

Findley, S. E., & Williams, L. (1990). *Women Who Go and Women Who Stay: Reflections of Family Migration Processes in a Changing World*. Working Paper Series. Geneva: ILO.

Ghana Home Page. General News. (2001, August 28). Brain drain affects health delivery in Ghana. Retreived from http://www.ghanaweb.com/GhanaHome Page/NewsArchive/.

———. (2001, September 10). Pharmacists Join Exodus for Greener Pastures. http://www.ghanaweb.com/GhanaHomePage/NewsArchive/.

———. (2002, January 21). 30 Nurses Flee KATH in a Month. http://www.ghanaweb.com/GhanaHomePage/NewsArchive/.

———. (2002, January 22). Brain Drain May Force Closure of Hospitals. http://www.ghanaweb.com/GhanaHomePage/NewsArchive/.

———. (2002, April 23). Brain Drain: Ghanaian Doctors Going to UK. http://www.ghanaweb.com/GhanaHomePage/NewsArchive/.

———. (2002, May 19). Brain Drain in the Health Sector: Ghanaian Doctors Going to UK. http://www.ghanaweb.com/GhanaHomePage/NewsArchive/.

Graham, Y. (1998). Where Have You "Been To"? *Orbit, 68*, 1.

Hotard, R. S., Denno, D. M., Adu-Sardokie, Y., Baffoe-Bonnie, B., Steele, R. W., & Bordes, I. D. (1998). AIDS in a Developing Country: Education to Prevent Spread of Disease. *The AIDS Reader, 8*(1), 12–16.

Konadu-Agyeman, K. (1999). Characteristics and Migration Experience of Africans in Canada. *Canadian Geographer, 43*(4), 400–414.

Kraus, J. (1991). The Struggle over Structural Adjustment in Ghana. *Africa Today, 38*, 19–37.

Manuh, T. (1994). Ghana: Women in the Public and Informal Sectors under the Economic Recovery Program. In P. Sparr (Ed.), *Mortgaging Women's Lives: Feminist Critiques of Structural Adjustments* (pp. 61–77). Geneva: Zed Books.

———. (1998, July–December). Ghanaians, Ghanaian Canadians, and Asantes: Citizenship and Identity among Migrants in Toronto. *Africa Today, 45*(3/4), 14, 481.

Nieswand, B. (2001). Ghanaians in Germany. Max Planck Institute for Social Anthropology, http://www.eth.mpg.de/.

Opoku-Dapaah, E. (1993). *Adaptation of Ghanaian Refugees in Toronto*. Toronto: York Lanes Press.

Oppong, J. R. (1998). A Vulnerability Interpretation of the Geography of HIV/AIDS in Ghana, 1986–1995. *Professional Geographer, 50*(4), 437–488.

Oquaye, M. (1995). Human Rights and the Transition to Democracy under the PNDC in Ghana. *Human Rights Quarterly, 17*, 556–573.

Owusu, T. (1994). *The Adaptation of Black African Immigrants in Canada: A Case Study of Residential Behavior and Ethnic Community Formation among Ghanaians in Toronto*. Unpublished doctoral dissertation, University of Toronto, Canada.

Parrillo, V. (2000). *Strangers to These Shores: Race and Ethnic Relations in the United States*. Boston: Allyn and Bacon.

Peil, M. (1995). Ghanaians Abroad. *African Affairs, 94*, 345–367.

Ramsey, F. J. (2001). *Global Studies: Africa*. Guilford, CT: Dushkin.

Rimmer, D. (1992). *Staying Poor: Ghana's Political Economy 1950–1990*. Oxford: Pergamon Press.

Schoorl, J. J., Heering, L., Esveldt, I., Groenewold, G., van der Erf, R. F., Bosch, A. M., de Valk, H., & de Bruijn, B. J. (2000). *Push and Pull Factors of International Migration: A Comparative Report* (Theme 1, General Statistics). Luxembourg: EUROSTAT.

SOPEMI. (2000). *Trends in International Migration*. Paris: OECD.

Statistics Canada. (2000, February 24). 1996 Census of Canada. http://www.statcan.ca.

Stock, R. (1995). *Africa South of the Sahara*. New York: Guilford.

Van Hear, N. (2000). People Abroad and People at Home in Societies under Strain. *Forced Migration Review*, 7. Retrieved from http://www.fmreview.org/fmr07.htm.

Vogel, R. J. (1998). *Cost Recovery in the Health Sector: Selected Country Studies in West Africa*. Technical Paper No. 82. Washington, DC: World Bank.

Weissman, S. R. (1990). Structural Adjustment in Africa: Insights from the Experiences of Ghana and Senegal. *World Development*, 18, 1621–1634.

Wong, M. (2000). Ghanaian Women in Toronto's Labor Market: Negotiating Gendered Roles and Transnational Household Strategies. *Canadian Ethnic Studies*, 32(2), 45–77.

World Bank. (1980). *Demographic Aspects of Migration in West Africa*. Staff Working Paper No. 414. Washington, DC: World Bank.

———. (2002). Country Briefs—Ghana. Retrieved from http://www.worldbank.org/afr/gh2.htm.

Zachariah, K. C., & Conde, J. (1981). *Migrations in West Africa: Demographic Aspects*. Oxford: Oxford University Press.

7

IRELAND

A Historical and Political Interpretation of the Irish Diaspora

Sean Kenny

INTRODUCTION

Profile of Ireland

Ireland is an island off the western coast of Europe, roughly the size of the state of Maine. In 1921, after five years of armed struggle, 26 of the island's 32 counties gained independence from Britain to form an Irish Free State, which would later become the Irish Republic. Northern Ireland, comprising about one-sixth of the island, remains part of the United Kingdom. The population of the Republic has risen from its low point of 2.9 million people about 50 years ago to about 3.85 million today, while Northern Ireland has had a more static total population that today stands at 1.64 million. Literacy in Ireland is in excess of 98 percent, one of the world's highest. The Irish economy has grown rapidly in the last decade, and agriculture, once the dominant economic sector, now accounts for only 4 percent of GDP, with manufacturing, mostly aimed at export markets, making up 38 percent and services the remaining 58 percent. Over 90 percent of the citizens of the Republic of Ireland are Roman Catholics, while the majority of the population of Northern Ireland is Protestant, and this has been at the root of the island's partition into two and the violence within Northern Ireland. A peace agreement signed in 1998 has taken hold and guarantees the rights of the minority Catholic population in Northern Ireland and may eventually lead to the peaceful reunification of Ireland.

Vignette

There are, quite literally, millions of individual stories of Irish migrants. Most, past and present, are completely undocumented, but it seems that in every generation a representative tale makes its way into Irish literature.

One of Australia's most famous authors is Thomas Keneally, who wrote *Schindler's List* and 20 other novels. In 1998, he published *The Great Shame*, a nonfiction account in which he describes the arrival of some of his antecedents from Ireland. Back in 1833, Hugh Larkin, a landless tenant farmer in Galway, took part in a protest against his landlord in which he and two other men, all in disguise, broke in the back door of the Big House and frightened the landlord's wife. They did her no harm and left as soon as they had made their point, but one of the servants recognized Hugh's voice and turned him in.

Larkin was convicted of Ribbonism[1] and sentenced to transportation for life to New South Wales. Of the 220 prisoners aboard the ship that carried him to Australia, over 60 had been involved in similar political acts with the remainder found guilty of crimes ranging from vagrancy to stealing—clothes, food, livestock—to manslaughter and murder. By the standards of the time the prisoners were well cared for on the voyage, which lasted 124 days.

On his arrival in Sydney, Larkin had the good luck to be assigned to a rancher who needed shepherds and was thus spared the short, harsh life of working on a chain gang. He was taken to Goulburn, 130 miles south, then sent further into the bush to live in a bark hut and tend his flock, a solitary existence that would test anyone's spirit and gave Larkin an understandable appetite for moonshine. He had left behind in Ireland his wife, Esther, and their two young children, and after nine years of good behavior he was allowed to petition to have them sent out at the government's expense. This he duly did, but the document appears to have been lost en route. Meanwhile, Esther also petitioned on her own behalf, but even if approved, she and her children could only travel free on a women's convict ship, and because of the success of the antitransportation movement in Britain, the last of these had now sailed.

Hugh would never see his wife and their two boys again. After 10 years in Australia, he met another Irish woman, Mary Shields, who had been transported from Limerick four years earlier for stealing clothes. She too had been married and had two children, a baby girl who either died or was handed over to some other relative before she left and a two-year-old son whom she had kept with her throughout the ordeal. Mary, too, was a first-time offender, not a habitual criminal, and after four years of exemplary behavior in a women's prison she made her way into service with Larkin's employer. By now Hugh had earned his "ticket of leave," which allowed him to live as a free man, and the pair settled down in Goulburn where they opened a hardware store. Mary died at the age of 36 while giving birth to their fourth child. Whatever demons haunted Hugh Larkin, he followed her to the grave three years later after apparently consuming "as much as two gallons of rum" (Keneally, 1998).

Overview of Migration Issues

Ireland has been continuously inhabited since the end of the last Ice Age, with one wave of invader after another mixing with the people already there, each bringing its own culture and technology with which to try to over-whelm the existing population. The most significant factor in shaping Ireland's violent history has been its proximity to the larger and more powerful island nation to the east, Great Britain.

Ireland has, however, retained a distinct culture and in the more recent past, as immigration gave way to emigration, its people have carried those ideas to many parts of the world, particularly to North America. This, and most other major historical events in Ireland, can be traced to the various migration patterns into and out of Ireland over the years. The use of the word "nation" in the Irish context is fraught with difficulty. On the one hand a sizable number of people living in Northern Ireland, who are indeed Irish people, are intractably opposed to the idea of Irish nationalism and would rather see themselves as British. On the other hand there is a diaspora of over 50 million people around the world—10 times the total population of the island of Ireland itself—who see themselves in various ways as being Irish.

This diaspora is the result of centuries of emigration motivated by political strife, the search for religious freedom and, since the middle of the nine-teenth century, harsh economic conditions and even survival itself. Ireland has been much more a sender of emigrants than a receiver of them, although it was the colonization of Ireland by England that brought about the social conditions that caused this enormous exodus.

HISTORY OF MIGRATION ISSUES

The history of migration into and out of Ireland goes all the way back to the first people who migrated there. About 5,000 years ago people crossed over from what is now Scotland and established themselves in the very northeastern part of Ireland. These first farmers colonized the northern half of the island, as evidenced by the "court-cairns" they built as burial chambers, whose ruins still abound. They were followed by a wave of "passage-grave" builders who came from northwestern France and who built even more elab-orate cemeteries, including the world-famous Newgrange, whose central chamber is still lit up today by the rising sun on the winter solstice.

About 4,000 years ago the concept of metallurgy reached Ireland, this

time possibly via nomadic traders called "Beaker People" after their distinctive pottery, and over the next couple of millennia the people developed the
ability to produce distinctive bronze tools, swords, and gold ornaments.
Then, some time between 2,200 and 2,600 years ago, the Celts arrived,
bringing with them iron tools and weapons. This was a civilization that at
its height dominated Europe, the Mediterranean, and Asia Minor. Today,
one usually associates the term "Celtic" with those people who ended up
speaking Gaelic or related languages: the Irish, Scottish, Welsh, and Bretons.
But the only nation that sees itself as truly Celtic today is Ireland.

This enduring Celtic legacy is largely a result of never having been colonized by the Romans. This allowed Irish society to evolve its own unique
culture with its own mythology, folklore, dancing, and music. Because it was
an oral society, traveling bards played an important role in preserving historical knowledge and Celtic Ireland even developed it own unique legal
system, known as the Brehon laws. So robust was this culture that even the
widespread adoption of Christianity from the fifth century A.D. onward had
little effect on it.

Around A.D. 800 the Vikings began to attack and plunder Irish monas-
teries in isolated raids, but over time they established permanent settlements
all along the east coast, most notably Dublin, the capital of Ireland today.
Then, in 1169, one local king, Diarmaid, in an effort to conquer the province
of Leinster, brought in mercenaries from England. But these were Normans,
the people who had conquered Britain over the previous century; they
brought with them awesome, new military technology, chain-mail armor,
and crossbows, and they seized the opportunity to conquer the entire country. They built new castles and tower houses and established new dynasties.

By the time Elizabeth I became England's first Protestant queen in 1558,
English power in Ireland had waned altogether outside of a small area
around Dublin. The Elizabethan strategy to reconquer Ireland revolved
around a concept called "surrender and regrant," which encouraged Irish
chieftains to give up their rights to their lands under the old Brehon laws
and have them deeded back by the crown. This had a certain appeal, since
under English law land ownership was hereditary and failure to comply
could mean that the land was granted to some other chieftain or even a rival
family member—which from the English perspective had the added benefit
of pitting the Irish against each other.

The enterprise worked up to a point, but the Irish had a way of backsliding
and to keep them loyal required a constant military presence. A major revolt
in the southern province of Munster was brutally squelched, and the confiscated lands were made available to English settlers, known as planters. The
Plantation of Munster failed, however, when it was overrun by the forces of
Hugh O'Neill, chieftain of the most powerful dynasty in the northern province of Ulster.

The Spanish had enough confidence in the Irish resistance to become involved and sent a force of 4,000 to occupy the port of Kinsale on the south coast, but an Irish attempt to break through the besieging English army failed, O'Neill and his allies were routed, and O'Neill went into permanent exile in 1607. This defeat had devastating and irrevocable consequences for the Irish. There was now no organized resistance to English rule and a whole new series of plantations was proposed. Not only were all of these settlers Protestants themselves, but they were also required to recruit at least 10 more British Protestant families for each thousand acres granted to them and to meet other stringently pro-English conditions.

No one knows for sure how many English and Scottish settlers came to Ireland in the seventeenth century, but it was certainly over 100,000 (Foster, 1989a). The Irish fought back sporadically but were crushed, first by Oliver Cromwell who set out to destroy every vestige of Catholicism through a combination of evangelization, banishment, and genocide, and then by the defeat of James II by William of Orange in what was really a European war fought on Irish soil. William's success was greatly facilitated by the new Ulster Protestants, who held out in the towns of Derry and Enniskillen until he arrived, and then fought alongside him at the Battle of The Boyne.

The natives and settlers might have over time, as had happened at other times, comingled, but events now raced in the opposite direction. In the eighteenth century a system of "Penal Laws" was enacted to crush the aspirations of the dispossessed Irish to reassert themselves and to dispossess the remainder. Catholics could not buy land or take out mortgages. They had to divide the land equally between all the sons. They could not vote or bear arms. Scottish Presbyterians, to whom the harsher of the Penal Laws did not apply, could hardly fail to exploit the opportunities on their doorstep. Fifty thousand more families poured into Ulster from Scotland in the quarter century after the Battle of The Boyne. Protestant Ulster today, with its Orange lodges (the Orange Order is named after King William of Orange), its parades commemorating the siege of Derry and the Battle of the Boyne, and its seemingly atavistic anti-Catholic elements, is a direct result of this migration. The Presbyterians coalesced into an exclusive society of their own, one that enjoyed remarkable economic success. Belfast grew into an important trading port. In 1921, when Ireland negotiated a treaty of independence with Britain, the six northeastern counties in which the majority population were descendants of those migrants opted to remain a part of the United Kingdom. This is what we know of as Northern Ireland today.

From the late eighteenth century onward, Ireland would become a source of emigration, a process that has gone on more or less continuously right up until the last decade when the Irish economy suddenly began to expand and immigration, still mainly of returning emigrants, began for the first time to outstrip emigration consistently.

The first major wave of Irish emigrants was Ulster Presbyterians, who went to North America in sufficient numbers to play a significant role in the

American War of Independence. These people would later rename themselves "Scots-Irish" to distinguish themselves from the masses of destitute Catholics crossing the Atlantic, before, during, and after the Great Famine of 1845–1852. Sailing to America in the eighteenth century was not for the fainthearted: The crowded wooden ships might get there in three weeks or they might take three months. They arrived in Pennsylvania and later Maryland, where the dream of the indentured servant was to pay off his master and head for the frontier, an area west of Philadelphia, where he could lay claim to land of his own. They eventually spread across the Susquehanna River and grew to dominate the Shenandoah Valley. The British apparently contrived to position the Irish in what was effectively a buffer zone between themselves and the Native Americans.

Once the Revolutionary War broke out, the Irish joined in, setting up Revolutionary Councils to take over Pennsylvania and Maryland. Five Ulstermen would eventually be among the signatories of the Constitution, including John Hancock himself, who was from Derry. These immigrants would continue to play a huge role in shaping the new country. These are also the Irish who brought with them what we know today as country and western music. Square dances are barely modified Irish jigs. The Irish found themselves on both sides of the Civil War, and after the war they were at the core of the push westward, of "Manifest Destiny."

Back in Ireland, by the end of the eighteenth century the treatment meted out to the indigenous Irish population was beginning to reach its inevitable conclusion. Virtually all of the arable land now belonged to Anglo-Irish landlords, many of whom lived elsewhere. The Catholic peasantry was concentrated into tiny farms, which had been subdivided to the point that potatoes were the only viable crop that would sustain an entire family. The west was particularly densely populated, and here there was no industry, and indeed social conditions were so backward that many people lived and died without ever tasting bread because there were so few flour mills (Woodham-Smith, 1962).

Emigration was encouraged and Irish Catholics began to arrive in America in large numbers. Ulster Protestants continued to emigrate, though in much smaller numbers, and they now began to see British North America, which would become Canada, as a more desirable destination. Then, in the middle of the nineteenth century, a cataclysmic event occurred in Ireland that sparked off a migration that would permanently and dramatically alter Irish demographics, both inside and outside Ireland.

In 1845 a mysterious disease attacked the potato crops across Europe. Ireland had 3 million of its poorest people entirely dependent on potatoes and the government, anticipating widespread hunger, instigated various relief works. This staved off the worst effects well into 1846, but then the blight, as it was now known, continued to reappear and a new government pursued a different strategy of importing and distributing Indian corn. By

1847 the policy had become one of placing the burden for relief on the local "unions," tax collecting entities that operated "work-houses" or "poor-houses." Income tax did not exist, so taxes were levied on landlords based on the number of tenants. This motivated the landlords to reduce that number, especially those tenants who could no longer pay rent, greatly exacerbating the problem. Some landlords even went so far as to pay the fares of their tenants to America to clear them off, but most simply evicted them, demolishing their hovels to prevent them from ever returning.

No one knows how many people perished in the years 1846–1852 as a result of the potato blight, but most historians agree that it was a million or more. At least another million emigrated and four out of five of those went to the United States. Approximately 369,000 people left Ireland in 1852 alone—over 5 percent of the total population (Kinealy, 1995). How was it possible for such a large number of poor people to cross the Atlantic back in those days? Essentially, this was because most bulk cargo was eastbound. In particular, there was a robust trade in timber from Canada after the Napoleonic Wars, when Britain sought to lessen reliance on continental Europe. These ships had now found a new cargo to carry westward: the Irish. Conditions on board were abysmal, slightly better on U.S. flagged ships, which were subject to more stringent laws. Nicknamed "coffin-ships," they were susceptible to outbreaks of disease that could contaminate everyone on board and for that reason were subject to quarantine when they reached North America. Most of those who made it ashore in good health made it their business to walk across the border into the United States, desperate to flee the British Empire in its entirety.

These people were, without doubt, some of the most wretched, ill-prepared immigrants ever to make their way to America, and they were treated accordingly. "No Irish Need Apply" signs became a common sight next to "Help Wanted" ones. The Famine Irish found themselves at the very bottom of the social totem pole. True, there were others there too, African Americans in the northeast and Chinese in the west, but in sheer numbers— the Irish constituted over 40 percent of all immigrants to the United States in the decade 1850–1859—these newcomers would come to dominate the low-end labor market. They worked as laborers on canals, railroads, and buildings and quickly took control of the labor unions in New York and Boston simply by being so numerous (Miller, 2001). One of the unique characteristics of this migration was that as many women as men arrived in the United States. Indeed, at the time, a quarter of all domestic servants in New York were Irish women.

Every one of these immigrants was destined to live some, if not all, of his or her life in squalor, and it is estimated that the average life expectancy after disembarkation was no more than about six years. But still they kept coming, steadily depleting Ireland's population, and slowly climbing the social ladder in the United States. Today about one in six Americans claims Irish descent.

The population of the United States however has grown to be 60 times that of Ireland, north and south, and although it continues to be a popular destination for Irish migrants, their numbers are now statistically insignificant.

Irish migration has not been exclusively to the United States. Large numbers of Irish moved to the burgeoning cities of England to work in steel, wool, and cotton mills, or as "navvies" working the building sites with their picks and shovels, to the point that about 10 percent of the population of Britain today claims Irish descent. Those who went to the United States always saw their journey as one-way and their departure was often accompanied by what was called an "American Wake," the same kind of celebration that would have taken place if they had died, as the remaining family members did not ever expect to see the departing relative again, unless they too followed across the ocean. Going to England, however, was viewed as reversible and yet very few ever did return.

After these two destinations comes Australia, but for those emigrating under their own resources and not being transported as convicts, Australia was four times as expensive to reach as America by boat, though by any other measure it was viewed as a highly attractive destination, and only this high cost limited the number of Irish and other Europeans who ended up there (Foster, 1989a).

One final trend in the history of Irish migration completes the picture of Irish society today: the movement of people within Ireland, particularly over the last 40 years. Up to that point the depopulation of rural Ireland was almost entirely caused by continuous and widespread emigration. The residual population was maintained first by remittances from America and Britain and later by government initiatives aimed at preserving the family farm, though half of all the people born into these farming communities in the twentieth century would die elsewhere. In the 1960s the Republic of Ireland finally began to industrialize, mostly by attracting investment from overseas companies who saw Ireland as a suitable location for supplying manufactured goods to Europe. This created opportunities in the major towns, and they began to grow again after decades of stagnation. Dublin, which had been growing continuously due to the fact that just about every government-related activity was centralized there, also experienced—and continues to experience—rapid growth.

Ireland also has a small nomadic population called "Travellers." They were once referred to as Itinerants, Gypsies, or Tinkers—the latter because they produced and repaired metal cans, pots, and buckets. Their genesis is still unclear, but by their own folklore they are descended from dispossessed Irish royalty. They certainly predate the Great Famine and possibly were a part of the upheaval of Cromwellian or Elizabethan times, but they may go back centuries before that. They tend to intermarry among themselves and have successfully resisted all efforts to integrate them into the "settled" community.

DIMENSIONS OF MIGRATION ISSUES

Political Dimensions

Although Irish migrants can be found all over the world, Ireland was never a colonial power. In fact, Ireland exhibited the same symptoms as other postcolonial nations. Following the euphoria of independence, there was an irrational civil war in which the die-hard revolutionaries refused to acknowledge the wishes of the majority, north or south. What these people failed to grasp was that the people who had migrated from England and Scotland to the six northeastern counties, who were dubious about the far less extreme politics of "home-rule" for Ireland within the United Kingdom, wanted no part of a breakaway state that quickly asserted itself as both Gaelic and Catholic. Within a generation the Dublin government had outlawed divorce, enshrined the Catholic Church in the new constitution, and, moreover, stated in that same constitution that it applied to all of Ireland.

Because of the enormous level of emigration, Ireland's demographics were unique in twentieth-century Europe. No other country had actually lost population in this way, and probably no other country in the world comprised a "residual" people whose most productive members, its young men and women, simply left permanently in deliberately high enough numbers to affect the lifestyles of those who remained and to allow the population not to rise. It may not be too surprising then that the country's political leaders, far from reaching out to the huge Irish diaspora, acted for the most part as if no such group existed (Lee, 1989).

The Irish who emigrated were universally successful wherever they went, and yet up to the present generation the country they came from never mustered the political will to make use of that fact. But that has not deterred the Irish elsewhere, particularly in the United States. The Irish have made their presence felt across the entire spectrum of American politics. The Ulster Irish who participated in The Revolutionary War would go on to dominate the White House in the nineteenth century. Jackson, Polk, Buchanan, and Grant were all presidents of Irish extraction. And the Irish Catholics who arrived in huge numbers immediately became active in local politics, in organizing unions, and in agitating for better pay and conditions for themselves. Female Irish domestic servants were famously assertive and played a major role in agitating for women's rights (Miller, 2001).

John F. Kennedy became the first American president of Irish Catholic descent and the first one to visit Ireland, an act that elevated him to legendary status. Ronald Reagan began his re-election campaign with a visit to his ancestors' village of Ballyporeen in County Cork to win Irish-American votes. And when he was re-elected, he made it a high priority to persuade the British Prime Minister, Margaret Thatcher, to make concessions to Irish Nationalists, which brought about the first Anglo-Irish power sharing agreement. Bill Clinton was equally committed to an Irish peace agreement, and he and a committee of U.S. politicians, headed by Senator George Mitchell, continued that effort, to the point where there is now a permanent ceasefire and an assembly in which both sides share power. None of this would have the same political importance if all of those emigrants had not made their way to America.

Social Dimensions

The impact of centuries of continuous emigration out of Ireland on Irish society itself is very much a question of what might have been. First of all, there is the actual size of the population. If emigration had been stemmed by industrialization, or by a more humane approach to the Great Famine, or even by a spirit of optimism about Ireland's future, instead of the population falling from over 8 million to under 5 million, what would it have risen to? This is very difficult to estimate other than by comparison with the experience in other European countries, which yields estimates of 12 million and above—up to three times the current population (Lee, 1989).

Second, there is the question of the relationship between the people who left and those who stayed. Though the Irish in Britain and America never forgot their heritage, the Irish in Ireland, other than being grateful for the remittances from relatives abroad, largely behaved as if those who left were no longer truly Irish or had simply ceased to exist. The Irish at home did not view those who left as a loss; quite the opposite. Politicians referred to the "safety valve" of emigration and worried more about what would happen if the doors to Britain and America were ever slammed shut than about stemming the exodus, let alone enticing the exiles home again (Lee, 1989).

Irish society throughout much of the twentieth century lapsed into isolation and intolerance. It is hard not to conclude that the dearth of ideas, the stagnation of society, was a result of the outflow of those with the most energy. In the last two decades this trend has reversed; the economy has taken off and unemployment has plummeted, and a very different attitude prevails. Ireland now proactively pursues immigrants to fill labor shortages. The Irish have stamped their ideas throughout the English speaking world. Ireland continues to be a well-spring of unique music, dance, literature, and performing arts, and the 70 million people of Irish descent remain a receptive audience for it, to the point that Irish culture is a pervasive part of Western culture, and ultimately of world culture today and for the foreseeable future.

Economic Dimensions

As above, the economic effects of the loss of so many people to emigration beg the question of what might have been. But here the results are clear and quantifiable. Because the people left and went to where the jobs were, there was no inflow of capital to Ireland itself in pursuit of cheap labor. And even with agriculture, the dominant export until 40 years ago though now far less important, the prevailing psychology was one of survival, not of investment and growth. In the 1960s some of Ireland's more astute economists and politicians began to understand the problem and devise ways to overcome it. They created government agencies whose function was to attract investment from abroad, and legislated tax incentives, government loans, and grants for buildings, machinery, and, most importantly, the training of employees. The economy began to grow. But Ireland itself was a tiny market for manufactured goods and realized that these multinational companies would only locate there as a means to access the enormous European market. Ireland joined what is now the European Community in 1973, and the trickle of foreign factories became a flood.

The policy had its ups and downs, but the idea that Ireland, with its tiny population, could only succeed in world terms by maintaining its attractiveness for business activities that would otherwise not take place there at all has firmly taken hold and drives much of the country's political, social, and economic thinking. Ireland continues to invest heavily in education, transportation, and telecommunications. It has embraced supply-side economics — steadily feeding capital into the economy with lower tax rates — to the point of attracting criticism from other European countries. Yet these same countries don't deny that Ireland has emerged from generations of unemployment and emigration as Europe's most successful economy.

THE FUTURE

The major social challenge for the Irish people today is the peaceful reconciliation of the Loyalist and Nationalist communities in Northern Ireland. With one of the world's most intractable conflicts and a legacy of the immigration of English and Scottish colonists, it still has the potential to return to chaos. There are still those people who want victory, not peace, and neither side can achieve what they would define as total victory. The current peace agreement has given the people of Northern Ireland their first taste of peace in a generation, and both sides have taken the opportunity to try to understand, and even solve, some of the hate crimes of the last 30 years.

A modern Irish migrant is as likely to leave Ireland simply to pursue some specialty or out of a healthy curiosity about the world as for monetary gain and is as likely to return as not. Joe O'Sullivan is a good example of this new type of Irish migrant. Born into a large Cork family in the 1950s, Joe grew up there and when he left school held down a number of construction jobs, erecting scaffolding and the like. But like so many young Irish people in the 1970s, Joe knew he was capable of more, and eventually he secured a position as a buyer with one of the many multinational manufacturing companies that were being attracted to Ireland at that time by a combination of tax incentives, Ireland's presence within the huge market of the European Union, and the availability of an eager, youthful, English-speaking workforce.

He job-hopped his way from buyer to senior buyer to purchasing manager, eventually becoming the European purchasing manager for Apple Computer Inc., which had established their European manufacturing in Cork, Ireland. But if Joe was to continue to grow in his career with Apple, he would have to leave Ireland, and this he did, accepting an assignment in Tokyo. After three years, the corporate headquarters beckoned and Joe, his wife, and three children moved to Cupertino, California. Then, with the opportunity of yet another promotion, Joe moved yet again, this time to Singapore where the company's Asian operations are located. Joe continues to prosper and has bought a house in a scenic fishing village on the Cork coast. The O'Sullivans will only return to Ireland when Joe retires from corporate life, and if they do they are likely to be part of a wave of such immigrants in the future.

Today anyone of Irish descent can piece together the trail as never before and can be as proud of what Ireland has finally become as of the courage of his or her own ancestors. Yet, maybe this is not the end but the beginning of a whole new migration into Ireland of people from less fortunate countries in pursuit of their own immigrant dreams.

NOTE

1. "Ribbonism" refers to the activities of an illegal secret society known as "The Ribbon Boys," which terrorized landlords to discourage them from evicting their tenants.

BIBLIOGRAPHY

Berleth, R. (1994). *The Twilight Lords*. New York: Barnes and Noble Books.
Central Intelligence Agency (CIA). Retrieved from http://www.cia.gov.
Foster, R. F. (1989a). *Modern Ireland 1600–1972*. London: Penguin Books.
———— (Ed.). (1989b). *The Oxford History of Ireland*. Oxford: Oxford University Press.
Hayden, T. (Ed.). (1997). *Irish Hunger*. Boulder, CO and Dublin: Roberts-Rinehart and Wolfhound Press.
Ignatiev, N. (1995). *How the Irish Became White*. New York: Routledge.
Keneally, T. (1998). *The Great Shame: And the Triumph of the Irish in the English-Speaking World*. Sydney: Serpentine Publishing.
Kenny, S. (1995). *The Hungry Earth*. Dublin: Wolfhound Press.
————. (1997). A Nightmare Revisited. In T. Hayden (Ed.), *Irish Hunger* (pp. 153–164). Dublin: Wolfhound Press.

———. (2001). Irish Spirit Now and Then. In P. Monaghan (Ed.), *Irish Spirit* (pp. 326–335). Dublin: Wolfhound Press.

———. (2002). *The Boy from America*. Unpublished manuscript.

Kiberd, D. (1995). *Inventing Ireland: The Literature of the Modern Nation*. London: Jonathan Cape.

Kinealy, C. (1995). *This Great Calamity: The Irish Famine 1845–1852*. Boulder, CO: Roberts-Rinehart.

Lee, J. J. (1989). *Ireland 1912–1985: Politics and Society*. Cambridge: Cambridge University Press.

Miller, K. (2001). *Journey of Hope: The Story of Irish Immigration to America*. San Francisco: Chronicle Books.

Monaghan, P. (Ed.). (2001). *Irish Spirit*. Dublin: Wolfhound Press.

Woodham-Smith, C. (1962). *The Great Hunger*. London: Hamish Hamilton.

8

JAPAN

Immigration In, Out, and Back and Forth

James Stanlaw

INTRODUCTION

Profile of Japan

If the word "immigration" is synonymous with the United States—or "emigration" with, say, China—people do not usually associate Japan with great mass movements of people. In fact, for the preceding two centuries before its doors were forced open by the Americans in the 1850s, Japan had effectively isolated itself from the rest of the world, with no one allowed to enter or leave the country. And if emigration between 1850 and 1950 is expressed as a percentage of population increase, England's rate of 74 percent or Italy's 47 percent far exceeds Japan's mere 1 percent (Kodansha Encyclopedia, 1993, Vol. I, p. 334). Yet, there have been significant numbers of people coming into the country, as well as sizable numbers of Japanese who have left. More importantly, however, is the kind of immigration and emigration found in Japan today: it is a microcosm of the transmigrations that the modern global economy is making increasingly common, not only for "developing" nations, but also for modern industrialized countries (Weiner, 2000).

Japan is one of the most important nations, economically, politically, and culturally, in Asia. With a 2000 population of more than 126 million people (about half the United States), it is the ninth most populous country in the world. With a real gross domestic product of more than $3 trillion, its economy is second only to the United States (with about $6 trillion). Geographically Japan is about the size of California or Montana, but over two-thirds of the land is occupied by rugged, mountainous terrain, making agriculture difficult and leaving vast areas uninhabited. Japan is also resource-poor, importing all of its oil, most of its minerals and ores, and much of its food.

Two factors have especially affected immigration to and from Japan: economics and citizenship—or notions of what it means to be Japanese. Economically, Japan is an affluent country with a per capita income of about US$24,500. However, since the late 1990s the Japanese economy has been in a slowdown, partly due to the Asian economic crisis in 1998 and, as alleged by the United States, some poor governmental fiscal policies. Real estate values have fallen, savings have decreased, and some of the "Japanese Miracle" of old—permanent job security, full employment, bonuses, and many fringe benefits—has been eroded. For example, the unemployment rate grew from 2.1 percent in 1991 to 3.4 percent in 1997. At the same time, declining birth rates, increasingly later marriages, and a sizable number of women who have delayed or avoided childbirth have caused something of a labor shortage in Japan, particularly in the less desirable or menial occupations. Thus, many foreigners from less-advantaged countries find that even the lowest of Japanese wages can be comparable to vast sums by the standards of their home country.

The second factor has to do with just who is Japanese. One reason this is rather complex is because of how Japan defines citizenship. Unlike the United States where birth within American territory grants American citizenship, Japan grants citizenship only to children of citizens, usually the father. Thus, children born of immigrant workers in Japan are citizens of the parent's home country in the eyes of the Japanese government. And it is extremely rare for a foreigner to obtain citizenship even if he or she is married to a Japanese citizen. Japan has often been accused if being xenophobic and excessively homogeneous, with little desire to change.

Vignettes

The Ins. These days there are many foreigners working in Japan, both legally and illegally. One such person is Ali, who is often seen on the street outside the Lasuca Department Store in a town just outside Tokyo. On his folding table and portable display case, he always has a variety of new things to sell to Japanese passersby. Sometimes it is exotic jewelry or glass goods; other times it is more practical items like watches, wallets, or pens. He is ambiguous about his legal status; though he has a city identification card (allowing him to peddle his wares), he does not particularly appreciate its close scrutiny. He is from "the Middle East" and is amused by Japanese schoolchildren and students practicing their limited English with him as they walk down the street.

The Outs. Around the turn of the twentieth century, Japan was undergoing the pains of modernization. Many rural villages were poverty stricken and thousands of Japanese people were going to Hawaii or Latin America to search for a better life. In 1920 a 19-year-old man named Naoichi arrived in Paramonga, Peru to work on a cotton plantation. Like many new immigrants, Naoichi did not plan on staying permanently; as soon as he was rich he would return to Japan with his fortune. However, as the cotton fields grew increasingly intolerable, he started a tailor shop and was moderately successful. Now in his 30s, he was anxious to get married and start a family. However, few local Japanese women were available. Thus, his adoptive father back in Japan arranged a marriage with a girl named Mutsue from his old village. This was quite fortunate for Naoichi, as otherwise he would have had to choose a "picture bride," a potential spouse whom he would only know through a photograph, and send for her from Japan.[1]

A midwife delivered their first son, Alberto, in 1938. By now it was clear to both Naoichi and Mutsue that their home was now Peru, not Japan. Gradually all talk of returning subsided, though Japanese customs and the Japanese language continued to be practiced at home. Alberto, however, was determined to learn native Spanish as well, after being ridiculed by other little boys.

World War II changed their lives forever. The Peruvian government sided with the Allies in the struggle against Japan and the personal freedoms of Peruvian Japanese were drastically curtailed. Almost 2,000 of them were sent, without charge or trial, to internment camps in the United States, along with the 110,000 Japanese Americans already there. They had no passports or documents, and they became stateless persons and refugees after the war.

Naoichi and his family were some of the more fortunate ones. Though Naoichi was arrested and held for a while, he was eventually released. Thus, he was able to stay with his family, though his business ventures continued to fail. In 1957, however, Alberto was one of only three people of Japanese descent to enter a university in Peru, where he graduated at the top of his class with a degree in agronomic engineering. This was only the first of many triumphs for Naoichi Fujimori's son; in 1990 Alberto Fujimori was elected president of Peru.[2]

The Back and Forths. Due to globalization, inexpensive and reliable transportation, and an increasingly international economy, the world is now a smaller place. For instance, there are hundreds of Japanese people living in central Illinois due to the presence of a major Japanese automobile manufacturing plant in the area. Entering the auto plant actually involves crossing a U.S. Customs border, in that there are restrictions on what one can take in or bring out. Besides the plant itself, there are dozens of ancillary Japanese companies catering primarily to the main corporation.

This town is not alone. There are now hundreds of Japanese companies in the United States making products of all kinds (see, for example, Graham, 1995, or Fucini and Fucini, 1990, who describe some other Japanese-American auto plants). Usually, there is at least a small Japanese management staff overseeing operations. In the case of a bigger company there may be

MIGRATION AND IMMIGRATION

engineers, designers, researchers, or other specialists present for various times as well. People can stay in the United States for anywhere from six months to three years or more. Some have stayed on for well over a decade or two, making them de facto, or at least semipermanent, residents. Actually, many of these workers are "transient salarymen,"[3] young engineers or technicians who spend six months or a year at a foreign location, and then go on to the next place. Often their job is troubleshooting.

The Dekasegi. Simply put, in the 1980s and early 1990s, the economies in some Latin American countries were in serious trouble. For example, the yearly inflation rate for Brazil in 1994 was 1,000 percent; the rate for Argentina in 1989 was over 200 percent. And Bolivia in 1985 had a staggering inflation rate of 11,700 percent. Thus, there were strong economic motivations for Latin Americans to seek employment elsewhere. Real economic growth in Japan during this period averaged over 4 percent a year (Central Intelligence Agency, 2000, pp. 68, 21, 59, 248), making it an attractive possibility.

At the same time, the birthrate in Japan began its steady decline. The "total special birthrate"—the average number of children a woman must bear in her lifetime to maintain the current population level—started to drop drastically. In 1975, the total special birthrate fell from 2.1 children per woman to 1.91. By 1985 it was 1.76, and by 1990 it was 1.54 (and continued to fall to 1.39 in 1997) (Asahi Shimbun Editorial Staff, 1999, p. 61). In other words, many factories in Japan were short of workers.

These economic conditions—that is, the push from Latin America and the pull to Japan—brought many people of Japanese ancestry back to Japan to seek work. The reason for this was that the Japanese government realized that it needed a large pool of foreign workers but, at the same time, it was hesitant to open its doors to full-blown immigration, American-style. A compromise of sorts was reached when it decided to revise the strict immigration laws to allow people of Japanese ancestry living overseas, *nikkei*, to come to work in Japan. These *nikkei* people, it was believed, shared linguistic, cultural, and especially racial affinities that would allow them to adjust easily to Japanese society and work styles (Sellek, 1997, pp. 201–204). Thus, the government issued special work permits to these *nikkei*-Japanese. These guest-workers of Japanese ancestry who "return" to Japan are commonly called *dekasegi*, literally "migratory earners" workers.

Since the early 1990s there have been many *dekasegi* Japanese-Brazilians working in Japan. Gabriella works in a small Brazilian grocery story in Hiratsuka, a midsized city near Yokohama. In this town there are many factories using *dekasegi* Japanese-Brazilian workers, such as a famous brand-name pen manufacturing corporation and several auto part manufacturers. Gabriella's husband worked in one of these factories, and she worked part-time in the store.

Overview of Migration Issues

All countries experience the benefits and the problems of immigration, but the process in Japan, for historical and cultural reasons, is different than in many other places of the world. Immigration to and from Japan can be looked at in many ways, but nine major kinds will be examined here: At the risk of oversimplifying, these will be roughly grouped as "the ins," "the outs," and the "back and forths."

The "ins" consist of the following three categories: (1) foreign workers in Japan, both legal and illegal (including the rising number of female entertainers or sex workers); (2) the sizable Korean permanent-resident population, and a few other ethnic minorities; and (3) official political refugees. The "outs" consist of the following three categories: (1) *nikkei-jin*, people of Japanese ancestry who now live outside Japan; (2) temporary overseas Japanese workers (transnational migrants, for example, working for Japanese or multinational corporations overseas); and (3) permanent overseas Japanese workers living in foreign countries.

The "back and forths" consist of the following three categories: (1) *dekasegi*⁴ workers, foreign nationals of Japanese descent who return to Japan and work temporarily to make money before they return home; (2) returnees from overseas activities, especially Japanese students and children who have lived or traveled abroad extensively and now face new challenges at home; and (3) Japanese nationals married to foreigners.

HISTORY OF MIGRATION ISSUES

Emigration

Population shifts in Japan have long been tied to historical developments. While there had always been immigration back and forth between Japan and the Asian mainland (especially Korea and China), Europeans began arriving in the fourteenth century during the western "Age of Exploration." The Tokugawa shoguns, however, after finally unifying Japan after centuries of intermittent civil war, closed the country around 1600 C.E., ostensibly to eradicate Christianity from the nation's shores. European traders and missionaries had brought their political and religious conflicts with them as they traveled throughout Asia, and the Japanese government lost patience trying to make sense of these differences. Also, the shoguns worried about how much influence the Europeans had over the local warlords and feared renewed uprisings if they became too powerful. In any case, the nation sealed it borders, preventing Japanese from leaving and foreigners from entering for the next 250 years. It was not until the American commodore Matthew Perry "opened" the islands in the middle of the nineteenth century that Japan again had legal intercourse with the rest of the world.

Soon after the period of national isolation ended, the "Japanese diaspora" began. Though not as well known as some of the other great migrations in world history—for example, the Jewish, Irish, African, or Chinese diasporas—the Japanese diaspora was nonetheless large and significant. As we saw in the case of former Peruvian President Fujimori's family, the instant contact with the West caused great social and economic upheavals in Japan around the turn of the twentieth century. Rural areas were especially hard hit, forcing many Japanese farmers to seek work overseas, particularly in Latin America, Hawaii, and mainland North America. The Japanese government even encouraged such migrations as a means to ameliorate population pressures and established organizations to facilitate it (Adachi, 1999).

Hundreds of Japanese left for work overseas. For example, over 180,000 went to Hawaii through the 1890s to the 1920s, making them the largest ethnic group in the islands. Some of these people went on to the American mainland, especially California. Records show some 275,000 Japanese directly entered the mainland United States from Japan by 1924,[5] and 15,000 went to Canada. Between 1899 and 1930, more than 20,000 Japanese went to Peru. By 1930 more than 100,000 Japanese went to Brazil, starting a trend that would last until the beginning of World War II. By 1940, there were 240,000 people of Japanese ancestry living in Brazil (Daniels, 2000, pp. 15–17).

American and Western immigration laws and the Second World War altered Japanese emigration patterns. The "Yellow Peril" threat at the turn of the twentieth century caused many governments to limit the number of Japanese who could enter their country. Australia closed its borders to Japanese in 1898, and Canada and the United States passed various "exclusion acts" in an attempt to curtail Japanese population growth. For example, American laws effectively barred people of Japanese ancestry from owning farmland in California by the 1920s. As a result, Japanese emigrants turned to Latin America as their new destination, particularly Brazil and Peru. Table 8.1 shows the numbers and destinations of Japanese emigrants in the years 1868–1941 and 1946–1989.

Immigration

After the opening of the country in the 1850s, there was not a tremendous influx of new immigration to Japan. There were, however, probably several thousand Westerners, who came for trade, fame, and fortune. The newly opened port cities, like Yokohama in 1859, were wild and woolly places: "[It is] a meeting place for merchants, sailors, missionaries, drifters, adventurers, and globetrotters from a score of nations" who mingled with "vendors, jugglers, samurai, farmers, [and] girls in bright kimono, many of them drawn from Tokyo or even points farther to do business, shop, and observe the odd behavior of the foreigners who [had] torn their nation from seclu-

Table 8.1
Number and Destination of Pre– and Post–World War II Japanese Emigrants

	1868–1941	1946–1989
Manchuria (Manchuko)[1]	270,007	na[2]
Hawaii	231,206	na
Brazil	188,985	71,385
United States (mainland)	107,253	135,084[3]
Canada	35,777	11,260
Paraguay	na	9,616
Bolivia	na	6,359
Peru	33,070	2,615
Mexico	14,667	na
Argentina	5,398	12,068
Russia/Soviet Union	56,821	na
Philippines and Guam	53,115	na
Singapore and Malaysia	11,809	na
Indonesia	7,095	na
New Caledonia	5,074	na
Hong Kong and Macao	3,815	na
Sarawak/North Borneo	2,829	na
Australia	3,773	1,558
India	1,885	na
New Zealand	1,046	na
Dominican Republic	na	1,390
Other	7,980	10,565
Total	1,041,605	261,900

1. Manchuria was a Japanese puppet state established after its annexation in 1931; these figures
   are based on 1932–1945 statistics.
2. "na" means unavailable or not applicable; only countries with more than 1,000 Japanese
   emigrants are listed; individual figures are not available for Europe, Africa, or western Asia.
3. This includes Hawaii.

Source: table based on figures taken from Kodansha Encyclopedia (1993), p. 335.

sion" (Rosenstone, 1988, p. 11). Yokohama was also home to some 1,500
Westerners, 3,000 Chinese, and 25,000 Japanese.

At the same time, the Japanese government of the Meiji Period (1868–
1912) imported hundreds of "foreign experts" to help modernize the country. They came for substantial periods of time, for high pay, to teach in the

universities, to advise businesses and the military, and to introduce techno-
logical innovations to the country. These included some of the best scholars
and scientists of the day. Though most stayed temporarily, some lingered
on in Japan for many years, effectively becoming permanent residents. So,
while Japanese farmers were leaving Japan for what they thought was a better
life overseas, Japan was industrializing rapidly and soon grew to become a
major world power.

In 1910 Japan annexed Korea after defeating China in the Sino-Japanese
War and later Russia in the Russo-Japanese War. At the time of annexation,
there were only 2,500 Koreans living in Japan, but World War II changed
this. Hundreds of thousands of Koreans were brought in as forced laborers
to help alleviate the manpower shortage caused by the war. They worked
largely in factories and coal mines; some young women were sent to work
as prostitutes at Japanese military installations at home and abroad. By 1945
there were about 2 million Koreans working in Japan. While most returned
home, many stayed on in Japan, as the division of the country due to the
Korean War in 1950 either made repatriation difficult or left some with little
economic opportunity back in their old country. Thus, they remained in
Japan and made a life for themselves as permanent residents, marrying and
raising families.

By the 1990s there were 688,000 people of Korean descent living in Japan—a number that remained relatively steady during the past decade. Koreans are the largest ethnic minority in Japan. Ninety percent are second- or
third-generation Japanese Koreans born in Japan. Most Japanese Koreans
these days have never been to Korea, and the vast majority do not speak
Korean. However, as mentioned, birth in Japan does not grant citizenship,
so these people are technically still foreigners. Though Koreans were Japanese nationals during the period of annexation through World War II, in
1952 a special law took away their citizenship, effectively making them foreign aliens. Those Koreans remaining in Japan endured economic hardships,
working in the service industries or as day laborers.

There is also the problem of different ancestries and political allegiances
for Koreans. It is commonly thought that there are 350,000 pro-South Koreans in the country and 250,000 pro-North Koreans. However, many Japanese Koreans are ambiguous about their affiliations or their heritage. Some
pay membership fees to both the North Korean and South Korean cultural
organizations, and others send their children to each other's schools. Still,
while the Japanese government has legally eliminated all distinctions between
North and South Koreans, the matter still lingers for many people (Ryang,
1997, p. 5).

The opening of Japan also brought in many Chinese, the second-largest
ethnic group in the country. Many entered Japan under the auspices of one
of the Western nations who brought their Chinese employees and servants
with them in the 1860s and 1870s. After the Sino-Japanese War, Japan

annexed Taiwan in 1895; since then, until the end of World War II, there was a constant flow of Taiwanese to Japan. Over 7,000 Taiwanese students were living in Japan to receive a higher education and Taiwan supplied 150,000 men for the Japanese military by 1943. Over 3,000 Taiwanese were actually in active Japanese military service at this time (Vasishth, 1997, p. 125).

There were thousands of Chinese of various backgrounds in Japan at the time of the Great Tokyo Earthquake in 1923; for example, there were 4,000 in Tokyo and 6,000 in Kobe—the majority being unskilled laborers brought in during the economic boom after World War I. However, rumors of arson, robbery, and rape during the earthquake caused hundreds of Chinese to be killed by Japanese mobs, even though the Yokohama Chinatown was completely destroyed and one-third of the Chinese in Tokyo and Yokohama had died in the disaster. Still, relations improved, and by 1930 there were again many Chinese (30,836) in Japan (Vasishth, 1997, p. 129).

DIMENSIONS OF MIGRATION ISSUES

Japanese emigration and immigration continue to this day, though in modified forms. Each of the nine categories mentioned in the beginning of this essay will now be examined in more detail.

The "Ins"

Foreign Workers in Japan, Both Legal and Illegal. The cover story of the February 2001 issue of *Japan Close-Up* asked, "Is Japan Ready for Foreign Labor?" There is no doubt that the number of foreign workers in Japan is rising significantly. In 1992, for instance, foreign workers accounted for 580,000 people out of a total work force of 65,780,000 (or 0.9% of the total Japanese work force). By 1997 these numbers increased to 670,000 out of a total work force of 67,930,000 (or 1.0%) (Japan Close-Up, 2001, p. 8). Over the past decade, a steady influx of about 90,000 people has entered the country for the first time to work each year (Komai, 1995; Mori, 1997). One big social dilemma, however, is illegal foreigners working in Japan. This number is also steadily increasing, from 166,080 illegal immigrants in 1989 to 416,040 in 1997. For the past ten years about 28 percent of all foreign workers in Japan have either been working on an expired visa or have entered the country illegally.

All foreign workers, to some degree, do the "dirty work" in Japan. In fact, the Japanese have a name for these kinds of occupations: "3K" jobs, taken from the words *kitsui* ("difficult"), *kitanai* ("dirty"), and *kiken* ("dangerous"). The illegal sojourners are especially at risk of being placed in the most difficult, dirty, and dangerous jobs, with little legal protection and no access to proper health care or areas of recourse in case of dispute or tragedy. As with

Table 8.2
Foreign Nationals Living in Japan by Country

	1990		1996	
Country	Number	Percent	Number	Perecent
Korea	687,940	64.0%	645,373	43.5%
China[1]	150,339	14.0%	252,164	17.0%
Brazil	56,429	5.25%	233,254	15.7%
Philippines	49,092	4.6%	93,265	6.3%
United States	38,364	3.6%	43,690	2.9%
Peru	10,279	1.0%	40,394	2.7%
United Kingdom	10,206	0.9%	14,438	1.0%
Thailand	6,724	0.6%	20,669	1.4%
Viet Nam	6,233	0.6%	11,897	0.8%
Canada	4,909	0.5%	na	na
Indonesia	na	na	11,936	0.8%
Iran	235	0.0%	8,418	0.6%
Australia	1,117	0.1%	6,290	0.4%
Other Countries	53,750	4.9%	100,919	6.8%
Total	1,075,317	100.0%	1,482,707	100.0%

1. Includes both Taiwanese and PRC nationals.

Sources: 1990 raw data based and modified on figures in Asahi Shimbun Editorial Staff (1993),
    p. 39 and Keizai Koho Center (1998), p. 108; 1996 raw data based and modified on figures
    in Asahi Shimbun Editorial Staff (1999), p. 63 and Keizai Koho Center (1998), p. 108.

such immigrants everywhere, they are at the mercy of their local hosts who might cut them loose at any moment.

One particular illegal activity should be mentioned, too: the phenomena of the *japa-yuki-san*,[6] Asian women migrants—mostly from Thailand and the Philippines—who come to work in the entertainment industry in Japan (Piper, 2000, p. 35). While many enter as singers or dancers, oftentimes they end up as bar hostesses, strippers, or prostitutes. Piper argues (2000, p. 36) that Japanese immigration laws were deliberately weakened to allow such women in on special visas so Japanese men would no longer have to go abroad on sex tours to Southeast Asia, a practice common in the 1970s and early 1980s. These laws are currently under pressure from feminist groups.

The Korean Permanent-Resident Population, and Other Ethnic Groups. Table 8.2 shows the number of foreign nationals living in Japan at various times in the 1990s. Koreans are on the top of the list, but as discussed, their status as "foreign nationals" is rather peculiar.

In 1982 the Japanese government granted permanent residence status to all persons of Korean ancestry, and their children, who had lived in Japan before the end of World War II. In 1992 all previous categories were abolished, and all Japanese Koreans were given the status of "special permanent residents." Thus, now—in theory at least—all Japanese Koreans enjoy the same rights as native-born Japanese (such as social security benefits). Also, Japanese Koreans no longer have to be fingerprinted as part of the alien registration process, an issue of contention for some three decades.

There are now also many Chinese living in Japan, as Table 8.2 shows. This is partly due to the decision by the Mombusho, the Japanese Ministry of Education, to increase the number of foreign students to 100,000 by the year 2000. International trade between Japan, Taiwan, and the People's Republic has increased tremendously this past decade; this has resulted in an increase in business exchanges. Also, there is now a firmly entrenched Chinese community in the country making life much easier for Chinese newcomers. In contrast to other minorities in Japan, the Chinese are characterized by their relative affluence, making them a "model minority." However, like the Koreans and others, it has not always been easy for these newcomers, and the early history of Chinese immigration to Japan is one marked by a fairly high degree of suspicion, prejudice, and discrimination.

Political Refugees. Japan has never been noted as a haven for political refugees, but by the 1980s the international community demanded that Japan take in at least a token number of "boat people" from Southeast Asia (mostly from Kampuchia, Laos, and Vietnam). By 1985, the Japanese government agreed to take 10,000 Southeast Asians under encouragement from the United States and the United Nations. However, there have been problems in implementing these protocols. First, Japan has always been somewhat reluctant to let foreigners into the country. Also, there is always the problem of determining who is an "economic" versus a "political" refugee. In the 1990s the large increase in the numbers of Chinese trying to enter or stay in Japan was another obstacle to implementing new policies. For example, Sassen (1993, pp. 82, 97–99) cites that the number of Chinese attempting to enter Japan illegally in 1991 (27,137) was almost triple that of 1989 (10,404). Some of these Chinese pose as Vietnamese refugees, and such incidents often get well publicized in the mass media, hurting public sympathy for both groups.

The "Outs"

Nikkei-jin. Today, as a result of the early Japanese emigration described above, there are substantial overseas Japanese populations in many countries in the world. As mentioned, these overseas Japanese are termed *nikkei* or

Table 8.3
Nikkei (Overseas Japanese) Populations in the Mid-1990s

Country	Total Population[1]	*Nikkei* Population[2]	*Nikkei* Population Per 100,000	Year of First Arrival[3]
Argentina	34,673,000	29,262	83.60	1907
Bolivia	7,165,000	7,986	111.70	1916
Brazil	162,661,000	620,370	381.20	1908
Canada	28,821,000	55,111	190.80	1891
Chile	14,333,000	2,292	15.30	1903
Colombia	36,813,000	1,106	0.32	1921
Costa Rica	3,463,000	57	0.17	na
Cuba	11,007,000	842	0.73	1907
Dominican Republic	8,089,000	583	0.74	na
Ecuadaor	11,446,000	152	0.13	na
Guatemala	11,278,000	113	0.10	na
Mexico	95,772,000	11,926	12.60	1892
Paraguay	5,504,000	6,054	109.00	1930
Peru	24,523,000	55,472	224.30	1899
Uruguay	3,239,000	436	1.23	1930
Venezuela	21,983,000	828	3.60	1931
United States	266,476,000	848,000	318.20	1868

1. *Source*: 1996 figures from the Wall Street Journal Staff (1998), pp. 501–502.
2. *Sources*: 1993 figures from "International Nikkei Demographics," The Japanese American National Museum, http://www.inrp.org/pre/english/demogrph.htm; and *Statistical Abstract of the United States 1996*, p. 31.
3. *Source*: "International Nikkei Demographics," The Japanese American National Museum, http://www.inrp.org/pre/english/demogrph.htm.

nikkei-jin, literally "persons of Japanese heritage"—this is the common term now often used in English as well. Table 8.3 shows the places in the world where there are now sizable *nikkei* populations, as well as their proportion of the total population of that country. Also included in the far right column, is the date of the first arrival of Japanese. For example, Brazil has the highest *nikkei* "population density," with almost 382 people of Japanese ancestry being found in any group of 100,000 Brazilians (see column labeled "*nikkei* population per 100,000" in Table 8.3).[7]

Temporary Overseas Japanese Workers. More than three-quarters of a million Japanese nationals were living abroad in 1996, more than a third in the

United States. The vast majority of these people were working in Japanese or multinational companies, or were family members of such workers. For example, to take just one industry, there are one hundred Japanese financial institutions in London, one of the world's major banking centers. Sakai (2000, pp. 62–65), in her ethnography of Japanese bankers in the city, estimates that they employ between 4,000–5,000 people. On the average, the typical Japanese London bank employs about 250 people, of which 30 to 40 are Japanese.

Permanent Overseas Japanese Nationals. Besides temporary overseas workers, there are almost three hundred thousand Japanese nationals who are permanent residents in other countries. More than a third of these people live in the United States, and about another third live in Brazil. A majority of other Japanese nationals live in Canada, Argentina, or Australia. About 1,500 Japanese women marry American men each year, a rate that has been fairly constant for the past several decades. What this means is that a majority of the Japanese permanent residents in the United States are probably wives of American husbands. There are very few Japanese husbands with American wives—no more than a few hundred each year.

The "Back and Forths"

Dekasegi Workers. While the term *dekasegi* literally means "temporary migrant worker" in Japanese, it is commonly restricted to foreign nationals of Japanese descent (*nikkei*) who return to Japan to work temporarily—usually in the unskilled employment sector—to make money before they return home. As mentioned, economic recessions in Latin America caused hundreds of thousands of *nikkei* from South America to come to Japan to seek work. At its peak in the early to mid-1990s, about 150,000 *dekasegi* workers came to Japan each year. About 90 percent came from Brazil, and about 7 percent from Peru (Mori, 1997, p. 108). Though the numbers now have decreased somewhat, there are still many *dekasegi* in Japan (Tsuda, 1999).

One other thing should be mentioned about *dekasegi* workers. Because of the labor shortage, the Japanese government relaxed some of its strict immigration laws in 1988. A new category of "long term resident" was introduced, allowing up to "third generation" *nikkei* Japanese and their spouses, regardless of nationality, to come to Japan to work (Sellek, 1997, p. 189).

Returnees. Ever since the "Japanese miracle" transformed a defeated country into a postwar superpower, probably several million Japanese have lived abroad for work or business. But for many of these people and their families, returning home can be quite problematic. First, while not meaning to overgeneralize, Japanese society tends to be more hierarchical and, in some ways, more age-conscious than Western societies. For example, there is a recruiting "season" for college graduates during which corporations hire en masse the new white-collar workers needed for the coming year. Often this cohort is promoted together on career paths that are remarkably stable and similar by American standards. Likewise, entrance to a college or university itself is generally restricted to a rather narrow window of four or five years just before or after one's twentieth birthday. When someone goes overseas, however, one's "place" in society is disrupted. Foreign assignments and responsibilities rarely correspond exactly to their Japanese counterparts. School systems abroad hardly ever match the Japanese curriculum. Spending time in another country, then, puts people at risk of being off the social escalator upon return.

Those who suffer the most often are the children of the Japanese workers overseas. More than 50,000 Japanese school-aged children lived abroad in the late 1990s. A majority of them lived in North America, though increasing numbers are now living in Asia. Only about 38 percent of them could attend a Japanese school—a full-time academic institution that follows the standard national curriculum of the Japanese Ministry of Education. The others attended only supplementary Japanese classes or were immersed in the local school system. The reason for these differences is that not every locale has the resources or the numbers to support a full-time Japanese school.

Political Dimensions

The political dimensions of immigration to and from Japan have always been paramount. The premodern Japanese government refused to allow any foreigners in or let the Japanese leave the country for some 250 years. The various discriminatory "Yellow Peril" laws at the turn of the twentieth century in the United States and Canada changed the flow of Japanese movement of people from North to South America. The views of the Japanese government on what constitutes a "Japanese citizen" and a "Japanese person" form the basis of current immigration law. Blood ties going back three generations are thought to be sufficient to carry enough remnants of Japanese memory and culture to create a selected unskilled labor pool of people who will fit into Japanese society with few problems of adjustment. Political beliefs, like cultural or religious beliefs, do not have to be logical or empirical to be accepted.

Social Dimensions

Japan has never seen itself as a heterogeneous society, nor does it really want to be one. In fact, Japanese leaders are often criticized by foreign countries when they make inadvertent comments about too much heterogeneity being the source of social problems in other parts of the world. The economic success of postwar Japan is in large part believed to be due to the unity and homogeneity of the Japanese populous. There at times appears to be in Japan a belief that Japanese culture, the Japanese language, and the Japanese "race" are three manifestations of the same trinity. All this points to a country that seems philosophically antagonistic to immigration or emigration.

Yet, we must also acknowledge an internationalized Japan, a country probably more open to new ideas than any other in the world. Taken in total, Western popular culture is more prevalent in Japan than even in many places in the United States. The multinational global economy and the international media are making Japan a major international focal point, both in business and culture. This means that more and more Japanese will be going abroad, and more and more foreigners will be coming into Japan.

Economic Dimensions

Finally, as with immigration and emigration everywhere, the influx of peoples in and out of Japan is closely tied to economic conditions, not only domestically but also globally. The labor shortage in the 1990s in Japan made the wage of the unskilled labor pool increase. By South American standards, even these low Japanese wages could be hundreds or thousands of times the local average wage or salary. This, of course, brought in a wave of *dekasegi* migratory workers to the islands. Likewise, the multinational economy has brought many educated Japanese professionals to venues overseas — not only to the United States and Europe, but also to Southeast Asia, Korea, India, and China. The transmigration of peoples, of all classes and backgrounds, ultimately relates to the world economy.

THE FUTURE

Japan is changing in many ways, and immigration lies at the heart of many of these shifts. Debates about whether or not to have foreign workers come into Japan are common in public media. Some, such as Taichi Sakaiya, former Director General of the Economic Planning Agency, claim that because of the population decline, it will be a necessity. Instead of lamenting the inevitable, he argues, Japanese need to take steps to make immigration work smoothly and orderly for both Japanese and foreign nationals. Foreign language training, medical care reform, and modifying the social welfare system will be necessary to avoid economic misery for some and social anguish for all (Sakaiya, 2001, p. 9).

However, others such as Takuro Morinaga, a Senior Research Fellow at the Sanwa Institute, argue that the coming immigration will pose a heavy burden for taxpayers. He suggests that Japanese companies only want foreign workers so they can maximize their profits by hiring the economically disadvantaged at low cost. While immigration may provide these businesses with short-term profits, the whole nation will pay because of increased pressures on the institutional infrastructure (schools, housing, hospitals, and so on). Also, these foreign immigrants will be the ones who need social services the most; that is, they will likely receive more in disbursements than they pay out in taxes, contributing to governmental debt. Also, as foreigners send money back overseas, this will result in a loss of capital leaving Japan, likely never to be recovered (Morinaga, 2001, p. 9).

At the same time, too, Japan is internationalizing in ways unanticipated even a few decades ago. Because of globalization, multinational corporations, and international development, more Japanese than ever before are going overseas, either as transmigrant workers or as spouses or children of these workers. These returnees will also present special challenges to Japanese social institutions that are geared toward an orderly progression throughout one's life—that is, things like promotions strictly by seniority, a narrow window of opportunity to go on to higher education, and little career mobility after starting with a company. Where does the middle-aged salaryman fit back in his home office in Tokyo after he has spent the last five years in the company's branches in Southeast Asia? How can the country best utilize a young woman who speaks native English, having spent her junior high school years in Canada or America, but who finds herself inadequately prepared for the picayune questions asked on Japanese university entrance examinations? What does the mother and housewife do back in the confines of the extended family in Japan after she has seen the world and been responsible for single-handedly running an international household?

And there have been new debates on what it means to be a *nikkei-jin* (overseas Japanese). *Nikkei* people are finding increasing dissatisfaction with being called "Japanese" at home and "Brazilian" in Japan. Several organizations are working on this problem. The International Nikkei Research Project at the Japanese American National Museum and the Asians in Latin America Working Group at Stanford University are just two such organizations in the United States.

The biggest organization is the La Asociación Panamericana Nikkei, the Association of Pan-American Nikkei—usually referred to by its common acronym, COPANI. This group was organized so *nikkei* people all over the world could get together and discuss common issues. The theme of the Fifth COPANI Meetings in 1989 was the issue of the *dekasegi* problem, and at the Eight Meetings in 1995 the definition of *nikkei* was discussed. This is actually not a trivial problem, as the Japanese government officially only recognizes as "Japanese" people who go back up to three generations (much to the dissatisfaction of overseas Japanese)

Increasing globalization guarantees that immigration to and from Japan will continue to be an important part of all discussions of international migration. The study of the Japanese diaspora and of immigration into Japan will help provide insights about the flow of peoples everywhere. Such an examination shows how problems of race and accommodation—and acculturation and acceptance—are used to demonstrate the way views of foreign "others" reflect and reify ideas of domestic "selves," even in an alleged "homogeneous" nation like Japan.

NOTES

1. The term "picture bride" actually came to be applied to any situation where a distant marriage was arranged, regardless of whether a photograph was involved or not.

2. This account is based on Kimura (1998).

3. This is a play on the common Japanese word *sarariman*, a neologism based on the English words "salary" and "man." This coinage means the male, salaried, white-collar worker.

4. As Adachi (2001) points out, when these returnee migrant workers became an international issue, the word *dekasegi* came to mean returnee guest worker for any nation. Note, too, that in such cases the Japanese word *dekasegi* can be spelled differently, such as *dekassegui* in Brazil and *dekasegui* in Peru.

5. However, Daniels (2000, p. 14) points out that this number is inflated, as repeated entries are included in these tallies.

6. This term was coined by analogy from *karayuki-san*, Japanese women who were forced to work as prostitutes overseas during World War II.

7. Some suggest that the numbers given in this table might be substantially higher in some cases. For example, Suzuki (1992, p. 169) claimed that the Japanese-Brazilian *nikkei* population in 1988 was actually 1.23 million and growing. He claimed that the generational breakdown was as follows (cited in Selleck, 1997, p. 187): first generation, 110,000, 8.9 percent; second generation, 450,000, 36.6 percent; third generation, 500,000, 40.7 percent; fourth generation, 80,000, 6.5 percent; fifth generation, 20,000, 1.6 percent.

BIBLIOGRAPHY

Adachi, N. (1999). Japanese Voices in the Brazilian Forest: Cultural Maintenance and Reformed Ethnic Identity in a Transplanted Community. *World Communication, 28*(2), 68–82.

———. (2001, November 28). *The "Imagined" Community: The "Real" and "Fake" Ethnic Identity Conflicts of Japanese-Peruvians.* Paper presented at the 100th Annual Meetings of the American Anthropological Association, Washington, DC.

Asahi Shimbun Editorial Staff. (1993). *Asahi Shimbun Japan Almanac 1993.* Tokyo: Asahi Shimbun.

———. (1999). *Asahi Shimbun Japan Almanac 1999.* Tokyo: Asahi Shimbun.

Central Intelligence Agency. (2000). *The World Fact Book 2000.* Washington, DC: Brassey's.

Daniels, R. (2000). The Japanese Diaspora: The New World, 1868–1990. *Pan Japan: The International Journal of the Japanese Diaspora, 1*(1), 13–23.

Fucini, J., & Fucini, S. (1990). *Working for the Japanese: Inside Mazda's American Auto Plant.* New York: Free Press.

Graham, L. (1995). *On the Line at Subaru-Isuzu: The Japanese Model and the American Worker*. Ithaca, NY: Cornell University Press.

Japan Close-Up. (2001, February). Will Japan Open Its Doors to Foreign Workers? *Japan Close-Up*, 6(26), 6–13.

Keizai Koho Center. (1998). *Japan 1998: An International Comparison*. Tokyo: Keizai Koho Center.

Kimura, R. (1998). *Alberto Fujimori of Peru: The President Who Dared to Dream*. Guildford, UK: Eyelevel Books.

Kodansha Encyclopedia. (1993). *Japan: An Illustrated Encyclopedia* (Vols. 1–2). Tokyo: Kodansha.

Komai, H. (1995). *Migrant Workers in Japan*. London: Kegan Paul International.

Mori, H. (1997). *Immigration Policy and Foreign Workers in Japan*. New York: St. Martin's Press.

Morinaga, T. (2001, February). Immigration Will Result in a Heavier Burden for the Taxpayers. *Japan Close-Up*, 6(26), 9.

Piper, N. (2000). Migration, Globalization and Gender: Japan's Sex Workers. *Pan Japan: The International Journal of the Japanese Diaspora*, 1(1), 24–48.

Rosenstone, R. (1988). *Mirror in the Shrine: American Encounters with Meiji Japan*. Cambridge, MA: Harvard University Press.

Ryang, S. (1997). *North Koreans in Japan: Language, Ideology, and Identity*. Boulder, CO: Westview Press.

Sakai, J. (2000). *Japanese Bankers in the City of London: Language, Culture and Identity in the Japanese Diaspora*. London: Routledge.

Sakaiya, T. (2001, February). Japan Has a History of Absorbing Immigrants. *Japan Close-Up*, 6(26), 9.

Sassen, S. (1993). Economic Internationalization: The New Migration in Japan and the United States. *International Migration*, 31, 73–99.

Sellek, Y. (1997). Nikkeijin: The Phenomena of Return Migration. In M. Weiner (Ed.), *Japan's Minorities: The Illusion of Homogeneity* (pp. 178–210). London: Routledge.

Suzuki, J. (1992). *Nihonjin Dekaseji-imin* [Japanese Dekaseji Immigration]. Tokyo: Heibon-sha.

Tsuda, T. (1999). The Permanence of "Temporary" Migration: The "Structural Embeddedness" of Japanese-Brazilian Immigrant Workers in Japan. *Journal of Asian Studies*, 58, 687–722.

Vasishth, A. (1997). A Model Minority: The Chinese Community in Japan. In M. Weiner (Ed.), *Japan's Minorities: The Illusion of Homogeneity* (pp. 108–139). London: Routledge.

Wall Street Journal Staff. (1998). *The Wall Street Journal Alamac 1998*. New York: Ballantine Books.

Weiner, M. (2000). Destination Japan: Migration in the Twentieth Century. *Pan Japan: The International Journal of the Japanese Diaspora*, 1(1), 49–74.

——— (Ed.). (1997). *Japan's Minorities: The Illusion of Homogeneity*. London: Routledge.

9

MEXICO

Mexican International Migration

Patricia Zamudio

INTRODUCTION

Profile of Mexico

Mexico is a democratic republic with 101 million people, 65 percent of whom are urban residents. It entered the modern world after the Mexican Revolution at the beginning of the last century and the Institutional Revolutionary Party (PRI) ruled the country until the year 2000 when presidential elections gave triumph to the candidate of an opposition party, the National Action Party (PAN). The official language of the country is Spanish, but over 6.5 percent of the population speaks an indigenous language, mainly Nahuatl. Mexico started a process of industrialization in the 1940s, which drove rural-to-urban migration, and since 1982, economic restructuring has liberalized the economy and deepened regional inequalities within the country. Mexico ranks fifth in Latin America in terms of income inequality. Almost 50 percent of the population over 12 years of age is economically active, but only half of those receive a salary. Women represent 36 percent of the economically active population. Over 90 percent of Mexicans over 15 years of age know how to read and write, over 91 percent of those between 6 and 14 go to school, and over 27 percent of all schoolgoers are enrolled at the tertiary level. About 8.5 million Mexicans live in the United States, the largest out-migration in the world.

Vignette

Mary Rosado was born 40 years ago in a rural town close to Xalapa, the capital city of Veracruz. She moved to Xalapa 20 years ago to work as a secretary so that she could raise her children comfortably. During the last five years, economics started to become a problem for Mary. So sometime in 1999, after feeling overwhelmed by debts, she decided to go north. She managed to get a leave of absence from her job and contacted a smuggler. Mary crossed the border in the winter of 2000, without documents, and after 15 days of journey arrived in Charlotte, North Carolina, where she has a niece. She found work and is sending part of her earnings to her three children and saving the rest. She hopes to be together with her children soon but is concerned that it might be a long time before they are reunited.

Overview of Migration Issues

Three key issues to address when thinking about Mexican migration are its causes, its changing trends, and the actors involved in it. Among the causes, economic conditions play an important role. The overwhelming majority of Mexican international migration is to the United States. According to the most recent Mexican census data, almost 99 percent of all Mexican international migrants go there (INEGI, 2001), almost 3 million of whom are undocumented (CONAPO, 2001). Supply of labor has become an increasingly important factor in Mexican migration to the United States, particularly since the mid-1980s, as a consequence of the rapid population growth in the 1970s, economic crises, and changes in economic policies in Mexico (SRE-CIR, 1997). And the United States has demanded large quantities of Mexican labor for different sectors of its economy since the 1940s, when the Bracero Program took place (see below). During the 1990s, sustained economic growth in the United States could incorporate a constant flow of Mexican immigrants. Salary differentials seem to drive the movement, but unemployment also plays an important role. In 1993–1997, 10.57 percent of Mexican migrants were not employed before leaving the country; in 1998–2000, the percentage increased to 17.3 percent (CONAPO, 2001).

In addition to economic factors, the development of social networks among Mexican migrants and their communities facilitates the movement, making it more accessible for potential migrants. New arrivals to the United States learn about the best ways to cross the border and get to their destinations, and many can also count on a place to stay when they arrive, help in finding a job, and the much needed community support to initiate their lives as immigrants. This process makes migration less costly and, over time, migration gains an important place within people's options when their homeland does not provide them with the resources to fulfill their needs or, simply, to develop their plans for building a better life.

The second important issue about Mexican international migration is the changing character it has acquired in the last two decades. This over-a-century-long movement is changing. It is diversifying more than ever, particularly with respect to demographics, places of origin, places of destination, and the occupations of migrants. The new trends in the demographics of the flow include a stronger presence of women—particularly among those who migrate legally—and an increase in the average age and in the average schooling of migrants (CONAPO, 2001; SRE-CIR, 1997).

The places of origin of migrants now includes the majority of Mexican municipalities. According to the National Council of Population (CONAPO, 2001), 869 municipalities in Mexico—about 30 percent of the total—have a medium, high, or very high international migratory intensity. With respect to destination places in the United States, there is still movement toward the traditionally concentrated areas of Mexican immigrants: Texas, California, Illinois, and Arizona. Increasingly, however, Mexican migrants are found in new destinations, spread all over the country, particularly in New York, Georgia, Colorado, Florida, and others.

The third issue to consider when approaching Mexican international migration is the way the different actors of the process see the phenomenon and implement actions to influence its dynamics. Besides the migrants themselves, their communities are important actors in the process in two ways. One is the way they experience migration. Considering international migration as a social process reflects much of what is involved. However, such an explanation of the movement fails to disclose the ways people experience the consequences of the separation from families and communities. Experiences are different for communities with a long history of migration than for those that are just beginning a movement. The former may have developed strategies to cope with the loss of its migrating population while the latter are just beginning to experience such a separation, with the suffering involved in the uncertainty about the destiny of migrants and the changes that the movement will very likely bring to their social relations.

The second way communities participate in the process is through the strategies they use to minimize the effects of migration on their families and social and economic conditions, particularly with respect to strengthening social links among those who stay and maintaining communication with those who leave. Though this can vary according to the migratory history of the community, there can be a learning process and a transmission process among communities, particularly when public policies help diffuse the implementation of successful strategies.

The Mexican federal government is another actor involved in migration. In 1989 it created the Programa Paisano to ensure a safe return of Mexicans to their homeland, and in 1990 it created the Program for Communities Abroad to promote communications with Mexicans in the United States. The new presidential administration has made migration a national priority, including it as a high issue on the bilateral agenda between Mexico and the United States. The United States is another actor involved in the process of Mexican migration, as its migratory policies have shown a pendular movement that goes from welcoming migrants to rejecting them, mainly according to the condition of the U.S. economy.

Non-governmental organizations (NGOs) are the last actors that need to be considered. They promote public policy and legislative change geared to ensure the respect for immigrants' human rights. They advise immigrants about migratory procedures and help the new arrivals with their various needs. Finally, they participate in efforts by communities of origin to maintain links with migrants and to develop actions geared toward diminishing the cost of losing population and increasing the potential benefits—economic or otherwise—of migration.

HISTORY OF MIGRATION ISSUES

The presence of Mexican populations in the United States has a long history. It started in 1848, when changes to the border "crossed" former Mexicans living in California, Arizona, New Mexico, and Texas, after the sale of Mexican territories to the United States through the Treaties of Guadalupe Hidalgo. The recruitment of Mexican workers by U.S. authorities started in the 1870s when companies needed people to work in southwestern rails and agriculture. Beginning at that time, the recruitment of Mexican labor through temporary migration agreements constituted a preferred option for employers. It had two advantages: Mexican labor filled low-skilled jobs and was flexible enough to be used in times of need and discarded when no longer needed.

Between 1901 and 1920, there were 268,646 Mexicans admitted legally into the United States (Tienda, 1989, p. 115). Those were times of civil war in Mexico, when the Mexican Revolution (1910–1917) strongly hit the economy of vast portions of the population. At the same time, the U.S. government implemented restrictive measures to limit Mexican migration, such as the Immigration Act of 1917, which required literacy and the payment of a fee. However, agribusiness and railroad contractors continued hiring Mexican immigrants who, without the means to meet the requirements of the act, were considered to have illegally entered the country (Betancourt, Cordova, & Torres, 1993). Such a condition of "illegality" translated into a condition of vulnerability for Mexican immigrants, who suffered abuses from their employers.

Besides the southern regions, other areas of the country also imported Mexican workers. For instance, during the second decade of the twentieth century and until 1929, there was an important migration of Mexican workers to the Chicago area, contracted by the Midwest Company to work on railroad tracks. The increasing migration of Mexican workers to this and other areas of the country was an important starting point in the development of strong Mexican-American communities. Over time, such communities have played an important role in attracting new immigrants of Mexican origin to the United States (see Kerr, 1976).

During the Depression years, there was a massive repatriation of Mexicans. In Illinois alone, between 1930 and 1932 over 14,000 people returned to Mexico. The number of Mexicans admitted into the United States legally between 1931 and 1940 was only 22,319 (Tienda, 1989, p. 115), a big difference compared to the over 250,000 admitted temporarily during the first two decades of the century.

THE BRACERO PROGRAM

The entrance of the United States into World War II offered another opportunity for Mexican migrants to enter the U.S. labor market. The structural conditions of Mexico were changing; between 1940 and 1980, the country's economy grew at a rate of 6.5 percent a year and it was a time of industrial modernization that increased the productivity of workers (Escobar et al., 1999). However, the growth did not benefit all Mexicans in the same way. On the contrary, the salary gap between urban and rural occupations grew, producing a continuous migration from the countryside to the cities. In addition, during that time, and until 1970, the Mexican population grew at an annual rate of 3.5 percent due to decreasing rates of mortality. There were almost 20 million Mexicans in 1940 and almost 50 million in 1970.

It was in this context that in the 1940s Mexico and the United States signed a series of bilateral agreements—the Bracero Program—which allowed thousands of agricultural Mexican laborers to work legally in the United States on a temporary basis. But the demand for braceros[1] surpassed the number allowed by the program and employers also engaged in the hiring of undocumented workers (Reichert & Massey, 1982; see also Betancourt et al., 1993).

During the 1950s employers in the United States continued recruiting Mexican workers directly, promoting the increase of the undocumented flow. The "wetbacks,"[2] however, enjoyed the opportunity to become legalized through programs implemented by the U.S. government. There were also those who became permanent immigrants. The possibility of being legalized created an incentive for potential migrants, further increasing the undocumented influx (Morales & Bonilla, 1993). By 1953, however, the alarm was sounded that illegal immigration was depressing wages and displacing U.S. workers. In response, "Operation Wetback" was launched, through which hundreds of thousands of undocumented workers were deported (see Calavita, 1992). For the rest of the decade, the Immigration and Naturalization Service (INS) provided U.S. growers with an ample supply of braceros as a substitute for the undocumented workers of the past.

The "Bracero Era" came to an end in 1964. The number of braceros that participated in the program from 1942–1964 was about 4.5 million. At the end of the 1950s, over 400,000 workers emigrated each year (Cornelius, 1978). Despite the end of the Bracero Program, there were over 200,000 emigrants to the United States between 1960 and 1970, most of them from the same origins as during the program. That number increased dramatically in the next decade to between 1.2 and 1.55 million people (Escobar et al., 1999, p. 37). Instead of stopping migration because of the end of the program, during the 1960s provisions made to migratory laws allowed the entrance of workers with close relatives in the United States or with certain needed skills (Calavita, 1992; Cornelius, 1978; Mines & Massey, 1985).

The Bracero Program was the real starting point of the massive process of Mexican migration to the United States, despite efforts by U.S. and Mexican governments to stop undocumented migration. During almost two decades, migrants acquired important knowledge about how to cross the border and where to find jobs, and they developed social networks that would be of help to plan and carry out the journey. Through this, they were able to migrate without the support of any program; they were also able to migrate without documents. Further, the formation of social networks promoted the continuing concentration of Mexican immigrants in their traditional destinations—Los Angeles and Chicago areas, and in Texas and Arizona. At the same time, some adventurous "pioneers" were slowly taking their chances in other states, such as Colorado, New Mexico, Washington, and Wisconsin.

The Immigration Reform and Control Act (IRCA)

The years following the end of the Bracero Program witnessed Mexican immigrants, mainly undocumented, continuing to be one of the main sources of cheap labor for U.S. employers. Structural conditions in Mexico help to explain it. In 1970, only 50.7 percent of the population was economically active (Escobar et al., 1999); that is, over 20 million people needed a job, with the majority still residing in the countryside, and the economy of the country could not create enough jobs to meet the demand. Despite the fact that entering the U.S. labor market located workers at the bottom of their occupational ladder, at least it offered them the possibility of accessing better paying jobs (Portes & Rumbaut, 1996).

But the United States would not always welcome Mexican workers. The phantom of a high unemployment rate after World War II led legislators to try to implement measures to stop immigration, working under the assumption that this was an important cause of perceived economic problems in the United States. Since 1971, several bills have been introduced in both houses of Congress to enact federal employer sanction laws (Calavita, 1992). They were never passed by the Senate. In 1975, there was an employer sanction bill presented in the House of Representatives; another attempt was made in 1977. In 1984, a second Simpson-Mazzoli bill was passed by both houses of Congress. This bill included employer sanctions to hiring undocumented workers, but it was very costly and was not approved (Ibid.).

In 1986, the United States implemented the Immigration Reform and Control Act (IRCA), which gave undocumented immigrants who had been in the United States for a certain number of years the opportunity to legalize their status (Cornelius & Bustamante, 1989). Besides the provisions for legalization, the act also imposed sanctions on employers who knowingly hired unauthorized workers (from US$250 to US$10,000). There were two programs for legalization, the General Legalization Program (LAW) and the Special Agricultural Worker Program (SAW). The act legalized over 2 million unauthorized residents—far more than policy makers had anticipated—the majority of whom came from Mexico (69.0% of LAW applicants; 81.9% of SAW applicants) (Calavita, 1994).

Instead of decreasing immigration, the act allowed many to bring their families legally into the United States through family reunification provisions in the law. Furthermore, social networks reinforced undocumented migration through the security of counting on the support of friends and relatives with a legal status. Before 1980, there were at least 2 million Mexicans in the United States (U.S. Census Bureau, 1990). In 1990, the U.S. Census reported over 4 million people who had been born in Mexico (U.S. Census Bureau, 1997).

By 1989 those businesses that traditionally depended on undocumented immigrant labor did not stop hiring this kind of worker (Cornelius & Bustamante, 1989) because they needed to fill vacant positions with cheap and vulnerable labor. At the same time, the law made the undocumented immigrant's economic situation less secure; the U.S. economy still provided them with opportunities to hold a job, but with the added risks and vulnerability that the law introduced into their migrant lives (Ibid.). Immigrants saw themselves taking longer to find jobs, and when they were hired it was usually under short-term conditions along with the constant threat of an INS inspection.

DIMENSIONS OF MIGRATION ISSUES

Mexico is the country with the highest proportion of its population residing in a foreign country. Almost 8 million Mexicans live in the United States, 3 million of whom are there without legal migratory documents. This information is not surprising if we look at the trends that have been discussed above. According to recent Mexican census information, more than 1.6 million Mexicans left the country in the last five years (INEGI, 2001).

The magnitude of such a migratory flow has been measured in relation to its impact on the Mexican economy. It is said that remittances of Mexican migrants in the United States account for the third largest source of foreign income in the country, behind oil and tourism. During the 1990s Mexico received over US$45 billion in remittances from immigrants in the United States. Last year alone, this income was over US$6.2 billion, that is, about US$17 million a day. Economic remittances are an essential source of income for over 1 million Mexican households.

Economic Dimensions

Mexicans and the United States: Context. In the 1990s the economic conditions of Mexicans did not improve significantly. On the contrary, recurring economic crises, particularly that of 1995, decreased already scarce job opportunities for the majority of Mexicans. Economic policies have not helped either. At the beginning of the decade, for instance, the government eliminated most input subsidies and price guarantees in agriculture and eased trade restrictions. The consequence was the eventual shrinking of the production of many commodities, notably corn, that today absorb a great deal of labor (Escobar et al., 1999). This situation has spread throughout the country in such a way that populations that formerly looked for alternatives for survival within their region, state, or country are resorting now to international migration. In a national context in which migration has become a common way for many to improve their lives, international movement to the United States occupies a top level in people's choices, despite its high costs, both human and economic.

In the United States, a sustained economy has provided new arrivals with opportunities to find jobs. There are changing trends in Mexican migration that correspond to changes in U.S. market labor, particularly the growth of the services industry and the decrease in agricultural work. Mexican workers are employed in the areas that have traditionally occupied them, such as southwestern agriculture, but they are also employed "in industries in the Midwest, the southeast, and the east coast, including construction, meat-packing, and services" (Escobar et al., 1999, p. 25). At the same time, the entire United States working population is currently distributed among industries as follows: agriculture, forestry, fishing, and hunting, 1,878,296; manufacturing, 18,500,186; and services, 54,007,143 (U.S. Census Bureau, 2000). Mexican migrants are incorporating into those labor markets that the U.S. population as a whole is incorporating as well. This does not, however, suggest equality in job holding between residents and immigrants. It is well known that immigrants hold lower-paid jobs and that their labor conditions are less secure and more subject to the impacts of economic changes. This is what defines migrant labor as a flexible labor force: It fills the demand for workers, but it is expendable when there is a scarcity of jobs.

The last decade witnessed contradictory trends in the way the United States addressed immigration. On the one hand, immigrants regularized during IRCA became eligible for citizenship during the 1990s. Between 1991 and 1995, 1.5 million people were admitted as legal U.S. residents. At the same time, the expansion of the U.S. economy allowed it to create a large number of jobs that could both absorb immigrants already in the United States and constitute an incentive for the incorporation of new arrivals. This situation has been connected to the flow of immigrants into new destinations: States that were previously characterized by certain underdevelopment, such as Mississippi or Louisiana, and that had not been preferred destinations for foreign-born population, have been receiving immigrants in the last decade.

On the other hand, the United States has implemented some policies that may deter immigration. Congress has passed legislation to implement more border and interior controls, like the Illegal Immigration Reform and Immigrant Responsibility Act of 1996 (IIRIRA). In addition, the Welfare Reform Act of 1996 was geared toward moving 2–3 million adult welfare recipients into jobs and toward creating jobs for the rapidly growing domestic labor force. Immigrants are therefore finding more competition in obtaining low-paying jobs.

There is also a new economic context as well, due to the deceleration the U.S. economy has suffered in the last few years. Such economic deceleration is also having significant effects on some industries in Mexico, especially on the maquiladora (assembly) industry, which very much depends on foreign investments. This situation is worrisome if we consider that many Mexicans see employment in the maquila as an alternative to migrating to the United States.

Social Dimensions

The Changing Trends of Mexican International Migration. Traditionally, Mexican migration to the United States has been predominantly temporal. The current trend, however, favors permanent migration, whereas Mexican migration had long been basically for seasonal and agricultural labor. The current jobs in manufacturing and the service industries that Mexican migrants hold allow them to stay in the United States longer, creating social and economic links to the society and including the possibility of a permanent residence there. According to the Binational Study of 1997 (SRE-CIR, 1997), the number of immigrants who are establishing U.S. residence is increasing: Between 1960 and 1970, 260,000–290,000 established permanent residence; this figure increased to 1.2–1.55 million between 1970 and 1980, and to 2.1–2.6 million between 1980 and 1990. The current status of Mexican immigrants is predominantly legal, however, over 37 percent of Mexicans residing in the United States remain undocumented.

Agriculture has been the main occupation for Mexican immigrants for many decades but in 2001 only 13.3 percent worked in this primary sector. The rest were distributed as follows: 36.2 percent worked in the secondary sector and 50.5 percent in the services sector. This is consistent with the origins of temporary migrants, which have changed from predominantly rural to urban. Between 1993 and 1997, the proportion was 54 percent urban to 46 percent rural; between 1998 and 2000, the proportion was 57.4 percent urban and 42.6 percent urban (CONAPO, 2001, p. 82). Immigrants of urban origin might see their probability of getting into the U.S. labor market and improving their economic conditions increase. However, immigrants who are arriving from new regions of origin in Mexico have yet to succeed in the construction and solidification of social links that will make the incorporation into the U.S. labor market and society less costly.

The increasing participation of women in the migratory movement is related to their growing legalized migratory status, since many women arrive as part of a reunification pattern. This is not true for all women, however. Ethnographic research has shown that women are increasingly migrating independently, without husbands or other male relatives, but these women may be less protected by family networks. Of the people residing permanently in the United States, 44.1 percent are women. Temporary migrants, however, show a different proportion: From 1993–1997, only 2.4 percent were women; from 1998–2000, the percentage grew to only 6.6 percent.

Despite the fact that Mexican immigrants have less schooling relative to the U.S. population and other immigrant groups, among those who reside in the United States 36.6 percent have over 12 years of schooling and 19.1 percent have between 9 and 11 years of schooling. Among temporary migrants, who tend to have less education, 34 percent have secondary school education or more (CONAPO, 2001).

Diversification of Origins

The traditional states in Mexico that have sent migrants to the United States have kept their predominant place, sending over 45 percent of all migrants. At the same time, other states and localities in Mexico are starting to participate in the migratory movement—96.2 percent of Mexican municipalities show some presence of international migration. The consequences for this can be analyzed at different territorial levels. At the national level, we see that the "process of international migration" has taken on a dynamic of its own. At the level of Mexican states, however, the process has a different character. The trend continues in the traditional sending states, suggesting that migrants may be enjoying well-developed social networks and other social knowledge that reduce the costs of migration. The situation is less certain for those immigrants from the new sending states, where there is very little or no social knowledge specific to migration.

The situation is even more dramatic at the municipal and local levels, and of great importance along human, family, and community dimensions. The localities that constitute the new origins of Mexican migrants to the United States are experiencing important changes in their social relations. All of the family and community disruption that migration from the Mexican western states experienced (Salgado, 1993) is happening in the new ones but at a seemingly much faster rate, given the fast growth of the movement in these new origins of immigration. Family and local economies suffer, particularly at the beginning of the migratory process. Families do not receive economic remittances immediately, and they have to pay the debts acquired to finance the migration of their relative(s).

Communities, too, change their way of life. Relations among people change, and expressions of solidarity acquire different forms as they become more monetized, less permanent (Zamudio, 1999). The uncertainty of the separation filters into peoples' expectations of one another, introducing suspicion, and the social fabric suffers (Zamudio, 2001). Communities lose people in their most productive years after having "invested" in them, emotionally as well as educationally and economically.

But not everything is bad news. Some communities are developing strategies to strengthen social links.

The Main Actors of Mexican International Migration

Getting into the United States and being incorporated into U.S. society and its labor market are not easy tasks, especially for those immigrants who do not have legal documents. The vulnerability of undocumented immigrants starts at the point of departure and increases during the crossing of the border (Zamudio, 2000). Many migrants are in the hands of the smugglers (also called *polleros*, or coyotes), who do not always comply with the conditions of the "crossing agreement." Others prefer to cross the border with experienced friends, subjecting themselves to the increasing dangers and controls of the U.S.-Mexico border. Some studies have shown that after crossing the border a couple of times, migrants develop a specific knowledge for migrating, thus, increasing their chances for success (Massey & Singer, 1998). At the same time, advisors, smugglers, and tourism and transportation agents have found migration to be a profitable business, and the migration infrastructure has become very sophisticated. Migrants have choices in deciding who will help them cross the border, in choosing how to finance the trip, and in finding employment in the United States.

In addition to the trauma of crossing, where many have lost their lives, there is still the need to find a place to stay and a job. If the migrant has friends, he or she can usually count on them, but that is not the case for everyone. Some migrants have to rely on people they barely know and take the risks that dealing with strangers implies. Finding a job is not easy for newcomers; the lucky ones can be recommended by a friend, but others go to job agencies or places known to be visited by employers or their intermediaries.

Over time, people who reside for longer periods in the United States develop relations and build or incorporate into a community. This can take years. Recent literature on international migration has paid attention to the construction of *paisano* communities in the host societies (see Goldring, 1998; Smith, 1998), showing that some immigrants organize in "clubs" (i.e., relatively formal associations constituted by those who come from the same municipality). Such clubs usually organize social gatherings in the United States to promote a sense of community among *paisanos* and, at the same time, collect funds to implement projects geared to improve social conditions in their municipalities or towns of origin (Goldring, 1998). However, despite the proliferation of such associations, the majority of Mexicans are still not organized in clubs.

The reception and use of remittances is important in maintaining family and community connections. Over a million households in Mexico depend on the remittances of their relatives in the United States. The way that money is spent can be an important factor in the duration and consequences of the migration. In the case where there is a "migratory project" (Zamudio, 2001), family members on both sides of the border have a relatively clear sense of how to spend the money, and the goals for the migration can more likely be attained within a certain amount of time. When there is no clarity over the way remittances should be spent, the money might be wasted and the migrant might have to remain abroad for a longer period of time, until the needs of the family are satisfied.

People in some communities of origin participate in an organized fashion in the maintenance of links with their members abroad. They do this both at the family and community levels. Some communities have developed organizations to promote continuous contact between family members — besides those practiced within the family — through phone calls at special occasions, such as baptisms and first communions, and through sending and receiving videos or other items. This way, contact is not lost.

Non-governmental organizations (NGOs) can play an important role in decreasing the costs of migration, human and economic, and otherwise. To start with, they not only focus on the organized groups but also on the ordinary migrant, particularly if he or she is a new arrival and needs emergency support of any kind. These organizations also develop networks that cross borders to provide immigrants, particularly those who are undocumented, with havens where they can have food and shelter and fulfill some other basic needs, even spiritual needs. Some of them allow immigrants to call home to ask for some money or simply to let their relatives know they are fine.

The involvement of the NGOs in migratory matters is not new in Mexico. Traditionally their role has been limited to assisting migrants in cases of emergency or need and to providing them with information regarding the networks of help they can find in their journey (mainly shelters at the border cities). Nowadays NGOs get involved in helping immigrants with legal counseling and job training, among other things. NGOs are also involved in the design of public policy and legislature. For example, the Catholic Church has played an important role in the protection of immigrants and emigrants in Mexico.

Political Dimensions

One important part of NGOs' recent participation has been the lobbying on legislative changes on migratory policy in Mexico. One of the basic assumptions that guides their work is the particular position of Mexico as a country of immigration, transit, and emigration. This position poses particular constraints on the actions that the Mexican government can take if it wants to maintain a coherent position on the issue of migration. The demand for respect of Mexican migrants' human rights has to be supported by a governmental policy of respect of human rights of undocumented immigrants in Mexico, either there to stay or on their way north to the United States. Unfortunately, the Mexican government has not maintained such coherence, posing an obstacle to the development of a culture of human rights that could strengthen Mexicans in their demand for respect of their rights both in Mexico and in the United States. The criminalizing approach that governmental authorities of both countries take toward undocumented migrants is a main concern of NGOs (CEMEFI, 2000; see also Zamudio, 2000). The level of vulnerability of undocumented migrants is such that these approaches make them the target of possible human rights violations. In response to such approaches, NGOs contend that Mexican state and municipal authorities should get involved in the provision of basic social services to migrants, such as health, education, justice, work training, a place to stay, transportation to their places of origin, and communication with their families (CEMEFI, 2000).

Since international migration involves more than one country, it should be treated as a bilateral and regional issue between Mexico, the United States, Canada, and the Central American countries. Within this topic, it is important to fight against the trafficking of migrants but without jeopardizing migrants' human rights. Issues related to corruption and the control of the borders are also important (Ibid.). Since migration means, fundamentally, the mobilization of people in search of better-paying jobs, it is also important that labor force mobility be included in the proposals for regional integration, such as the 1993 North American Free Trade Agreement, signed by Mexico, the United States, and Canada.

Besides economic policies that seem to be helping the movement, the Mexican government at its federal, state, and local levels has developed policies directly related to migratory issues. At the federal level, three main agencies deal with international migration: the National Institute of Migration, the Secretariat of Foreign Affairs, and the Office for Attention to Mexican Migrants Abroad.

The National Institute of Migration deals mainly with foreigners who enter the country. It also gets involved in the protection of migrants who try to cross the border, either from the south or north. The institute has created so-called "Beta Groups," made up of personnel trained to assist Mexican and foreign migrants in situations of emergency during their border-crossing attempts. In some states the institute participates in the return of the bodies of Mexicans who die abroad.

The Secretariat of Foreign Affairs has two important programs. One is the Paisano Program, created in 1989, which coordinates several governmental agencies that support and protect the return of Mexican migrants in order to ease administrative work and avoid mistreatment from the part of authorities. The other is the Program for Mexican Communities Abroad (PMCA), implemented in 1990 with the purpose of improving and increasing relations with Mexicans who live abroad. The importance of the PMCA is that it promotes social organization of Mexican communities in the United States. This, in fact, has helped develop communication among paisanos. By October 2000, there were about 680 clubs of Mexican paisanos in the United States: 57 percent of the clubs are in California, 25 percent are in Texas, 9 percent are in Illinois, and 7 percent are in Arizona.

However, despite these apparently neutral efforts on the part of the Mexican government to maintain a presence and help Mexican communities, immigrants are suspicious about the government and community leaders' intentions. Some of the leaders of the clubs are seen as pursuing personal economic and/or political advantages by organizing their fellow countrymen. Others think that it is the Mexican government that has political and economic interests toward them, such as gaining their votes in favor of specific parties or collaboration in the improvement of their communities of origin. Such suspicions discourage people from actively participating in the organizations.

The Office for Attention to Mexican Migrants Abroad was created by the new presidential administration under Vicente Fox, given the current significance of the issue. It seeks to inform migrants about the rights they have and to monitor the respect of such rights. It also looks for opportunities to generate productive projects in the communities of origin and to help improve communication between people on both sides of the border. In addition, state governments in Mexico are also developing some strategies for dealing with international migration. At least 18 states have created an office for protection of their people.

THE FUTURE

Mexican international migration has entered into a dynamic that suggests that the movement north might get even stronger. Mexican economics do not show signs of improvement, and the working-age population is expected to grow considerably during this decade. The social infrastructure that has sustained and developed the migratory flow is maturing. However, economic conditions and other political concerns of the United States might make it more difficult for people to find a job there and be incorporated into the society. Border control might tighten, making it more expensive and dangerous to cross the border without documents. It is necessary for Mexico and the United States to engage in the design of policies that take a comprehensive approach to the issue.

Experience has shown that the probability of success of migration increases with the clarity and precision of a "migratory project." Access to information will be decisive in people's process of deciding whether to migrate and how to do it. It is necessary to inform the population about possible alternatives to undocumented migration to the United States, such as the temporary work programs that Canada is implementing.

For Mexicans already in the United States, it is important that Mexican legislation allows them to acquire U.S. citizenship so that they can fully enjoy the rights they are entitled to, without losing their rights in Mexico or being considered traitors. And because these people maintain their attachments to their homeland and even contribute to its survival, there must be a commitment from the Mexican state to implement measures that allow them to vote in the next presidential elections, just as any other Mexican citizen would.

NOTES

1. "Bracero" refers to the fact that agricultural workers work with their "brazos" (arms).

2. "Wetback" makes reference to the fact that the undocumented migrants used the Río Grande to cross the border, getting their backs wet by the water.

BIBLIOGRAPHY

Betancourt, J., Cordova, T., & Torres, M. A. (1993). Economic Restructuring and the Process of Incorporation of Latinos into the Chicago Economy. In R. Morales & F. Bonilla (Eds.), *Latinos in a Changing U.S. Economy: Comparative Perspectives on Growing Inequality* (pp. 135–163). Newbury Park, CA: Sage Publications.

Calavita, K. (1992). *Inside the State: The Bracero Program, Immigration and the INS.* New York: Routledge.

———. (1994). U.S. Immigration and Policy Responses: The Limits of Legislation. In W. Cornelius, P. L. Martín, & J. F. Hollifield (Eds.), *Controlling Immigration: A Global Perspective* (pp. 55–82). Stanford, CA: Stanford University Press.

CEMEFI (Responsible). (2000). *Reporte Final. Conclusiones y Propuestas de la Mesa de Diálogo entre las Organizaciones de la Sociedad Civil y el Equipo de Transición en las Areas Social y Política del Gobierno del Presidente Vicente Fox Quesada*. México: Centro Mexicano para la Filantropía, CEMEFI.

CONAPO. (2001). *La Población de México en el Nuevo Siglo*. México: CONAPO.

Cornelius, W. (1978). *Mexican Migration to the United States: Causes, Consequences and U.S. Responses* (Migration and Development Monograph C/78–9). Cambridge, MA: Centro MIT for International Studies.

Cornelius, W., & Bustamante, J. A. (Eds.). (1989). *Mexican Migration to the United States: Origins, Consequences, and Policy Options*. San Diego: Center for U.S.–Mexican Studies, University of California.

Escobar, A., Bean, F. D., & Weintraub, S. (1999). *La Dinámica de la Emigración Mexicana*. México: Ciesas and Porrua.

Faist, T. (2000). *The Volume and Dynamics of International Migration and Transnational Social Spaces*. Oxford: Clarendon Press.

Goldring, L. (1998). The Power of Status in Transnational Social Fields. In M. P. Smith and L. E. Guarnizo (Eds.), *Transnationalism from Below* (pp. 165–195). New Brunswick, NJ: Transaction Publishers.

INEGI. (2000). *XII Censo de Población y Vivienda*. México: INEGI.

———. (2001). Cuestionario Ampliado-Migración. Tabla 13. Población Migrante Internacional Según Lugar de Destino y su Distribución Porcentual Según Entidad Federativa Expulsora. *XII Censo de Población y Vivienda*. México: INEGI.

Kerr, L.A.N. (1976). Assimilation Aborted: Chicanos in Chicago, 1939–54. In M. G. Holli & P. d'A. Jones (Eds.), *Ethnic Chicago* (pp. 270–298). Grand Rapids, MI: W.B. Eerdmans.

Massey, D. S., & Singer, A. (1998). The Social Process of Undocumented Border Crossing. *International Migration Review, 32*, 561–592.

Mines, R., & Massey, D. S. (1985). Patterns of Migration to the United States from Two Mexican Communities. *Latin American Research Review, 20*, 104–124.

Morales, R., & Bonilla, F. (Eds.). (1993). *Latinos in a Changing U.S. Economy: Comparative Perspectives on Growing Inequality*. Newbury Park, CA: Sage Publications.

Portes, A., & Rumbaut, R. G. (1996). *Immigrant America: A Portrait*. Berkeley: University of California Press.

Reichert, J. S., & Massey, D. S. (1982). Guestworker Programs: Evidence from Europe and the United States and Some Implications for U.S. Policy. *Population Research and Policy Review, 1*, 1–17.

Salgado, N. (1993, August). Family Life Across the Border: Mexican Wives Left Behind. *Hispanic Journal of Behavioral Sciences*, 391–401.

SRE-CIR (Secretaría de Relaciones Exteriores–Commission for Immigration Reform). 1997. *Binational Study on Migration Between Mexico & the United States*. Mexico and Washington, DC: Authors.

Smith, R. (1998). Transnational Localities: Community, Technology and the Politics of Membership within the Context of Mexico and U.S. Migration. In M. P. Smith & L. E. Guarnizo (Eds.), *Transnationalism from Below* (pp. 196–238). New Brunswick, NJ: Transaction Publishers.

Tienda, Marta. (1989). Looking to the 1990s: Mexican Immigration in Sociological Perspective. In W. Cornelius & J. A. Bustamante (Eds.), *Mexican Migration to the United States: Origins, Consequences, and Policy Options* (pp. 109–150). San Diego: Center for U.S.–Mexican Studies, University of California.

Tuirán, R. (2001). Intervención en la ceremonia de presentación del Programa de Trabajo de los 210 Consejos Municipales de Población. *Xalapa*, Ver. 15 de agosto.

U.S. Census Bureau. (1990). Table 1. General Characteristics of Foreign-Born Persons, by Nativity, Citizenship, and Year of Entry. *1990 Census*. Washington, DC: U.S. Government Printing Office.

————. (1997). Table 3-4. Country or Area of Birth of the Foreign-Born Population from Latin America and Northern America: 1997 [Electronic Version]. *March 1997 Current Population Survey*. Washington, DC: U.S. Government Printing Office.

————. (2000). Table 3. Profile of Selected Economic Characteristics. *Census 2000 Supplementary Survey Profile for the United States*. Washington, DC: U.S. Government Printing Office.

Zamudio, P. (1999). *Huejuquillense Immigrants in Chicago: Culture, Gender, and Community in the Shaping of Consciousness*. Unpublished doctoral dissertation, Northwestern University, Evanston, IL.

————. (2000). *A Subjective Experience of Migration: The Uncertainties of the Border Crossing*. Paper presented at the SECOLAS 48th Annual Conference: Challenges of the Américas in the New Millenium, Veracruz, México.

————. (2001). *La Migración Internacional de los Veracruzanos: Un Diagnóstico Preliminar*. Veracruz, México: CIESAS-Golfo and the Gobierno del Estado de Veracruz.

10

THE NETHERLANDS

The Myth of Ethnic Equality

Twanna A. Hines

INTRODUCTION

Profile of the Netherlands

The Netherlands is one of Europe's smallest countries and one of the world's most densely populated. Home to over 16 million residents, 94 percent of the population is of native Dutch or other European ancestry. The majority of the migrants to the Netherlands are fellow European Union (EU) nationals—mostly from Germany and the United Kingdom (Anderson, 1998). Size, proximity, and language may account for this migration trend. Germany and the United Kingdom are two of the largest countries in Europe. Geographically, Germany borders the Netherlands to the east. Crossing the English Channel, England is northwest of the Netherlands. Linguistically, German, English, and Dutch are in the same family of language. While Dutch is the official language of the Netherlands, English is widely spoken and many Dutch students learn German while they are in school. About six percent of the migrant population is comprised of individuals with backgrounds that span beyond EU borders. The four chief migrant groups in the Netherlands come from Surinam, Turkey, Morocco, and the Antilles.

Eighty-nine percent of the Netherlands' population resides in urban areas, with the majority residing in the *Randstad*. The *Randstad* is the densely populated area between four major cities located in the west of the country: Amsterdam, The Hague, Utrecht, and Rotterdam. A former colonizing nation, the Netherlands has been ruled by and has ruled other nations. Granting sovereignty to Indonesia in 1949 and Surinam in 1975, other former Dutch colonies include Aruba and the Antilles. Currently a parliamentary democracy under a constitutional monarch, the Netherlands has two capitals. The national capital is Amsterdam, while the seat of government is located in The Hague. A prosperous and open economy, the Netherlands ranks third worldwide, behind the United States and France, in the value of agricultural exports.

Vignettte

Bicycles are very much a part of the Dutch culture and many refugees, like the majority of the population in the Netherlands, use bicycles as their primary mode of transportation. One of the stereotypes that some people hold about refugees is that they have stolen the bikes on which they ride. To reduce this stereotype the national association for asylum seekers, the Central Organization for the Care of Asylees (COA), thought it would be a good idea to require asylum seekers living in the Netherlands to buy and attach red stickers to their bicycles. The stickers would serve as proof that the refugees did not steal the bikes they were riding.

Some refugees found the stickers to provide a sense of relief. Visual proof that a bike was purchased and not stolen, the stickers eliminated the need for the refugees to attest verbally to their innocence. Language barriers often make it difficult for native speakers and people who are new to learning the language to communicate. Joao, a refugee currently living in the Netherlands, stated, "My Dutch is not very good. It is aggravating when I have to convince the neighbors that come looking for their stolen bikes that this bike is really mine. With such a sticker, it is immediately made clear without an argument."

However, not all refugees were keen on the idea of buying the stickers. Because individuals held stereotypes about the immigrants stealing bikes, the COA required the refugees to buy stickers to prove their innocence. Therefore, many migrants—as well as many Dutch natives—believed the rationale behind the stickers was that the refugees were guilty until proven innocent. Omar, also a refugee living in the Netherlands, stated, "Do you know what the worst part of it is? You must pay five guilders [approximately US$2.00] to show that you are not a thief."

Soon after the COA began requiring the stickers, the media began to make connections with similar instances in Dutch history of singling out ethnic minorities. An article in the *Volkskrant*, a national daily Dutch newspaper, ran the headline, "Asylum Seeker Center Bicycle Sticker Resembles Star of David." The Netherlands was one of the first nations toppled by Nazi Germany during World War II in the early and middle years of the twentieth century. Dutch Jews were required to wear the Star of David to make themselves more easily identifiable as Jewish.

Following an inundation of negative press, a leader of the COA stated that he believed what started out as a good intention had the wrong effect, because the stickers stigmatized the refugees. "If you make a comparison with [World War II]," he said, "you know that something has to change." Amid enormous pressure and immense societal and political criticism, the COA eventually stopped requiring asylum seekers to buy the stickers.

Although the refugees in this vignette experienced mixed reactions to the COA's initial decision to require the red stickers for the bicycles, a lack of social integration is apparent in each instance. Like other immigrants, refugees are often conspicuous due to differences in language, clothing, and other audio and visual cultural clues. Already highly visible, the stickers had the added effect of stigmatizing the immigrants.

Overview of Migration Issues

The Netherlands is rapidly transforming due to international migration (Anderson, 1998; Bax, 1995; Lucassen & Penninx, 1997). Currently, the bulk of the minority and immigrant populations in the Netherlands consists of three groups: guest workers recruited to fill low to unskilled occupations starting after World War II, migrants from former colonies, and post–Cold war refugees from newly independent Eastern European states (Bax, 1995). The three groups' combination of skin color, culture, and religion often set them apart and make them more conspicuous than previous waves of immigrants.

Significantly employed by many European nations beginning in the 1940s with the conclusion of World War II, the process of guest worker recruitment involved bilateral agreements that arranged for less developed nations to supply Europe's labor force (Castles, 1993; Martens, 1999; Veenman & Roelandt, 1994). Guest workers in the Netherlands included individuals recruited from countries located in the eastern and southern regions of Europe as well as individuals from North Africa (Lucassen & Penninx, 1997). In eastern and southern Europe, the Netherlands drew mostly laborers who were from Turkey. In North Africa, the laborers mainly came from Morocco.

In addition to actively recruiting newcomers from Turkey and Morocco, the Netherlands saw an increase in individuals from former colonies after decolonization in the middle and latter segments of the twentieth century (Bax, 1995). The bulk of postcolonial immigrants are individuals such as Surinamers, Moluccans, Indonesians, Antilleans, and Arubans. Migrants from these countries have historical, social, cultural, and political relationships with the Netherlands due to its colonial past.

If migrants are individuals and groups of people who leave their country of origin to reside—temporarily or permanently—in another country, refugees are migrants who flee their home countries in fear of persecution. Representing a small percentage of the Dutch population, the largest numbers of refugees come from Afghanistan (5,055), Yugoslavia (3,850), and Iraq (2,773) (Anderson, 1998; European Commission, 2000).

Today, the Netherlands continues to experience influxes of migrants from former colonies, relatives of guest worker recruits, and refugees. While the Netherlands has the second highest growth rate of all the European countries, the native Dutch population is barely increasing at all (Lucassen & Penninx, 1997; Melich, 1997). The migrants appear to fill demographic gaps posed by Dutch fertility trends (Lucassen & Penninx, 1997).

HISTORY OF MIGRATION ISSUES

Throughout modern history, immigration to the Netherlands has traditionally occurred during eras of great national prosperity, while emigration has occurred during periods of economic hardship and war (Bax, 1995; Lucassen & Penninx, 1997). The first period of mass immigration occurred from 1585–1670, a period in Dutch history known as the Golden Age. Located at the crossroads of Europe and operating the busiest seaport in the world, Rotterdam, the Dutch established themselves as a trading nation. Location, however, was not the sole factor contributing to Dutch domination of the sea. As the Netherlands is below sea level, the Dutch have regarded their tremendous adeptness at defending against the waters as a necessity for their survival. The Netherlands was also able to capitalize on its trading prowess and seafaring skills during the Golden Age by exploring and conquering distant territories (Bax, 1995).

Expanding their empire, the Dutch established and commandeered trading stations in Africa, Southeast Asia, and the Americas. Riches obtained from Dutch colonies yielded tremendous prosperity in the Netherlands. The country's relative prosperity and tolerance of religious freedom attracted economic migrants and political refugees from various parts of Western Europe (Lucassen & Penninx, 1997; Martens, 1999; Veenman & Roelandt, 1994). Many of the migrants temporarily resided in the Netherlands while others made the country their permanent home. Keeping in fashion with the rules of colonization, inhabitants of Western European countries settled into various lands at this time but were unaccustomed to others, in turn, settling on their own soil. The economic tide shifted by the nineteenth century (Bax, 1995). The Dutch economy began to stagnate, and the number of immigrants decreased. Dutch farmers, craftsmen, and artisans began to emigrate to the plentiful soils of North America due to bad harvests. During this time, the revolving door to the Dutch border witnessed more exits than entries.

The two world wars during the first half of the twentieth century tremendously affected Western Europe's ethnic landscape. During World War I, Germany's effort to conquer France and its invasion of Belgium sent Belgian refugees across the Dutch border. Immediately preceding and during World War II, Jews and other Nazi adversaries from Eastern Europe, Germany, and Austria sought refuge in Dutch tolerance. When Germany invaded the

Netherlands in 1940, many Dutch nationals, including the Queen, fled to England. The Germans declared the Dutch fellow Aryans under Nazi law. Many Dutch people remained in the Netherlands and formed active resistance parties against the Nazis. Others willingly joined *National-Socialistische Beweging* (NSB), the Dutch Nazi Party that had already developed and thrived in the Netherlands in the 1930s, prior to German invasion. The supporters of the NSB began voluntarily turning over their non-Aryan compatriots to the German occupying forces. Paradoxically, Anne Frank was both a beneficiary of tolerance in the form of those who hid her and a casualty of the bigotry of those who informed the Nazis of her family's whereabouts.

At the conclusion of World War II, the Netherlands was war-torn and it needed to rebuild, but out-migration and human casualties had significantly reduced its population and labor force. Fueled by rapid economic growth as service industries expanded, the Dutch economy experienced structural shortages in the labor market during the 1960s and early 1970s. In short, Dutch nationals began moving into the service sector, and laborers were needed to fill the low and unskilled sectors of the economy.

The Dutch government regulated the recruitment of foreign laborers (*gastarbeiders*), primarily from Turkey and Morocco (Brubaker, 1996; Castles, 1993; Lucassen & Penninx, 1997; Zimmermann, 1995). This process, widely employed by European nations after World War II, was called the "guest worker program." The term "guest worker" was used because the assumption was that the workers would simply be "guests" who would rebuild the host country and then return to their homelands after a short amount of time. The primary goal of the guest worker program was to ensure that the laborers contributed to the Dutch economy while maintaining strong ties with their home countries (Bax, 1995). As such, social and cultural integration programs to assure the possibility of increased socioeconomic standing for the migrants, such as language acquisition initiatives, were not enacted. The workers resided in poor living conditions and generally had to restrict their expenditures in order to send money to support their family members back in their home countries.

Active labor recruiting decelerated after the oil crisis in the mid-1970s due to economic stagnation; nevertheless, a steady migration stream remained (Brubaker, 1996; Castles, 1993; Lucassen & Penninx, 1997; Zimmermann, 1995). The waves of guest worker migrants primarily began with Turkish and Moroccan men who came to the Netherlands looking for work. However, family reunification, a process of issuing visas to immigrants' family members still living in the immigrants' countries of origin, implanted immigrant women. Thus, instead of returning to their home countries, many of the laborers remained in the Netherlands and were reunited with their family members on Dutch soil.

In conjunction with postwar economic restructuring, the restructuring of former colonies also introduced waves of migrants to the Netherlands (Lucassen & Penninx, 1997). Like many other former colonizing nations, Dutch officials chose to permit migration and draw pools of labor from former colonies because this ensured that the immigrants had already gained exposure to Dutch language, culture, and institutions. These territories would later become independent lands such as Aruba, Dutch Antilles, Surinam, New York City (originally New Amsterdam), Indonesia, South Africa, and others. Migration from many of these lands increased during the years immediately preceding and following the countries' quasi-independence. Ultimately, the migrant annals of the Netherlands have primarily resulted in four minority populations: Antillean, Surinamese, Turkish, and Moroccan. (Bax, 1995; Mattheijer, 2000; Sociaal-Economische Raad (SER), 2000; Zorlu, 2000). The Turkish and Moroccan migrants are former guest worker recruits. The Antillean and Surinamese migrants are postcolonial nationals.

Political refugees and asylum seekers increasingly dominate the present immigration streams (Mattheijer, 2000; SER, 2000; Zorlu & Hartog, 1999). The Netherlands has been second only to Switzerland, which has the highest number of asylum seekers and refugees in Western Europe. Over the last two decades, there seems to have been a marked change in the composition of this particular pool of migrants fleeing persecution and seeking a better way of life (Bax, 1995). In the 1980s and into the 1990s, many of the refugees arrived in the Netherlands from African nations such as Ghana and Somalia. Currently, the majority of the refugees come from the Middle East, post–Cold War nations, and the newly independent states, such as Bosnia and Afghanistan (Mattheijer, 2000). The trend seems to indicate that tensions between east and west have thawed while resistance to welcoming large numbers of refugees from the south remains frozen.

DIMENSIONS OF MIGRATION ISSUES

Political Dimensions

Loosely integrated into Dutch society, culture, and economy, immigration policy toward these migrants has been exceedingly restrictive (Brubaker, 1996; Castles, 1993; Lucassen & Penninx, 1997; Zimmermann, 1995). Nevertheless, the Netherlands did not explicitly make immigration a dominant policy concern at the national level. Furthermore, Dutch political leaders were reluctant to speak out against immigrants and minorities in the manner in which other Europeans leaders such as Strauss (Germany), Chirac (France), and Thatcher (England) have done. Then Pim Fortuyn, an openly gay politician and former sociology professor, stepped onto the political stage and campaigned for closing the nation's doors to immigrants.

Shocking the nation by seizing 35 percent of the vote in the local elections in Rotterdam, one of the four major Dutch cities with large immigrant communities, Fortuyn shook up Dutch politics by supporting taboo causes such as increasing corporate welfare, toughening up on crime, and ceasing immigration. Following Fortuyn's success, other political parties in the Netherlands fell into step and vowed to revisit Dutch immigration laws. On May 7, 2002, an animal rights activist made history by gunning down Fortuyn just days before the general election. Upon his death, the Dutch populace elected Pim Fortuyn's party, Pim Fortuyn's List, into the national government.

At first glance, Fortuyn's anti-immigrant platform seemed out of place in the Netherlands, which has a reputation for being tolerant and embracing liberalism. The Netherlands was the first European country to sanction same-sex marriages, regulate prostitution, legalize euthanasia, and tolerate the sale of marijuana over the counter in thousands of infamous "coffee shops." Supporting each of these causes, Fortuyn disassociated himself from other European right-wing leaders. Therefore, his proclamation that Islam is a "backward" culture and other negative statements about immigrants and minority communities seemed contradictory. Illuminating remarkable inconsistencies in modern politics, Fortuyn's campaign tolled the same historically contradictory tone in which nations professed all men are created equal while systematically enslaving ethnic groups. Likewise, Dutch tolerance seemingly excluded equality for migrants and ethnic minorities. Believed to be one of the most astonishing killings of a European politician since Swedish Prime Minister Olof Palme was murdered in Stockholm in 1986, the rise of Pim Fortuyn's List signals a revival of right-wing parties in the Netherlands and throughout continental Europe.

Prior to the political gains of Pim Fortuyn's List, Dutch support for far-right and extremist parties had been on a continual downward spiral and open violence and hate crimes committed against minorities were much less prevalent in the Netherlands than in many of its continental neighbors, including France and Germany. Indeed, in recent years, the Dutch government has made concerted efforts to socially, economically, and politically integrate ethnic minorities living in the country by establishing targeted integration policies. Implemented by local authorities, the goal of the programs has been to attempt to correct the ill treatment of migrants. The policies fall into three categories: social integration, education, and labor market policies.

As Dutch is not a major international language, most of the social integration policies focus on language acquisition (SER, 2000). Targeting newcoming refugees and individuals related to the former guest worker recruitment program, these programs are not as useful for postcolonial migrants, as many of them already know the Dutch language.

Education policies were erected because many minority children begin their schooling with educational deficiencies due to their arrival in the Netherlands in the middle of their school career (Bax, 1995; Leman, 1991). Social inequality also affects their performance such that educational gaps between minority and native Dutch children tend to persist throughout the duration of a child's schooling.

Labor market policies have included training programs that focus on the attainment of marketable skills (Clark, Dutt, & Kornberg, 1993; Hartog & Vriend, 1989; Lucassen & Penninx, 1997; Penninx, Schoorl, & van Praag, 1993). Targeting postcolonial nationals and former guest worker recruits' relatives, these programs are not completely suitable for refugees (SER, 2000). The Dutch central institute for refugees, Vluchtelingenwerk Nederland, maintains that highly-educated individuals with asylum status encounter barriers to entering the workforce because they must go through a laborious procedure to receive permits to work.

According to the Social and Economic Council (2000), an advisory body to the Dutch government, Dutch government and employment agencies neither fully nor consistently implement any of the policies aimed to integrate minorities, and this problem should be rectified before instituting any new policies on migration. Sociaal-Economische Raad (2000) claims current workforce, language acquisition, and educational initiatives have been ineffective due to: (1) a lack of cooperation and a "take it or leave it" attitude among government and employment agencies; (2) integration and education policies not being closely tailored to the backgrounds of the minorities; (3) companies' lack of cooperation; and (4) minorities' restricted use of the opportunities offered. Whether or not these targeted policies represented genuine tolerance of migrant groups or a facade masking the Dutch population's indifference toward minorities and migrant participation in mainstream society is debatable.

Social Dimensions

Current social integration of guest workers, migrants from former colonies, and refugees is deeply rooted in Dutch *pillarization* (Bax, 1995; Zorlu, 1999). Although the protestant Dutch Reformed Church has been the dominant religious group throughout the country's history, the Netherlands never experienced the violent persecution of religious minorities in the manner that other European countries did. Therefore, Europeans fleeing religious persecution often went to the Netherlands. During the nineteenth century, in order to manage the increasing religious diversity in the Netherlands, the Dutch government institutionalized *pillarization*, a method by which religious and secular group-specific interest groups formed the pillars of society, and were entitled to set up their own associations, schools, political parties, trade unions, and social service and social work agencies, as well as their own broadcasting and mass media mechanisms for radio and television. These interest groups engulfed all spheres of public life and pillarization remained the chief system to ensure the social and political integration of various secular and religious groups.

Because of pillarization's relative success rate in managing religious diversity, it has also been employed as a method of integrating recent migrants (Bax, 1995; Zorlu, 1999). The Dutch government began aiding the establishment of separate interest groups for ethnic minorities and newer immigrants in the Netherlands. Because social, religious, and cultural distinctions did not overlap with economic divisions historically, pillarization created separate but equal horizontal boundaries in Dutch society. After World War II, however, the Dutch society experienced significant changes. The gap between the rich and the poor began to widen. The pillars in society now consisted of ethnic rather than strictly denominational divisions. Furthermore, because migrants were typically recruited to fill very specific gaps in the Dutch workforce, the social, religious, and cultural pillars of society began to form along vertical economic lines of inequality. In this respect, pillarization has come to resemble another Dutch construction — apartheid, which is a Dutch word that literally translates as "apartness."

Pillarization has been effective in managing religious diversity but not ethnic diversity. Therefore, pillarization has yielded mixed outcomes in the case of Turkish and Moroccan Muslims who were recruited during the guest worker program (Lucassen & Penninx, 1997; Shadid, 1991). While practicing Christians are somewhat scarce in the Netherlands, Islam is becoming a dynamic religious force. Due to pillarization, the Dutch government has experienced relative success in integrating these migrants' religion into the national culture. For example, the Dutch government has subsidized the construction of prayer halls and there is judicial consideration for practicing Muslims (Shadid, 1991). Both of these occurrences would be unlikely in other European countries. However, pillarization has accomplished nothing in terms of aiding in the social integration of these and other migrants. Indeed, pillarization seems to hurt migrants more than help them.

The social integration of migrants in the Netherlands is relatively weak, especially in schooling (SER, 2000; UN, 2000b). Chided by the United Nations (2000b) for high levels of de facto segregation, educational levels for the four main immigrant groups in the Netherlands lag behind those of the native Dutch population's. Schools in the Netherlands are openly labeled "black" or "white," a phenomenon that is very uncommon on the European continent, and pillarization has resulted in a degree of separation of immigrant and nonimmigrant children (Lucassen & Penninx, 1997). Turkish and Moroccan migrants' average educational level ranges between no schooling and primary education. Surinamese and Antillean migrants' average educational level ranges between lower/preparatory vocational education to university preparatory education. The average native Dutch population's educational attainment is senior secondary vocational education, senior general secondary education, or university preparatory education.

As the job market turns sour and the Dutch economy stagnates again, xenophobia is on the rise (Bonnett, 1998; Brubaker, 1996; Hagan et al.,

1999; UN, 2000b). This sentiment is especially common among the lower class as these individuals are often in direct competition with immigrants for low to unskilled jobs and cheaper housing (Bax, 1995; Lucassen & Penninx, 1997). Most of the anti-immigrant sentiment in the Netherlands seems to be directed at refugees and the former guest worker recruits more so than against individuals from the former Dutch colonies, whose culture is more closely aligned with Dutch culture. As demonstrated by the brief bike sticker requirements, refugees have a precarious position in society. Turkish and Moroccan individuals have also become the subject of increasing hostilities and hate crimes, especially in the aftermath of the terrorists attacks on September 11, 2001 at the World Trade Center in New York City.

Economic Dimensions

In addition to the relatively weak social integration of migrants, they are also poorly integrated into the Netherlands economically (Clark et al., 1993; Hartog & Vriend, 1989; Lucassen & Penninx, 1997; Penninx et al., 1993). Unemployment rates among minority groups are roughly three times that of the native Dutch population. Developments in the Dutch economy that have significantly affected the economic well-being of migrants include the restructuring of the postwar economy, the signing of the Treaty of Maastricht, and women entering the Dutch work force. Social factors that affect the migrants' economic standing include the Dutch language's lack of prominence as a world language and discrimination against ethnic minorities.

The Dutch economy evolved from a manufacturing to a service economy during the late 1970s to the early 1990s (Hartog & Vriend, 1989; Lucassen & Penninx, 1997; Penninx et al., 1993). During this time, the share of low-skilled jobs in the economy decreased by approximately one-third (Bax, 1995). Guest workers have not survived the intense restructuring and skill upgrading of the Dutch economy. Their economic status resembles that of low-skilled elderly Dutch persons. Unemployment and early retirement are common occurrences for these groups. Due to skill upgrading, the guest workers that were employed in this sector continue to experience high levels of unemployment as jobs continue to disappear.

The signing of the Treaty of Maastricht has also affected migrants economically. Signed by EU member-states in 1997, the treaty created the European Common Market and stipulated that nationals from fellow European Union countries were permitted free mobility. Therefore, European labor migrants can leave their country of residence to seek employment in other EU nations, and employers must not discriminate between the native population and fellow EU job seekers. Migrants from outside the EU no longer compete solely against nationals in their home countries; they now potentially face competition from other EU-nationals who are given priority in the labor market.

The final economic factor affecting migrants is the increased participation of Dutch women in the work force since 1995 (Melich, 1997; Zorlu, 2001). The Netherlands has historically had one of the lowest percentages of women in the workforce; however, as Dutch women enter the workforce, they are acquiring jobs that have typically been filled with migrant and minority women such as low-paying, part-time positions. Consequently, minority women's labor force participation in these sectors of the economy is beginning to stagnate.

Dutch is the official language of the Netherlands. While migrants who do not originate from former colonies may have had the opportunity to learn more than one language such as French or English, the overwhelming majority does not have access to the Dutch language prior to arrival in the Netherlands. Therefore, poor facilities for Dutch language especially affect the former guest worker recruits and refugees (Lucassen & Penninx, 1997; Shadid, 1991). Postcolonial migrants' exposure to the Dutch language prior to their arrival in the Netherlands has a positive effect on their employment opportunities. Employment rates for Surinamese migrants, for example, approach the general average of the native Dutch population's. The former guest worker recruits, Moroccans and Turkish migrants, have the worst opportunities in the Dutch labor market, as they experience the intersection of industry restructuring, discrimination, and language's effect on employment opportunities.

Although social and economic factors account for a portion of the low employment rates for migrants, other factors such as low levels of educational attainment contribute to the migrants' disadvantaged position. However, migrants whose skills and education are comparable to that of a native Dutch person still experience barriers that obstruct their entry into the workforce (SER, 2000). The United Nations Committee on the Elimination of Racial Discrimination (United Nations, 2000a) expressed concern at Dutch minorities' low labor force participation rate, and asserted that sufficient protection against discrimination in the Dutch labor market does not exist. The International Labor Organization (2001) studied discrimination against migrants in the Netherlands and determined that discrimination during the recruitment and selection processes was extremely common. During the study, individual migrants and native Dutch persons were matched on important criteria significant to employers' particular vacancies. The study revealed that employers frequently barred migrant candidates from proceeding beyond initial inquiry telephone conversations after they heard foreign names or accents. In the study, discrimination was fairly indirect as employers never confessed to refusing to employ migrants; rather, they stated that the vacancies had already been filled.

THE FUTURE

In many ways, the Netherlands is able to proudly assert with pride a tolerant political climate in the areas of legalization of drugs, sex workers, same-sex marriages, and religious freedom that is unparalleled in other European countries. There has also been a certain amount of lenience in allowing immigrants to enter the country, as the Netherlands has been one of the major recipients of migrants in Europe, from post–World War II migration waves to the present. In fact, the Netherlands has the highest percentage of naturalized immigrants in all of Europe (11%). Therefore, the Dutch case of immigration seems to include promoting cultural pluralism and tolerance while granting residency, citizenship, and voting rights to immigrants.

While the Netherlands has accepted many migrants and granted them increased political rights, these developments have not been coupled with substantial and effective efforts to assure socioeconomic parity for the migrants. Furthermore, pillarization appears to have taken on a form of neo-apartheid, where migrants and the native Dutch population live separately in one nation. While the former group may have made some socioeconomic progress in recent decades, it clearly remains in a disadvantaged position.

Migration is likely to remain a key issue in the Netherlands for years to come. As Dutch nationals are living longer, delaying starting their families, or opting not to have children at all, the Netherlands may experience economic strains and a decline in its overall population size if additional migrants are not attracted to the country. As one of the most densely populated countries in the world, a decline in population may appear to be a positive and welcomed outcome. However, while trimming the number of migrants may assist in reducing the strains of overpopulation, replacement migration may be necessary to ensure that the economic stability of the current worker-to-retiree ratio is not threatened.

The next test of the infamous Dutch tolerance may be the full political, social, and economic integration of current and future migrants into the fabric of the country. Making strides in this sphere may prove difficult as far right-wing parties in the Netherlands and other European countries begin to storm the political scene and reject the indifference of yesteryear's politicians. Nevertheless, minorities of the Dutch population are likely to grow, irrespective of immigration policy, due to the demographic trends of the migrants already residing in the country. In the future, this growing proportion of minorities in the Dutch population may find strength in numbers. Until then, migrants precariously await the unfolding of new policies that may directly affect them.

BIBLIOGRAPHY

Anderson, N. (1998). *World Directory of Minorities* (2nd ed.). London: Minority Rights Group Press.

Bax, E. H. (1995). *Cleavage in Dutch Society: Changing Patterns of Social and Economic Discrimination*. Paper presented at the Conference of Political, Economic and Social Racism, Thessalonica, Macedonia, Greece.

Body-Gendrot, S. (1992). Immigration, Marginality, and French Social Policy. In A. M. Messina (Ed.), *Minorities in Advanced Industrial Countries* (pp. 571–583). Westport, CT: Greenwood Press.

Bonnett, A. (1998, November). Who Was White? The Disappearance of Non-European White Identities and the Formation of European Racial Whiteness. *Ethnic and Racial Studies, 21*(6), 1029–1055.

Brubaker, R. (1996). *Nationalism Reframed: Nationhood and the National Question in the New Europe*. New York: Cambridge University Press.

Castles, S. (1993). Migrations and Minorities in Europe. Perspectives for the 1990s: Eleven Hypotheses. In S. Solomos & J. Wrench (Eds.), *Racism and Migration in Western Europe* (pp. 17–35). Providence, RI: Berg Press.

Clark, H. D., Dutt, N., & Kornberg, A. (1993, November). The Political Economy of Attitudes Toward Polity and Society in Western European Democracies. *Journal of Politics, 55*(4), 998–1021.

European Commission. (2000). Official Web Page of the European Union. Retrieved from http://europa.eu.int/.

Hagan, J. et al. (1999). *The Interest in Evil: Hierarchic Self-Interest and Right-Wing Extremism Among East and West German Youth*. N.p.

Hartog, J., & Vriend, N. (1989). Post-War International Labor Mobility: The Netherlands. In A. Thirlwall & I. Gordon (Eds.), *European Factor Mobility: Trends and Consequences*. London: Macmillan.

Leman, J. (1991, June). The Education of Immigrant Children in Belgium. *Anthropology and Education Quarterly, 22*(2), 140–153.

Lucassen, L., & Penninx, R. (1997). *Newcomers: Immigrants and Their Descendants in the Netherlands 1550–1995*. Amsterdam: Het Spinhuis. (Original work published in Dutch, 1994, Nieuwkomers, Nakomelingen, Nederlanders.)

Martens, E. (1999). *Minderheden in Beeld (SPVA '98)*. Rotterdam: ISEO.

Mattheijer, M. (2000). *De toelating van vluchtelingen in Nederland en hun integratie op de arbeidsmarkt* (AIAS Report No. 2). Amsterdam: University of Amsterdam.

Melich, A. (1997). Eurobarometer 47.1. Images of Switzerland, Education Throughout Life, Racism, and Patterns of Family Planning and Work Status. N.p.

Penninx, R., Schoorl, J., & van Praag, C. (1993). *The Impact of International Migration on Receiving Countries: The Case of the Netherlands* (NIDI CBGS Publications No. 28). Amsterdam: Swets & Zeitlinger.

Shadid, W. A. (1991, Summer). The Integration of Muslim Minorities in the Netherlands. *International Migration Review, 25*(2), 355–374.

Sociaal-Economische Raad (SER). (2000). Kansen Geven, Kensen Nemem: Advies bevordering arbeidsdeelname Ethnische Minderheden.

United Nations. (2000a). *Conclusions on Report of the Netherlands*. Committee on the
    Elimination of Racial Discrimination. 57th Session. New York: United
    Nations.
————. (2000b). *Population Report*. New York: United Nations.
Veenman, J., & Roelandt, T. (1994). Ethnic Minorities in the Dutch Labor Market:
    An Overview of Facts and Theories. In H. Entzinger, J. Siegers, & F. Tazelaar
    (Eds.), *Immigrant Ethnic Minorities in the Dutch Labor Market: Analysis and
    Policies*. Amsterdam: Thesis Publishers.
Zimmermann, K. (1995). Tackling the European Migration Problem. *Journal of Eco-
    nomic Perspectives*, 9(2), 45–62.
Zorlu, A. (2000). Illegalen in Nederland. *Economische Statistische Berichten, 4282*,
    956–958.
————. (2001). *Ethnicity and Gender in the Dutch Labor Market*. Mimeo, University
    of Amsterdam.
Zorlu, A., & Hartog, J. (1999, October 10). The Amsterdam Labor Market: A
    Problem Posed. Paper presented at *Marginal Labor Markets in Metropolitan
    Areas*, a conference conducted at the meeting of the CEPR, Dublin, Ireland.
————. (2001). *Migration and Immigrants: The Case of the Netherlands*. Amsterdam:
    University of Amsterdam, Institute for Migration and Ethnic Studies.

11

THE PHILIPPINES

The Dilemma of Philippine International Labor Migration

James A. Tyner

INTRODUCTION

Profile of the Philippines

Situated between the South China Sea and the Philippine Sea, the Philippines is an archipelago of over 7,100 islands. A colony first of Spain (1521–1898) and then of the United States (1898–1946), the Philippines is an ethnically diverse country of over 70 million people. It is the only Catholic-dominated country in Asia; approximately 90 percent of its citizens are Catholic, with the remainder either Muslim or Animist. Over 150 languages are spoken throughout the country; Tagalog, however, is the official language and English is its lingua franca.

The Philippines has a relatively high rate of natural population increase. Each year the population of the Philippines increases by approximately two percent. This increase is attributable to both a youthful age structure (38% of its inhabitants are under 15 years of age) and a high birth rate. Economically, the Philippines remains less developed than many of its neighbors (e.g., Singapore, Malaysia, and Thailand). The confluence of a high population growth rate and stagnant economy contributes to widespread poverty. In 1997, for example, an estimated 37 percent of all Filipinos were living below the poverty line. The per capita GNP in the Philippines stands at only US$1,050 compared to a per capita GNP of US$26,000 in the United States.

Poverty often serves as a push factor for migration. And indeed, the Philippines is a significant country of emigration. Currently, between 4 million and 5 million Filipinos reside in over 160 countries and territories. Each year, approximately 1 million Filipinos move to other countries in search of economic opportunities. The majority of Philippine international migration is temporary contract labor migrants—approximately 85 percent. This type of migration can be distinguished from other forms of emigration because systems of contract labor migration are, in theory if not in practice, circulatory (Skeldon, 1992, p. 37). Migrants are deployed on specific labor contracts, generally of either two-year or six-month durations, depending on the type of job. Upon completion of their contracts, these migrants—unlike traditional settlement migrants—are expected to return to their country of origin.

Vignettes

Just as many of the first settlers to the United States came from England as contracted laborers (also called indentured servants), many Filipinos migrate as contract laborers. As implemented in the Philippines, the system of overseas contract work entails an elaborate procedure of recruitment and deployment. This separates the Philippines' system of international labor migration from other systems, such as the migration of Mexican workers into the United States. In the Philippines, the government actively supports— indeed encourages—the out-migration of its citizens. And Filipino labor migrants, similar to the English indentured servants who arrived in North America, migrate in search of economic opportunities. Many of these migrants hope to earn enough money for investment purposes, perhaps to start their own business or to pay off debts. However, overseas employment is a politically contested issue in the Philippines. There are many social costs associated with overseas employment, and these costs often affect women more so than men. In essence, the dilemma of Philippine international labor migration is a balance between capital accumulation and the provision of basic human rights. The following vignettes will help illustrate the different experiences.

Imelda's Story. Imelda lived with her father in a southern province of the Philippines; her mother had disappeared shortly after giving birth. When Imelda was in the sixth grade, she was raped by her father's best friend. She was told not to say anything or else she would be hurt. For a month Imelda was raped repeatedly, until her father found out and killed his best friend. In turn, Imelda's father was killed by relatives of the rapist. Just 15 years old, Imelda found herself alone and responsible for the upbringing of her brothers and sisters.

Within a month of her father's death, Imelda was approached by four men: two Filipinos and two Japanese. These men spoke of unlimited economic opportunities in Japan and the potential to earn considerable sums of money. Having nowhere else to turn, Imelda accepted an offer to work as a waitress in a Japanese nightclub. The men arranged and paid for the documentation of a passport, visa, medical/police clearances, and processing fees. Imelda did not know, however, that the men had bypassed the legal licensing procedures for overseas contract work. Imelda did not know that she had been illegally recruited and trafficked to Japan.

Once in Japan, Imelda's passport was taken away and she was locked in a windowless room, chained to a bed. There she remained—forced into prostitution—until she was able to escape three years later (interview with author, Manila, June 1993).

Nelia's Story. Nelia grew up in Olongapo, near the United States naval base at Subic Bay. One day, after completing high school, she was approached by two Filipinos. These men identified themselves as "talent scouts"; they were working for a Manila-based labor recruitment agency. The men asked Nelia if she wanted to earn money by working in Japan. The men arranged for a bus ticket to Manila and told Nelia to meet them at the studio the following morning.

With her parents' approval, Nelia moved to Manila where she learned dance routines and choreography. She lived in a small apartment above the training studio with other women and men; all were training for work in Japan. After two years in Manila, Nelia was told to attend a booking at the studio. She, along with a handful of other women and men, performed a series of dance routines behind a mirrored room divider. On the other side of the divider were club managers from Japan. After the audition, Nelia was offered a six-month contract to work as a dancer in a nightclub in Okinawa, to which she agreed.

Nelia worked in Japan for a number of years, each time on a six-month renewable contract. During her sojourns, she was able to send back substantial sums of money to her relatives in the Philippines. Only after meeting her future husband, a U.S. seaman who was stationed in Okinawa, did Nelia quit her job in Japan (interview with author, Ohio, December 2000).

Overview of Migration Issues

Both Imelda and Nelia are part of a large-scale system of out-migration from the Philippines. Patterns of Philippine international labor migration exhibit two significant and interrelated trends. Geographically, the majority of Philippine overseas contract workers (OCWs) are deployed to employment sites in Asia. Indeed, 1997 marks the first time since the program's inception in 1974 that Asian destinations surpassed Middle Eastern destinations. In 1984, for example, Middle East destinations accounted for 83 percent of all deployed land-based Philippine contract workers; by 1997 this region accounted for only 45 percent. Conversely, the Asian share of Philippine workers increased from 13 percent to over 48 percent during the same period (see Table 11.1), with Hong Kong, Taiwan, and Japan emerging as principal destinations. Saudi Arabia, however, remains the largest single des-

Table 11.1
Deployed Land-Based Philippine OCWs to the Middle East and Asia, 1984–1997

Year	Total	Middle East	Asia	Other
1984	300,378	250,210 (83.3%)	38,817 (12.9%)	11,351 (3.8%)
1985	320,494	253,867 (79.2%)	52,838 (16.5%)	13,789 (4.3%)
1986	323,517	236,434 (73.1%)	72,536 (22.4%)	14,547 (4.5%)
1987	382,229	272,038 (71.2%)	90,434 (16.7%)	19,757 (5.2%)
1988	385,117	267,035 (69.3%)	92,648 (24.1%)	25,434 (6.6%)
1989	355,346	241,081 (67.8%)	86,196 (24.3%)	28,069 (7.9%)
1990	334,883	218,110 (65.1%)	90,768 (27.1%)	26,005 (7.8%)
1991	476,693	302,825 (63.5%)	132,592 (27.8%)	41,546 (8.7%)
1992	517,632	340,604 (65.8%)	134,776 (26.0%)	42,252 (8.2%)
1993	509,653	302,975 (59.4%)	168,205 (33.0%)	38,473 (7.5%)
1994	517,662	286,387 (55.3%)	194,120 (37.5%)	37,155 (7.2%)
1995	436,884	234,310 (53.6%)	166,774 (38.2%)	35,800 (8.2%)
1996	424,259	221,224 (52.1%)	174,308 (41.1%)	28,727 (6.8%)
1997	486,627	221,047 (45.4%)	235,129 (48.3%)	30,451 (6.3%)

Source: POEA (1987); POEA special tabulations for the author.

tination of Philippine OCWs, receiving approximately 200,000 migrant workers each year (see Table 11.2). These geographic trends have resulted from broader structural changes in the global economy, and especially of the rapid industrialization that has occurred throughout parts of Asia.

A second important trend has been the increased feminization of Philippine international labor migration. Again, 1997 marked the first time in the history of the Philippines' overseas employment program that female migrants outnumbered their male counterparts. This observation clearly contradicts the long-established and erroneous assumption that women only migrate with or to join husbands or fathers. In the Philippines, women often take the initiative to migrate.

The existence of geographic gender segregation also is apparent in patterns of Philippine international labor migration (see Table 11.3). In 1997 female workers were concentrated overwhelmingly within the service sector (89.5 percent) whereas male workers were more likely to be employed within the production/construction sector (82.4 percent). Women also find employment in the "entertainment" sector, as dancers, singers, and musicians. These jobs are often associated with sex work. Women, such as Imelda in the opening vignette, may ultimately work as strippers, masseuses, or even prostitutes.

Table 11.2
Leading Destinations of Philippine OCWs, 1995–1999

Country	1995	1996	1997	1998[1]	1999
Saudi Arabia	168,604	155,848	160,302	193,698	198,556
Hong Kong	51,701	43,861	78,513	122,337	114,779
Taiwan	50,538	65,464	72,747	87,360	84,186
Japan	25,032	20,183	33,226	38,930	46,851
United Arab Emirates	26,235	26,069	25,579	35,485	39,633
Singapore	10,736	15,087	16,056	23,175	21,812
Italy	5,829	6,780	8,915	20,233	21,673
Kuwait	9,852	10,802	10,205	17,372	17,628
Brunei	6,807	7,651	9,594	16,264	12,978
Qatar	9,691	7,889	8,294	10,734	7,950

1. The POEA adjusted its counting procedures in 1998. Data for 1998 and 1999 indicate departures as opposed to individual migrants leaving. As such, the last two years of data are inflated owing to returning migrants.

Source: Scalabrini Migration Center, *Asian Migration Atlas 2000*, http://www.scalabrini.asn.au/atlas/amatlas.htm.

The gender division of labor has a clear geographic dimension. Labor-importing countries of the Middle East have historically employed male workers within construction and production sectors, whereas Asian import-ers have employed female workers within either the service sector (as maids) or the entertainment sector (as performing artists). Within Asia, the leading destinations of female Philippine domestic workers include Hong Kong, Sin-gapore, and Taiwan. Japan, conversely, accounts for the largest share of Phil-ippine performing artists. In 1997, for example, out of a total of 30,114 female Philippine migrant performing artists deployed, Japan accounted for 29,890 (99.3%). Viewed from another perspective, of the 31,315 deployed Philippine migrant workers to Japan, 29,890 (95%) were female performing artists.

These gender-spatial patterns, coupled with the vignettes of Imelda and Nelia, are an indication of the problem. Overseas contract workers find em-ployment in foreign countries to better their lives, as well as the lives of their families. Why do governments, though, encourage the out-migration of their citizens? There are three main reasons. First, it is thought that overseas em-ployment will reduce, albeit temporarily, domestic labor pressures. Many countries throughout the Third World, including the Philippines, suffer from high unemployment. Second, contract labor migration is presumed to facil-

Table 11.3
Occupational Segregation of Philippine Migrant Workers by Sex, 1997

Occupation	Total	Female	Male
Administrative, Managerial	555 (100%)	112 (20.2%)	443 (79.8%)
Agricultural	538 (100%)	40 (7.4%)	498 (92.6%)
Clerical	3,534 (100%)	1,483 (42%)	2,051 (58%)
Production, Construction	83,560 (100%)	14,703 (17.6%)	68,857 (82.4%)
Professional	51,228 (100%)	37,222 (72.7%)	14,006 (27.3%)
Performing Artists	31,656 (100%)	30,114 (95.1%)	1,542 (4.9%)
Sales	2,560 (100%)	1,121 (43.8%)	1,439 (56.2%)
Service	76,402 (100%)	68,370 (89.5%)	8,032 (10.5%)
Not Classified	3,027 (100%)	441 (14.6%)	2,586 (85.4%)
Total	221,404 (100%)	123,492 (55.8%)	97,912 (44.2%)

Source: Unpublished data, POEA; special tabulations for the author.

itate skills transfer from more developed to less developed countries. Third, and among the most important, is the role of remittances (money sent back home to the Philippines by Filipino migrants as they work abroad). In 1999, for example, Filipino migrant workers remitted nearly US$7 billion.

International labor migration, however, does not occur without risks. The problem is that migrants, living and working in foreign countries, and denied equal treatment under the law, are exceptionally vulnerable. Migrant workers are subject to various forms of oppression and exploitation, including illegal recruitment, nonpayment of contracts, physical and sexual abuse, rape, and murder. In short, the human rights of migrant workers are placed in jeopardy. As one analyst explains: "Migrants enjoy human rights as human beings, not primarily as migrants. However, their situation as migrants qualifies them as particularly vulnerable persons in a society where the condition of workers in a foreign country carries an institutional weakness, determined by the fluctuating nature of migration policies, normally crafted from the perspective of the interest of the country of employment" (Battistella, 1993, p. vi).

While working in the host society, migrants may not enjoy full political rights or have access to legal and welfare assistance if they have been wronged. In some countries, migrant workers are denied their basic human right to practice freedom of religion. They may be susceptible to immediate and uncontested repatriation. Critics of the Philippine overseas employment program, consequently, claim that the government is sacrificing its workers for profit. In its endeavor to garner profits for economic growth and development, the Philippine state is viewed as not providing adequate welfare and protection for migrant workers and their families. Before addressing the current political, social, and economic dimensions of the dilemma in further detail, however, let us first look more closely at the emergence of the Philippine's overseas employment program.

HISTORY OF MIGRATION ISSUES

Although emigration from the Philippines can be traced back to Spanish colonial times, the Philippines' governmental overseas employment program began only in 1974. Initially the program was formed as a component of a broader national development effort during the dictatorial regime of former Philippine President Ferdinand Marcos. The program, considered a model by the International Labor Organization (ILO) for overseas employment, was designed to satisfy the three aforementioned goals: a reduction in unemployment, an increase in skills acquisition, and an increase in foreign capital through mandatory remittances.

Since its inception the Philippines' overseas employment program has undergone a series of institutional transformations. From 1974 to 1982 the program was composed of three separate agencies: the National Seaman Board (NSB), the Overseas Employment Development Board (OEDB), and the Bureau of Employment Services (BES). This period established the basic working relationships between government agencies and the private sector.

The migration of Philippine labor migrants is highly organized. The private sector itself is composed of thousands of labor recruitment agencies, distinguished primarily by the type of worker recruited and deployed. Recruitment agencies may specialize, for example, in the migration of nurses or domestic workers. Many of these agencies maintain Web sites.

In 1982 the NSB, BES, and OEDB were merged to form a giant governmental conglomerate: the Philippines Overseas Employment Administration (POEA). An attached agency to the Department of Labor and Employment (DOLE), the POEA is the principal government agency involved with Philippine labor migration. Currently the POEA is composed of four divisions: Pre-Employment Services, Licensing and Regulation, Adjudication, and Welfare and Employment. The basic tasks of the POEA are to (1) promote and develop overseas employment opportunities, (2) establish an environment conducive to the legitimate and responsible operation of private recruitment agencies, (3) provide protection to Filipino workers and their families, and (4) develop and implement programs for returning contract workers in the areas of retraining and reemployment.

As indicated in these four tasks, the POEA is mandated to facilitate overseas employment, provide for the reintegration of returning workers, and offer protection and welfare to workers and their families. The track record of the POEA, however, has been called into question. To what extent can, or does, the POEA provide for its workers?

DIMENSIONS OF MIGRATION ISSUES

Social Dimensions

Overseas employment is well entrenched in Philippine society. In Manila, approximately 11 percent of all families receive their main source of income from abroad whereas only 14 percent of families receive their main source of income through entrepreneurial activities (Tyner & Donaldson, 1999, p. 220). What are the social costs and benefits associated with overseas employment?

Research has questioned the impacts of overseas employment on families. Overall, marriage and family life have remained relatively stable (Vasquez, 1992, p. 60). Concern, though, is raised when one or more parents obtain overseas employment. Although parents' migration and overseas employment is generally perceived as beneficial, questions are raised as to the long-term effects on children. When both parents are abroad, the children are left in the care of relatives and concern is raised over the family-building, emotional impact on the children (Gonzalez, 1998, p. 97).

Labor migration may have a detrimental effect on marriages. Physical separation over long periods, coupled with difficulties in maintaining communication via telephone or mail, places strains on marriages. Consequently, various non-governmental organizations have been established to provide counseling, such as KAKAMMPI (*Kapisanan ng Kamag-anakan ng Mang-gagawang Migranteng Pilipino*, or Association of Relatives of Pilipino Migrant Workers).

Overseas employment also has facilitated changed gender roles in the household. Women, in particular, have been found to gain a large measure of independence and freedom and to play a greater role in the managing of household resources. Indeed, whether it is the wife who migrates, or her husband, existing research indicates that these women "manifest a clear appetite for a more diversified role leading to a greater space for self-determination and a freer decision-making process" (Cruz & Paganoni, 1989, p. 101).

One of the most significant aspects of overseas employment, however, is the prevalence of exploitation and abuse. Although both male and female migrants encounter abuse, women are more likely to be the victims of abuse. Consider, for example, the gender differences of reported welfare cases (see Table 11.4). Cases involving female migrants outnumber male migrants in all but one category. The gender-segregation of employment opportunities

Table 11.4
Reported On-Site Welfare Cases of Philippine OCWs, 1994

Nature of Case	Middle East		Asia		Europe and Americas		Total		Grand Total
	Male	Female	Male	Female	Male	Female	Male	Female	
Maltreatment	549	1,645	41	684	—	—	590	2,309	2,899
Physical Abuse	156	254	2	35	—	—	158	289	447
Rape/SexualAbuse	—	47	—	9	—	—	—	56	56
Sexual Harassment	—	153	—	24	—	—	—	177	177
Mentally Ill	—	18	—	4	—	—	—	22	22
Health Problems	28	140	6	42	—	2	34	184	218
Contract Substitution	361	1,040	51	125	4	17	416	1,182	1,598
Salary Nonpayment	310	799	37	385	7	27	354	1,211	1,565
Salary Underpayment	—	—	—	478	—	—	—	478	478
Poor Work Conditions	25	260	11	429	—	—	36	689	725
Pregnant	—	30	—	34	—	—	—	64	64
Repatriation	—	—	—	344	2	9	2	353	355
TNT	97	88	—	—	—	—	97	88	185
Other	318	1,011	160	3,772	23	61	501	4,368	5,345
Total	2,024	5,465	308	6,365	36	116	2,188	11,946	14,134

Source: adapted from DOLE (1995), Table 17.

contributes to the increased susceptibility of female migrants. For the most part, female migrant workers are more vulnerable because they often labor in isolated work sites. This is especially the case for live-in domestic workers. Performing artists, on the other hand, are employed within the "entertainment" or "sex" industry; as such, they are particularly at risk of physical and sexual abuse.

As the story of Imelda illustrates, overseas contract migration is often a cover for the illegal trafficking of women. Women may be illegally recruited for overseas employment and, once in the host society, forced into prostitution. As "undocumented" migrants, these women are especially vulnerable to further abuse. And because the Philippine state and other governments encourage—indeed facilitate—overseas employment, they are perceived as being compliant in the trafficking of women. For example, it has been asserted that "the Japanese government, the Philippine government and the other governments sending their women provided the legal cover within which trafficking can occur" (De Dios, 1993, p. 43).

Economic Dimensions

As indicated earlier, overseas employment programs are an integral part of national development strategies to reduce unemployment levels, increase human capital as migrant workers return with skills acquired abroad, and increase foreign revenues through remittances. It is therefore appropriate to consider the success or failure of the Philippines in reaching these objectives, while keeping in mind the aforementioned social dimensions.

Unemployment has been, and continues to be a severe problem of the Philippine economy. With continued high population growth, there remains a need to create new jobs domestically in the Philippines. This has not, however, happened. Overseas employment thus provides temporary relief to the domestic labor market. The effects of overseas employment, though, have been limited. At most, the export of labor merely serves as a stopgap measure in that overseas employment alone is insufficient to meet the labor demands of the Philippines. It has been estimated that contract migration absorbs only about 35 percent of the estimated 750,000 annual entrants to the labor force (Vasquez, 1992, p. 51). Nevertheless, the Philippine economy would be in worse shape if overseas employment were not permitted. Therefore, without other structural changes in the economy, the Philippines must continue its policy of encouraging temporary overseas contract work as a supplementary means to achieving full domestic employment (Gonzalez, 1998, p. 70).

Overseas employment also has injected substantial sums of money into the Philippines. Between 1975 and 1999 Philippine OCWs remitted over US$44 billion. These remittances, sent through the Philippine commercial banking system, help earn the necessary foreign exchange to balance the country's financial accounts (Gonzalez, 1998, p. 70). As Vasquez (1992,

p. 51) concludes, annual remittances through financial institutions have substantially contributed to improving the country's balance of payments. Remittances also contribute to the economic well-being of households. Remittances are used for children's education, household expenses, property acquisition, entrepreneurial ventures, and savings (Gonzalez, 1998, pp. 70–71). Other funds, however, are utilized to acquire consumer goods such as stereos and televisions rather than long-term investment alternatives, thus calling into question the overall benefits of remittances (Gonzalez, 1998, p. 104).

Critics of overseas employment call into question the perceived gains of skills transfer. In particular, findings suggest that migrant workers do not learn new skills while abroad. This is because foreign employers prefer to hire workers already skilled for the tasks needed. Indeed, most migrants from the Philippines are not uneducated or unskilled; they are also not the most impoverished (Tyner, 2001). Indeed, many migrant workers are college educated. However, because of deficiencies in the Philippine economy, some Filipinos are able to earn more money as domestic workers in foreign countries than as teachers or other professional occupations in the Philippines. Paradoxically, migration may thus entail an upward mobility in terms of wages, but a downward mobility in social status and skills.

Overseas employment does provide, though, a hidden benefit to the Philippine economy. Workers in the Philippines are trained to perform the jobs left by those workers who migrate overseas (Vasquez, 1992, p. 47). Moreover, many Filipinos continue their education, or attend technical schools, in the hope of gaining overseas employment. As such, the prospect of contract labor facilitates educational advancement and skills acquisition in the Philippines. Indeed, it is no coincidence that the Philippines has one of the world's most educated populace.

Political Dimensions

As illustrated in Table 11.4, Filipino OCWs are susceptible to many forms of abuse and exploitation, ranging from illegal recruitment and nonpayment of contracts, to forms of physical abuse. Clearly, migrant workers occupy precious legal positions in the global labor market; their vulnerability is augmented when they, as noncitizens, do not receive all levels of assistance and protection. How can the Philippine state provide protection to its overseas workers? Former Philippine President Fidel Ramos outlined the following conditions that labor-importing countries must observe (Gonzalez, 1998, p. 131):

1. The host country must have labor and social laws protecting the rights of migrant workers; and declarations or resolutions for the protection of these workers.
2. The host country must be a signatory to multilateral conventions.

3. The host country must have concluded a bilateral agreement or arrangement with the Philippine government regarding the protection of the rights of overseas workers.

4. The host country must have taken concrete measures to protect such rights.

The Philippine government does not have sufficient leverage on the international political stage to demand that these conditions be met. Attempts to establish bilateral agreements, for example, have been rather futile. Labor-importing countries, by and large, do not want to enter into any binding agreement. Host countries object to the establishment of bilateral agreements for two reasons, according to one source (Gonzalez, 1998, p. 133). First, it is claimed that OCWs are subject to the same laws and regulations that nationals receive; second, terms of employment are negotiated between the migrant workers and employers, hence the state should not become involved. Thus, although some arrangements have been reached with nine countries, the Philippines has tried, without success, to establish bilateral agreements with many of the top labor-importing countries of Filipino OCWs, including Saudi Arabia, Japan, Singapore, and the United Arab Emirates. Moreover, with its economy so fragile, the Philippine government is in a weak position to make demands on labor-importing countries. Should the Philippines, for example, adopt a hard-line approach and threaten to restrict the out-flow of migrant workers, labor-importing countries would simply recruit workers from other countries (e.g., Indonesia and Sri Lanka). This poor bargaining position, of course, contributes to the perspective that the Philippine government is willing to sacrifice its workers rather than risk losing its share of the global labor market.

The Philippine government has also sought to provide protection for its workers through multilateral arrangements and other international conventions. It has, for example, ratified the 1990 International Convention on the Protection of the Rights of all Migrant Workers and Members of Their Families, and in 1994 the Philippine United Nations delegation initiated and lobbied successfully the 38th Session of the UN Commission on the Status of Women into passing Resolution 38/7 on "Violence Against Women Migrant Workers." Many of these international agreements, however, have not been ratified by all labor-sending or -receiving countries and, even more important, are generally unenforceable.

The lack of formal agreements or adherence to common instruments, consequently, leaves the action for protection of migrant workers in the hands of labor attachés stationed within the embassies (Battistella, 1992, p. 123) as well as non-governmental organizations (NGOs) in both sending and receiving countries. These organizations, such as Batis Center for Women, the Center for Overseas Workers, and the National Center for the Protection of Overseas Pilipino Workers (NCPOPW), while often understaffed and underfunded, provide an invaluable service in the protection and assistance of migrant workers and their families. Among the objectives of the NCPOPW, for example, are the following:

1. Strengthen the coordination of governmental and non-governmental organizations involved with contract workers;
2. Analyze the situations of contract workers in the Philippines and abroad;
3. Monitor governmental policies and operations;
4. Develop policies that will address the protection and welfare of contract workers;
5. Give recommendations on legislative measures; and
6. Develop recommendations regarding the future prospect of contract work at the international level.

THE FUTURE

The year 1995 marked a crucial period in the history of the Philippines' overseas employment program (Tyner, 2000). In that year Flor Contemplacion, a female domestic worker employed in Singapore, was scheduled for execution for the alleged 1991 murder of another Filipina domestic worker and a four-year-old Singaporean boy. Questions arose as to Contemplacion's guilt. Protests were held, but to no avail, and on March 17 Contemplacion was executed. During the summer of 1995, just months after the execution of Contemplacion, another Filipina domestic worker, Sarah Balabagan, went on trial for murder. She was a 15-year old girl who had entered the United Arab Emirates on a forged passport to bypass POEA regulations. In July 1994 she was allegedly raped by her 85-year-old employer and, in self-defense, Balabagan killed her employer. The court trial was highly publicized. First she was sentenced to seven years' imprisonment on charges of manslaughter. She was also, however, to receive US$27,000 as compensation for being raped. A second trial convened; this time, she was sentenced to death. Finally the president of the United Arab Emirates intervened and had the sentence reduced to one years' imprisonment and 100 cane lashings. In return, the relatives of the slain employer received US$41,000 in compensation.

These two cases are not isolated events but rather testify to the widespread existence of abuse. Throughout the previous decade numerous trials and tribulations were played out. In 1989, for example, Jocelyn Guanezo, a Filipina performing artist, returned home to the Philippines after having worked in Japan since 1985. Upon her return, however, she was "in a state of shock, apparently a victim of physical and mental abuse" (Philippine Senate, 1991, p. 20). In 1989, the Philippine government also addressed the case of 300 Filipinas who, while in Lebanon, had their passports confiscated and were forced into prostitution. What these cases illustrated was the existence of a global problem of abuse and exploitation. Rather than isolated cases, these cases of abuse and murder of migrant workers—and especially of female migrant workers—proved to be the tip of the iceberg.

In 1995 Republic Act 8042, the "Migrant Workers and Overseas Filipinos Act," was signed into law by then-President Fidel Ramos. Hailed by many as the "Magna Carta" of labor migration, the future of the Philippines overseas employment program will, to a considerable degree, be determined by how this piece of legislation is implemented. RA 8042 is laden with many wide-reaching provisions. These include:

• Establishment of Migrant Workers and Other Overseas Filipinos Resource Centers in countries with large concentrations of Philippine migrants; these are to be open 24 hours a day, seven days a week;

• Provision of lawyers and social workers in countries with high concentrations of Philippine migrants;

• Creation of the position of Legal Assistant for Migrant Workers Affairs who is responsible for the provision and overall coordination of overseas Filipinos in distress;

• Establishment of a Legal Assistance Fund to provide legal services to overseas Filipinos;

• Issuance by POEA of travel advisories;

• Creation of Emergency Repatriation Fund;

• Establishment of Replacement and Monitoring Centers to facilitate reintegration of returning Filipinos;

• Creation of a Migrant Worker Loan Guarantee Fund to be used for predeparture loans and family assistance loans for migrant workers; and

• Deregulation of the POEA.

Despite the apparent comprehensiveness of RA 8042, many critics remain unsatisfied. In particular, concern exists that the policy does not address the increasing deployment of skilled laborers (doctors, nurses, engineers), ensuring the optimal use of remittances, increasing the number of personnel in diplomatic posts, and the promotion of migrant worker "unions" (Gonzalez, 1998, pp. 129–130). Moreover, there exists considerable consternation over the intent of the provision calling for the deregulation of the POEA. Does this imply that the POEA will be abolished, or simply that its functions will be reduced? Until the details of RA 8042 are fully ironed out, the Philippines' overseas employment program will continue to be subject to considerable debate.

What is clear, however, is that the POEA has refocused its mission in light of these controversies. Unlike earlier statements that stressed the market promotion functions, the POEA now claims to "manage" migration. One observer asks, however, "How far can the Philippine Government implement the principles [of RA 8042] both domestically and internationally and how

[will] the current declaration respond to the constantly changing and complex realities of contract migration?" (Gonzalez, 1998, p. 128). Indeed, until long-term structural inequities in the Philippines' political economy are addressed, Filipinos will continue to search for better opportunities on other shores. As such, the dilemma of Philippine international labor migration will likewise continue.

BIBLIOGRAPHY

Battistella, G. (1993). The Rights of Migrants, NGOs and the Vienna Declaration. In G. Battistella (Ed.), *Human Rights of Migrant Workers: Agenda for NGOs* (pp. i–xii). Quezon City, Philippines: Scalabrini Migration Center.

Cruz, V. P., & Paganoni, A. (1989). *Filipinas in Migration: Big Bills and Small Change*. Quezon City, Philippines: Scalabrini Migration Center.

De Dios, A. (1993). Issues Without Borders: Understanding Trafficking and Sexual Exploitation of Asian Women. In N. Sancho & A. G. Layador (Eds.), *Traffic in Women: Violation of Women's Dignity and Fundamental Human Rights* (pp. 38–47). Quezon City: Asian Women Human Rights Council.

Department of Labor and Employment. (1995). *White Paper on Overseas Employment*. Manila: Department of Labor and Employment.

Garming, M. B. (1989). *Protection of Overseas Pilipino Workers Legislative Agenda*. Manila: Friedrich Ebert-Stiftung.

Gonzalez, J. L., III. (1998). *Philippine Labour Migration: Critical Dimensions of Public Policy*. Singapore: Institute of Southeast Asian Studies.

Philippine Senate. (1991). On the Death of Maricris Sioson and the Plight of the Filipina Entertainers in Japan. *Senate Committee Report No. 1681*. Manila: Senate Archives.

Skeldon, R. (1992). International Migration Within and from the East and Southeast Asian Region: A Review Essay. *Asian and Pacific Migration Journal, 1*(1), 19–63.

Tyner, J. A. (2000). Migrant Labor and the Politics of Scale: Gendering the Philippine State. *Asia Pacific Viewpoint, 41*(2),131–154.

———. (2001). Regional Origins of Philippine Overseas Contract Workers. *International Journal of Population Geography, 7*, 173–188.

Tyner, J. A., & Donaldson, D. (1999). The Geography of Philippine International Labor Migration Fields. *Asia Pacific Viewpoint, 40*(3), 217–234.

Vasquez, N. (1992). Economic and Social Impact of Labor Migration. In G. Battistella & A. Paganoni (Eds.), *Philippine Labor Migration: Impact and Policy* (pp. 41–67). Quezon City, Philippines: Scalabrini Migration Center.

12

PUERTO RICO

Between the Nation and the Diaspora—Migration to and from Puerto Rico

Jorge Duany

INTRODUCTION

Profile of Puerto Rico

Puerto Rico has a peculiar status among Latin American and Caribbean countries. On July 25, 1898, U.S. troops invaded the Island during the Spanish-Cuban-American War. In 1901, the U.S. Supreme Court defined Puerto Rico as "foreign to the United States in a domestic sense" because it was neither a state of the union nor a sovereign republic (Burnett & Burke, 2001). In 1917, Congress granted U.S. citizenship to all persons born in Puerto Rico, but the Island remained an unincorporated territory of the United States. In 1952, Puerto Rico became a commonwealth (or Associated Free State, in Spanish) with limited self-government in local matters such as taxation, education, health, housing, culture, and language. However, the U.S. federal government retains jurisdiction in most state affairs, including immigration, citizenship, customs, defense, currency, transportation, communications, and foreign trade. In particular, the commonwealth government lacks the power to establish its own immigration policies and laws. Today, the Island's electorate is almost evenly divided between supporting commonwealth status and becoming the fifty-first state of the union; only a small minority advocates independence.

In addition to its unresolved colonial dilemma, Puerto Rico is increasingly a nation on the move: a country whose porous borders are incessantly crisscrossed by migrants coming to and going away from the Island. Since the 1940s, more than 1.6 million people have moved from the Island to the

U.S. mainland. Today, nearly half of all persons of Puerto Rican origin live in the continental United States. At the same time, the Island has received hundreds of thousands of immigrants since the 1960s, primarily returning Puerto Ricans and their descendants, and secondarily citizens of other countries, especially the Dominican Republic and Cuba. By the year 2000, approximately 9 percent of the Island's residents had been born abroad, including those of Puerto Rican parentage born on the U.S. mainland. This combination of a prolonged exodus, together with a sizable influx of returnees and foreigners, makes Puerto Rico a test case of multiple population movements. Few other countries in the Caribbean region—or indeed, the entire world—have experienced such massive displacements of people in such a short span of time. The growing diversity in the migrants' origins and destinations undermines the ideological premises of traditional discourses of the nation based on the equation among territory, birthplace, citizenship, language, culture, and identity.

Vignette

Benjy López is the pseudonym of a Puerto Rican man who was born in Vieques in the 1920s, moved to the U.S. mainland in the 1940s, and returned to the Island in the 1960s (Levine, 1980). After joining Puerto Rico's National Guard and serving in the U.S. Army in the mainland, St. Thomas, Panama, and Germany, López settled in New York City. There he graduated from high school, went to college, and worked as a merchant marine, racketeer, pimp, house painter, taxi driver, and rental agent. He finally resettled in San Juan, where he became a successful salesman working for a friend's company. Although López's life history is by no means typical, it illustrates the increasingly mobile livelihoods of Puerto Ricans, Dominicans, and Cubans. Constant movement has become a way of life for many people in search of upward social mobility.

Overview of Migration Issues

Table 12.1 presents a rough estimate of the net migration between Puerto Rico and the continental United States throughout the twentieth century.[1] These figures show that Puerto Rican emigration acquired massive proportions during the 1940s, expanded during the 1950s, tapered off during the 1970s, and regained strength during the 1980s. Between 1980 and 1989, net migration to the mainland was estimated to be 490,562 persons, compared with 446,693 persons between 1950 and 1959. According to these figures, the contemporary Puerto Rican diaspora has surpassed the one that took place in the two decades after World War II. Almost 8 percent of the Island's inhabitants moved to the continental United States during the 1990s.

Table 12.1
Net Migration from Puerto Rico, 1900–1999

Years	Net Migration to the U.S. Mainland	Total Passenger Traffic
1900–1909	2,000	2,000
1910–1919	11,000	11,000
1920–1929	35,638	35,638
1930–1939	12,715	12,715
1940–1949	145,010	145,010
1950–1959	446,693	460,826
1960–1969	221,763	151,770
1970–1979	26,683	85,198
1980–1989	490,562	287,451
1990–1999	325,875	–226[1]
Total	1,717,969	1,191,382

Note: the available figures for 1900–1949 are for total passenger traffic only.
1. The minus sign (−) indicates a net movement of passengers to the Island.

Sources: for 1900–1919, Vázquez Calzada, "Demographic Aspects of Migration" (1979); for 1920–1949, U.S. Commission on Civil Rights, *Puerto Ricans in the Continental United States* (1976); for 1950–1989, Junta de Planificación de Puerto Rico, *Balanza de pagos* (1978–1999) and *Estadísticas socioeconómicas* (1972–1989); for 1990–1999, Junta de Planificación de Puerto Rico, "Movimiento de pasajeros entre Puerto Rico y el exterior" (2001).

As the exodus to the mainland has accelerated, immigration to the Island has continued unabated. In 1994–1995 alone, 53,164 persons left the Island, while 18,177 arrived to reside there. Nearly 95 percent of those who moved to the Island were return migrants and their children (Olmeda, 1998). Furthermore, thousands of Puerto Ricans have engaged in multiple moves between the Island and the mainland. In a recent survey, nearly 20 percent of all the respondents had lived abroad and returned to the Island, while another 3 percent had moved back and forth at least twice (Duany, 2002). In short, contemporary Puerto Rican migration is best viewed as a "revolving-door" movement, in which thousands of people are leaving the Island while others are returning from the mainland.

Table 12.2 shows the growth of the Puerto Rican population in the continental United States between 1900 and 2000. The exodus was relatively small until about 1940, when it began to expand quickly. Since 1960 the mainland Puerto Rican population has grown more slowly, but faster than on the Island. Today, the number of stateside Puerto Ricans closely approx-

Table 12.2
Puerto Rican Population in the Continental United States, 1900–2000

Year	Number	Percent Increase	As Percent of Entire Population of Puerto Rican Origin
1900	678	—	0.0
1910	1,513	223.2	0.1
1920	11,811	680.6	0.9
1930	52,774	346.8	3.3
1940	69,967	32.8	3.6
1950	301,375	330.7	12.0
1960	892,513	196.1	27.5
1970	1,429,396	60.2	30.9
1980	2,013,945	41.0	38.7
1990	2,727,754	35.4	43.6
2000	3,406,178	24.8	47.2

Note: Between 1910 and 1940, the available figures refer to persons of Puerto Rican birth only; after 1950 they include persons of Puerto Rican parentage, and after 1970 they include all persons of Puerto Rican origin.

Sources: for 1900, Gibson and Lennon, *Historical Census Statistics on the Foreign-Born Population of the United States* (1999); for 1910–1950, U.S. Census Bureau, *U.S. Census of Population: 1950* (1953b); for 1960–1980, U.S. Census Bureau, *U.S. Census of Population: 1960* (1963) and *Persons of Spanish Origin by State: 1980* (1982); for 1990, U.S. Census Bureau, *Profiles of General Demographic Characteristics* (2001d); for 2000, U.S. Census Bureau, *The Hispanic Population* (2001a).

imates those on the Island. According to the 2000 census, about 47 percent of all Puerto Ricans lived in the continental United States. Because of continued emigration, Puerto Ricans abroad will probably outnumber islanders in the next decade.

The geographic distribution of Puerto Ricans in the U.S. mainland has changed. Although Puerto Ricans still concentrate in the state of New York, their proportion decreased from nearly three-fourths of the total in 1960 to less than one-third in 2000. For the first time ever, the number of persons of Puerto Rican origin in New York declined in the 1990s. Still, New York City has the largest number of Puerto Rican residents in the mainland— 789,172 in 2000. Correspondingly, the proportion of Puerto Ricans has increased in other states, especially in Florida, which recently displaced New Jersey as the second largest Puerto Rican concentration. Other states with sizable increases in their Puerto Rican population include Pennsylvania,

Massachusetts, Connecticut, and Texas. Overall, the figures document the growing dispersal of the Puerto Rican diaspora in the continental United States over the past few decades (U.S. Census Bureau, 1963, 1982, 2001d, 2001e).

At the same time, the Island's population has become increasingly diverse with regard to nativity. On the one hand, the Island's foreign residents diminished greatly between 1899 and 1940, largely as a result of the decline in Spanish immigration (Department of Commerce, 1913, 1921, 1932; War Department, 1900). After 1940, especially between 1960 and 1970, the foreign-born population increased rapidly, primarily as a consequence of immigration from Cuba and the Dominican Republic. Smaller numbers of people have also come from Spain, Colombia, Mexico, Venezuela, Argentina, China, and several other countries. In the 2000 census, nearly 140,000 Island residents claimed to have a non-Puerto Rican Hispanic origin. (U.S. Census Bureau, 1943, 1953a, 1961, 1973, 1984, 1993, 2001e).

On the other hand, the U.S. mainland-born population in Puerto Rico has increased spectacularly since the beginning of the twentieth century. Most of this growth has been due to the return of Puerto Ricans and their offspring born in the continental United States. Between 1991 and 1998, Puerto Rico received 144,528 return migrants (Junta de Planificación de Puerto Rico, 2000). By the end of the twentieth century, mainland-born residents of Puerto Rican descent were one of the fastest-growing sectors of the Island's population. A smaller number of Americans have also moved to the Island. In 1990, the census found 16,708 persons born in the continental United States, whose parents were also born there, living in Puerto Rico (U.S. Department of Commerce, 1993). In short, the Island is simultaneously undergoing three major types of population movements: emigration, immigration, and return migration.

HISTORY OF MIGRATION ISSUES

Since the first decades of the twentieth century, the Puerto Rican government assumed an active role in promoting and managing migration to the United States (Lapp, 1990). This public policy was based on the widespread perception that Puerto Rico was a poor and overpopulated country. Early efforts focused on recruiting agricultural workers from the Island to Hawaii, the Dominican Republic, Cuba, and the U.S. Virgin Islands, especially St. Croix (Rosario Natal, 1983). However, the massive relocation of Puerto Rico's population gained impetus during the 1940s. In 1948, the Puerto Rican government established the Bureau of Employment and Migration in New York City, which became the Migration Division of the Department of Labor in 1951. In 1989, this office was renamed the Department of Puerto Rican Community Affairs in the United States and elevated to the governor's executive cabinet. The department was eliminated in 1993 because pro-statehood leaders, then a majority in Puerto Rico's legislature, believed that the department represented an unwarranted instance of applying public policy in another jurisdiction. Still, the commonwealth government maintains a formal presence in the mainland through the Puerto Rican Federal Affairs Administration.

The project of organizing and supervising migration from Puerto Rico was first elaborated by the American sociologist Clarence Senior, who also served as director of the Migration Division (1951–1960). In an influential book, Senior (1947) advocated establishing an emigration office attached to the governor's executive staff and working closely with the Island's Department of Labor. The main function of this office would be to recruit workers from Puerto Rico to the United States and Latin America, especially Venezuela. The office would provide migrant workers with information on job openings, training, transportation, settlement, and insurance, as well as promote further emigration from the Island. Although the plan to relocate Puerto Ricans in Latin America proved too expensive, the idea of finding jobs for them in the United States, primarily in New York City, later crystallized in the Migration Division.

Senior's blueprint for planned emigration was well received by Luis Muñoz Marín, then president of the Puerto Rican Senate (1941–1948) and later the Island's first elected governor (1948–1964). Muñoz Marín agreed that it was "necessary to resort to emigration as a measure for the immediate relief to the problem posed by our surplus population, while we seek permanent solutions in the long run" (Muñoz Marín to Egloff, September 28, 1946; author's translation). An economist working for the Office of Puerto Rico in Washington, D.C., Donald J. O'Connor, also urged the resettlement of Puerto Ricans in the United States and other countries such as the Dominican Republic and Brazil. According to O'Connor, "migration can accomplish what economic programs on the island cannot do quickly"—that is, create jobs and sources of income, while reducing population growth (O'Connor to Piñero et al., August 10, 1948). High-ranking members of the ruling Popular Democratic Party (PDP), such as Antonio Fernós-Isern, Teodoro Moscoso, and Rafael Picó, concurred with O'Connor's optimistic assessment. Thus began a government-sponsored program of large-scale migration as a safety valve for Puerto Rico's demographic and economic pressures.

On May 12, 1947, the Puerto Rican legislature passed Public Law 25, creating the Bureau of Employment and Migration. From its inception, the Bureau (and its heirs, the Migration Division and the Department of Puerto Rican Community Affairs in the United States) sought "to follow its migrant citizens to facilitate their adjustment and adaptation in the communities in which they chose to live" (Estado Libre Asociado de Puerto Rico, 1972–1978, p. 1; author's translation). According to Public Law 25, "the Government of Puerto Rico does not stimulate or discourage the migration of

Puerto Rican workers to the United States or any other foreign country; but it deems its duty to duly orient [them] regarding the occupational opportunities and adjustment problems in ethnologically strange settings" (Estado Libre Asociado de Puerto Rico 1977–1978, p. 6; author's translation). The public policy of "following migrant citizens" to the United States, while officially neither "stimulating nor discouraging" their departure, seems to have paid off in the short run. Population control was a key ideological element in the PDP's development strategy between the 1940s and 1960s (Pantojas-García, 1990). Postwar Puerto Rican migration has ebbed and flowed according to the stages of the Island's industrialization program, Operation Bootstrap, as well as to changes in the U.S. economy, particularly in the large urban centers of the northeast (Rivera-Batiz & Santiago, 1996; Rodríguez, 1989; Whalen, 2001). Although the factories sponsored by Operation Bootstrap created thousands of jobs, they could not absorb the labor force displaced by a swift agricultural decline. Between 1945 and 1965, Puerto Rico's development strategy expelled a large share of its population, primarily to mainland cities that required cheap labor, such as New York City, Chicago, and Philadelphia. Afterwards, Puerto Ricans tended to move abroad when job opportunities were more attractive on the mainland and returned when economic conditions improved on the Island. Today, many people move back and forth in search of jobs, higher wages, and better standards of living, as well as to reunite with their families, to study, or to retire on either the Island or the mainland. U.S. citizenship, cheap air transportation, and far-flung social networks facilitate such comings and goings.

During Muñoz Marín's tenure as governor, more than a half million Puerto Ricans moved abroad. Defining himself as a return migrant, Muñoz Marín (1958, 1960) advised mainland Puerto Ricans to adapt themselves to their new environment, especially by learning English and registering to vote in local elections. At the same time, he encouraged the migrants to preserve their cultural identity, proudly assert their Puerto Rican origin, and return to the Island when socioeconomic conditions improved there. At the tenth anniversary of the Migration Division in New York, Muñoz Marín (1958) proclaimed, "I envisage, not immediately or soon, but in the not too distant future, the time in [which] more citizens, of Puerto Rican origin or not, will follow my second example and migrate to Puerto Rico." The number of returnees began to surpass those leaving for the United States in the early 1970s, especially as a result of minimum wage hikes on the Island and the financial crisis of New York City, which was the traditional core of the Puerto Rican diaspora (Meléndez, 1993; Santiago, 1993). The shift from manufacturing to high-technology and service industries further eroded the socioeconomic position of mainland Puerto Ricans.

Today, Puerto Ricans constitute one of the most disadvantaged groups in the United States. Most socioeconomic indicators place Puerto Ricans in the lowest rungs of the U.S. social structure, below African Americans and other

Table 12.3
Basic Socioeconomic Indicators of Puerto Ricans and Other Ethnic and Racial
Groups in the Continental United States, 2000 (in Percentages)

	Puerto Ricans	Cubans	Mexicans	Non-Hispanic Whites	Non-Hispanic Other
College graduates	13.0	23.0	6.9	28.1	23.2
Unemployment	8.1	5.8	7.0	3.4	6.9
Below poverty level	25.8	17.3	24.1	7.7	20.9
Households with annual income above $35,000	41.6	44.6	43.0	60.4	46.4
Female-headed households	35.8	18.3	21.1	12.7	36.7
Managerial and professional occupations	17.1	23.5	11.9	33.2	26.4

Source: U.S. Census Bureau, *Current Population Survey, March 2000* (2001c).

Hispanics such as Mexicans and Cubans. According to the 2000 Current
Population Survey, Puerto Ricans are more likely to be unemployed and
poor, and to live in female-headed households, as well as to have lower levels
of income, educational attainment, and occupational status than all the other
major ethnic and racial groups (see Table 12.3). These figures document the
persistent material deprivation of Puerto Ricans on the mainland, especially
in New York City, six decades after the takeoff of massive migration. The
deteriorating living conditions of Puerto Ricans in the United States are
basically due to the economic restructuring of New York City, Philadelphia,
Boston, and other industrial centers, as well as the increasing polarization
between well-paid skilled jobs and low-paid unskilled jobs, particularly in the
service sector. The automation, computerization, suburbanization, overseas
relocation, and decline of entire manufacturing sectors like the garment industry have displaced many Puerto Rican workers, who were heavily concentrated in such sectors (Rodríguez, 1989).

Meanwhile, the Island became an attractive destination for return migrants
as well as for foreign immigrants. The massive influx of Cubans and Dominicans to Puerto Rico dates to approximately 1960. Two major political
events in neighboring Caribbean countries signal the beginning of this period: the triumph of Fidel Castro's Cuban Revolution in 1959 and the as-
sassination of Rafael Leonidas Trujillo, the dictator of the Dominican
Republic, in 1961. Furthermore, U.S. marines invaded Santo Domingo in
April 1965, after a coup d'état and civil war. These events set in motion a
complex series of socioeconomic forces leading to the exodus of 33,463

Cubans and 114,895 Dominicans to Puerto Rico between 1960 and 2000, according to official figures. The Island's rapid economic growth during the 1960s, as well as political turmoil and material hardship in the sending countries, brought many immigrants to Puerto Rico.

Cuban immigration to Puerto Rico grew rapidly between 1960 and 1970, but trickled down after 1980 (U.S. Department of Justice, 1960–1977, 1978–2000). Although thousands of Cubans left their country through the Mariel boatlift, few of them came to Puerto Rico, and fewer still did so in the following years. In contrast, legal Dominican immigration has increased steadily since 1966, reaching unprecedented levels in the early 1990s. In addition, an unknown number of undocumented immigrants have crossed the Mona Channel between the Dominican Republic and Puerto Rico (Duany et al., 1995). In 1996, the Immigration and Naturalization Service estimated that 34,000 undocumented immigrants, mostly Dominicans, were living in Puerto Rico (*Migration News*, 1997). Thus, the Puerto Rican situation presents the apparent paradox of a growing immigrant population—one of the largest in the Caribbean—along with sustained emigration to the United States. It has been argued that the Island has become an international migrant crossroads, "the scene of multiple, cross-cutting, back-and-forth geographical displacements of people of different national origins" (Martínez, 1998, p. 1).

DIMENSIONS OF MIGRATION ISSUES

Economic Dimensions

The main economic impact of the Puerto Rican exodus has been to reduce the growth rate of the Island's labor force, especially between 1945 and 1965. Had it not been for the migration of 325,000 workers to the mainland, the local unemployment rate would have almost doubled to 22.4 percent in 1960 (Pantojas-García, 1990, p. 82). To this extent, the export of surplus labor helped to trim down the country's high population density and unemployment levels. As government planners predicted in the 1940s, migration has become a livelihood practice for thousands of Puerto Rican families. As a survival strategy, it has allowed many people to increase their earnings and pool resources across several localities.

The economic significance of the diaspora can be gauged through the migrants' money transfers to their relatives on the Island. Although much smaller in volume than in neighboring countries like the Dominican Republic and Cuba, personal remittances to Puerto Rico increased more than tenfold, from approximately $47 million in 1960 to nearly $549 million in 1999 (Junta de Planificación de Puerto Rico, 1978–1999). Together with the larger amounts of transfer payments from the U.S. federal government, remittances are a growing source of support for the Island's population. They represented about half of the net income generated by the tourist industry in 1997 (Junta de Planificación de Puerto Rico, 1998).

In the long run, exporting labor has not been a viable development strategy. Despite decades of uninterrupted outmigration, unemployment rates on the Island remain unacceptably high (even when they reached a relatively low 11 percent in 2000). Living standards have deteriorated over the past two decades. Three out of five persons still live under the poverty level. An increasing proportion of the population depends on transfer payments from the federal government, particularly for nutritional and housing assistance. With the elimination of section 936 of the Internal Revenue Service code, which provided tax exemptions for U.S. companies located in overseas territories, the Island's economic outlook seems bleak (Martínez, 1999). Consequently, migration to the mainland will most likely increase.

One issue of public concern has been the so-called "brain drain," that is, the outflow of professionals, technicians, and managers. Although recent data do not support the idea of a massive brain drain, they reveal that Puerto Rican migrants have become more educated and skilled over time (Meléndez, 1993; Rivera-Batiz & Santiago, 1996). The continued export of relatively young, well-educated, and highly trained workers represents a serious loss of the country's human resources. In particular, a growing number of medical doctors, nurses, engineers, schoolteachers, and university professors have sought better working and living conditions abroad, especially in states like Florida and Texas. For instance, in the early 1990s, almost 40 percent of all the physicians who graduated from the Island's medical schools were living in the continental United States.

The economic outcomes of return migrants to Puerto Rico have shifted over time. During the 1950s and early 1960s, returnees (like Benjy López, mentioned at the beginning of this chapter) competed favorably with nonmigrants for better-paid jobs. Many migrants acquired useful linguistic skills and occupational experiences on the mainland and, upon returning to the Island, had moderate economic success. According to one expert, return migrants constituted a well-educated, middle-class elite during that period (Hernández Alvarez, 1967). However, later returnees did not fare as well in the local labor market. At least since 1980, reverse migration to the Island has been associated with high unemployment and poverty rates, as well as low educational and occupational status (Muschkin, 1993; Rivera-Batiz & Santiago, 1996). In 1990, three-fifths of recent return migrants were employed as blue-collar and service workers, especially as operators, fabricators, and laborers. Compared to nonmigrants, the returnees were underrepresented in upper-status jobs such as managers, professionals, and technicians. This occupational profile has remained constant in the 1990s (Olmeda, 1998).

The economic effects of foreign immigration in Puerto Rico have been twofold. On the one hand, most Cubans have joined the middle and upper ranks of the Island's labor force. In 1990, nearly four out of five Cuban workers in Puerto Rico had white-collar jobs. About 43 percent were employed in technical, sales, and administrative support occupations, especially as sales persons; another 36 percent were managers and professionals. Only about 21 percent were employed as blue-collar and service workers, and as farmers. In San Juan, Cuban entrepreneurs tend to play the role of a middleman minority specializing in the distribution of goods and services within the Puerto Rican economy. Many of them have established small businesses or work for other compatriots, especially in retail trade, construction, real estate, insurance, and communications. Cuban-owned businesses have created new sources of income and employment for Puerto Ricans as well as for Cubans. In short, Cubans in Puerto Rico have largely entered the primary labor market, characterized by relatively high wages, educational levels, and occupational prestige, as well as good working conditions, fringe benefits, and opportunities for upward mobility.

On the other hand, Dominican immigration has tended to increase the supply of cheap labor in Puerto Rico. In 1990, almost half of all Dominican workers were employed as unskilled service workers (about 31%) — especially as domestics, cleaners, and waiters — and blue-collar workers (about 16%). Nearly 14 percent were semiskilled craft and repair workers, including tailors, mechanics, carpenters, masons, and electricians. While almost 24 percent were employed in technical, sales, and administrative support occupations, only 13 percent were managers and professionals. The majority of Dominican immigrants have come to fill a void created by relative labor scarcity in certain niches of Puerto Rico's economy, such as domestic service, the construction industry, and coffee agriculture (Pascual Morán & Figueroa, 2000). In sum, most Dominicans have incorporated into Puerto Rico's secondary labor market, characterized by low wages, occupational status, and educational levels, as well as poor working conditions, few fringe benefits, and limited opportunities for upward mobility.

Social Dimensions

Social relations between Puerto Ricans and Americans on the mainland have been strained at least since the beginning of the great diaspora after World War II. When Benjy López arrived in New York City in the 1940s, he found that whites scorned all Puerto Ricans as inferior (Levine, 1980). Because of their racial mixture and heterogeneity, Puerto Ricans were often treated as blacks. Regardless of their skin color, lower-class immigrants tended to settle in segregated inner-city neighborhoods like Spanish Harlem, the Lower East Side of Manhattan, and the South Bronx. U.S. public opinion highlighted the negative effects of Puerto Rican migration on housing, education, and welfare. The immigrants were stigmatized as lazy, ignorant, criminally prone, sexually obsessed, physically unfit, culturally inassimilable, and dark-skinned aliens (even though they were U.S. citizens). Language and cultural differences increased the social distance between Puerto Ricans and other ethnic groups, including African Americans (Mills et al., 1950). Nonetheless, because of their physical and social proximity, Puerto Ricans and African Americans developed a close interaction, especially in New York City, where they became the two leading minority groups. More recently, relations between Puerto Ricans and Dominicans in the city have been marked by cooperation as well as some tensions resulting from competition for scarce resources.

In Puerto Rico, return migrants are commonly called Nuyoricans, regardless of their place of birth or upbringing. The term is often used pejoratively to imply that Nuyoricans are somehow less Puerto Rican than Island-born-and-bred residents are. In San Sebastián, a small northwestern town, the returnees are disdained as *los de afuera* (those from outside) because they do not conform to local standards of behavior (Pérez, 2000). The popular stereotype of Nuyoricans contains several negative attributes derived from their supposed Americanization, including their way of speaking, dressing, walking, and relating to others. Not only do islanders perceive Nuyoricans as a different group; Nuyoricans also tend to view themselves distinctly from both Island-born Puerto Ricans and Americans (Hernández Cruz, 1994; Kerkhof, 2000; Lorenzo-Hernández, 1999; Rodríguez-Cortés, 1990). Many Puerto Ricans from the Island consider the Spanish language as a key symbol of their national identity, whereas Puerto Ricans in New York City may prefer to speak English or switch between Spanish and English without feeling any less Puerto Rican (Zentella, 1997). Typically, islanders consider Nuyoricans to be more pushy, aggressive, and disrespectful than themselves. In turn, Nuyoricans often perceive themselves to be more cosmopolitan, sophisticated, and independent than islanders. Daily interaction between Nuyoricans and islanders frequently resembles the tense relations between different and opposed ethnic groups.

The public image of Cubans in Puerto Rico is highly ambivalent. In the 1960s, Cubans were frequently accused of displacing professional and semi-professional workers, such as medical doctors, engineers, architects, lawyers, teachers, and entertainers (see González, 1970). One seldom hears such charges today. In a recent survey, most Puerto Ricans in San Juan praised Cubans' contribution to the local economy, especially in commerce, but many respondents thought that Cubans were prone to fraud and corruption (Duany, 1999). Although the majority of the Puerto Ricans acknowledged that Cubans are hardworking and independent, they continued to characterize Cubans as dishonest and stingy. Moreover, Cuban contributions to Puerto Rican culture and politics are not well known or appreciated. The immigrants are still perceived as upwardly mobile but unwanted strangers who harbor attitudes popularly associated with the white elite of San Juan (the so-called *blanquitos* and *riquitos*). Even today, Cubans are thought to be unconditionally pro-American and more racist than Puerto Ricans. Nationalist groups have rejected Cuban immigrants because many of them advocate statehood for Puerto Rico. Contemporary writers have tended to represent Cubans as foreign to the national imaginary of Puerto Ricans, despite their cultural and linguistic affinities. In sum, the dominant perception of Cuban immigrants on the Island is that of shrewd but arrogant merchants. As Benjy López quips, Cubans have often been dubbed "the Jews of the Caribbean" (Levine, 1980, p. 127).

Compared to Cuban immigration in Puerto Rico, Dominican immigration has generated much more hostility. A recent survey found the highest levels of intolerance against gays, ex-convicts, and Dominicans in Puerto Rico (Benítez, 2001). This widespread anti-Dominican prejudice has several sources. To begin, as noted before, many of the immigrants are undocumented. Second, the majority is black or mulatto in physical appearance. Third, the bulk of the immigrants belong to the working class and many are of rural origin. Finally, most are women. Hence, Dominicans in Puerto Rico represent a disadvantaged minority in legal, racial, economic, and gender terms. Despite evidence to the contrary, Puerto Ricans routinely complain that Dominicans are taking away their jobs and blame the immigrants for increasing unemployment, crime, prostitution, and drug trafficking. In numerous ethnic jokes and riddles, the figure of the Dominican—especially the illegal alien—appears as the "Other" *par excellence*: a strange, dangerous, and incomprehensible outsider who occupies a marginal and clandestine status. Ironically, the Puerto Rican stereotype of Dominicans as dumb, ignorant, dirty, disorderly, and violent recalls that of Haitians in the Dominican Republic as well as that of Puerto Ricans in the United States.

Political Dimensions

Like many transnational migrants, mainland Puerto Ricans retain close political ties to their home country. Currently, voting in Puerto Rican elections, referenda, and plebiscites is restricted to Island residents. However, the majority of Puerto Ricans in the continental United States is keenly interested in Puerto Rican politics. Recent polls have found that most migrants support the current commonwealth status, while a sizable minority prefers statehood and a small but vocal minority advocates independence (Falcón, 1993). Benjy López was a nationalist sympathizer when he returned to the Island, but he soon became disillusioned with the lack of popular support for independence (Levine, 1980). Incorporating the Puerto Rican diaspora into public debates about the Island's relations with the United States remains an unmet political challenge. As in the Dominican Republic, many residents of Puerto Rico do not consider those living outside the Island as part of their nation and therefore do not wish to extend them the right to vote.

In turn, despite their U.S. citizenship, islanders cannot vote for the president of the United States nor elect their own voting delegates to Congress (the Island's Resident Commissioner is a nonvoting member of the House of Representatives). As a result, elected officials of Puerto Rican origin on the mainland often behave like transnational politicians with a special stake in Island issues. In May 2000, two of the three Puerto Rican delegates to the U.S. House of Representatives, Luis Gutiérrez and Nydia Velázquez, were detained during a peaceful demonstration in Vieques, a small island off the east coast of Puerto Rico used by the U.S. Navy as a military training ground. The third, José Serrano, was arrested inside the White House while protesting the Navy's bombing of the island. Many other Puerto Rican leaders from New York have publicly expressed their support for the peace movement in Vieques. Thus, several decades of unceasing migration to the United States have transnationalized Puerto Rican politics.

Return migrants to Puerto Rico do not differ greatly from nonmigrants in their political participation. In a recent survey of a random sample of the municipality of Aguadilla, nearly 52 percent of the returnees supported Commonwealth, while 39 percent supported statehood and 9 percent advocated independence or some other status. A similar proportion of nonmigrants supported each option. Moreover, about two-thirds of both groups identified with the New Progressive Party (NPP), which advocates statehood for the Island (Vargas-Ramos, 2000). Apparently, return migration to Puerto Rico has not had a substantial impact on status politics.

The political participation of foreign immigrants in Puerto Rico has not been well documented, partly because the Island's Electoral Commission does not release breakdowns of voting patterns by national origin or birthplace. However, one survey found that two-thirds of the Cubans in Puerto Rico supported the NPP during the 1980s (Cobas & Duany, 1997, p. 64). Between 1960 and 2000, 22,163 Cubans were naturalized as U.S. citizens in San Juan (U.S. Department of Justice, 1960–1977, 1978–2000). This figure represents two-thirds of all Cuban immigrants admitted to the Island during that period. However, Cubans have had little influence on Puerto Rican elections. No Cuban has ever gained a seat in Puerto Rico's legislature, and only one Cuban has been elected to a municipal assembly. The exiles' conservative, anti-communist, and anti-independence ideology has had a stronger impact on public opinion, as a result of their control of important sectors of the mass media, including newspapers, radio, and television.

Until recently, Dominican immigrants were primarily concerned with the politics of their homeland rather than with Puerto Rican politics. Accordingly, they were basically organized around the major political parties of the Dominican Republic (the Dominican Revolutionary Party, the Dominican Liberation Party, and the Social Christian Reformist Party). However, members of the Dominican community have begun to participate actively in Puerto Rican electoral campaigns, supporting both PDP and NPP candidates

(Iturrondo, 2000). At this point, the political preferences of Dominicans in Puerto Rico seem divided. In any case, most of them are not yet U.S. citizens and therefore cannot vote in local elections or plebiscites. Between 1972 and 2000, only 11,547 Dominicans were naturalized in San Juan (U.S. Department of Justice, 1978–2000). This figure represents one-tenth of all Dominicans admitted to the Island during that period. However, the 1996 approval of dual citizenship by the Dominican legislature may well increase the naturalization rate of Dominicans in the continental United States and in Puerto Rico. It remains to be seen whether Dominicans will have a decisive impact on municipal politics, especially in San Juan, where they concentrate.

THE FUTURE

Massive migration to and from Puerto Rico will undoubtedly continue and probably increase during the first few decades of the twenty-first century. Deteriorating living conditions on the Island have already intensified the outflow of people to the U.S. mainland, similar in scale to the great exodus of the 1950s. At the same time, the return flow of Puerto Ricans is likely to persist, as well as the circulation between the Island and the mainland. While Cuban immigration to Puerto Rico has practically stopped, Dominican immigration shows no signs of containment. At the same time, smaller groups of people from other countries will continue to move to the Island. The future of Puerto Rico's population seems increasingly transnational in its geographic and cultural locations. Should current trends continue, settlement patterns on and off the Island will become more mobile and diverse than before. The crucial challenge posed by the increasing dispersal of people in the diaspora is nothing less than imagining a nation whose territorial and symbolic borders are constantly transgressed and redrawn.

NOTE

1. The estimate is based on the difference between outbound and inbound passengers between the Island and the mainland, as reported by Puerto Rico's Planning Board. Currently, the Immigration and Naturalization Service does not keep statistics on population movements between Puerto Rico and the continental United States.

BIBLIOGRAPHY

Benítez, J. (2001). *Reflexiones en torno a la cultura política de los puertorriqueños (entre consideraciones teóricas y la evidencia empírica)*. San Juan: Editorial del Instituto de Cultura Puertorriqueña.
Burnett, C. D., & Burke, M. (Eds.). (2001). *Foreign in a Domestic Sense: Puerto Rico, American Expansion, and the Constitution*. Durham, NC: Duke University Press.

Cobas, J. A., & Duany, J. (1997).*Cubans in Puerto Rico: Cultural Identity and Ethnic Economy*. Gainesville: University Press of Florida.

Duany, J. (1999). Two Wings of the Same Bird? Contemporary Puerto Rican Attitudes Toward Cuban Immigrants. *Cuban Studies, 30*, 26–51.

———. (2002). *The Puerto Rican Nation on the Move: Identities on the Island and in the United States*. Chapel Hill: University of North Carolina Press.

Duany, J., Angueira, L. H., & Rey, C. A. (1995). *El Barrio Gandul: Economía subterránea y migración indocumentada en Puerto Rico*. Caracas: Nueva Sociedad.

Estado Libre Asociado de Puerto Rico, Departamento del Trabajo, División de Migración. (1972–1978). *Informe anual. Archivos Históricos de la Migración Puertorriqueña*. New York: Centro de Estudios Puertorriqueños, Hunter College.

Falcón, A. (1993). A Divided Nation: The Puerto Rican Diaspora in the United States and the Proposed Referendum. In Edwin Meléndez & Edgardo Meléndez (Eds.), *Colonial Dilemma: Critical Perspectives on Contemporary Puerto Rico* (pp. 173–180). Boston: South End Press.

Gibson, C. T., & Lennon, E. (1999). *Historical Census Statistics on the Foreign-Born Population of the United States*. Electronic document. http://www.census.gov/population/www/documentation/twps0029.html.

González, A. J. (1970). Estudio sobre el impacto de la inmigración en Puerto Rico: Julio de 1967. *Revista del Colegio de Abogados de Puerto Rico, 31*(4), 619–647.

Hernández Alvarez, J. (1967). *Return Migration to Puerto Rico*. Berkeley: Institute for International Studies, University of California.

Hernández Cruz, J. E. (1994). *Corrientes migratorias en Puerto Rico/Migratory Trends in Puerto Rico*. San Germán, PR: CISCLA, Universidad Interamericana.

Iturrondo, M. (2000). *Voces quisqueyanas en Borinquen*. San Juan: Camila.

Junta de Planificación de Puerto Rico. (1972–1989). *Estadísticas socioeconómicas*. San Juan: Junta de Planificación de Puerto Rico.

———. (1978–1999). *Balanza de pagos*. San Juan: Junta de Planificación de Puerto Rico.

——— (Ed.). (1998). *Informe económico al gobernador, 1997*. San Juan: Junta de Planificación de Puerto Rico.

———. (2000). Migración de retorno en Puerto Rico. In *Informe económico al gobernador, 1999* (pp. 1–16). San Juan: Junta de Planificación de Puerto Rico.

———. (2001). Movimiento de pasajeros entre Puerto Rico y el exterior. Años fiscales. Unpublished document. San Juan: Junta de Planificación, Programa de Planificación Económica y Social, Subprograma de Análisis Económico.

Kerkhof, E. (2000). *Contested Belonging: Circular Migration and Puerto Rican Identity*. Unpublished doctoral dissertation, University of Utrecht, the Netherlands.

Lapp, M. (1990). *Managing Migration: The Migration Division of Puerto Rico and Puerto Ricans in New York City, 1948–1968*. Unpublished doctoral dissertation, Johns Hopkins University, Baltimore.

Levine, B. B. (1980). *Benjy Lopez: A Picaresque Tale of Emigration and Return*. New York: Basic Books.

Lorenzo-Hernández, J. (1999). The Nuyorican's Dilemma: Categorization of Returning Migrants in Puerto Rico. *International Migration Review, 33*(4), 988–1013.

Martínez, F. E. (Ed.). (1999). *Futuro económico de Puerto Rico: Antología de ensayos del Proyecto Universitario sobre el Futuro Económico de Puerto Rico*. Río Piedras, PR: Editorial de la Universidad de Puerto Rico.

Martínez, S. (1998). Identities at Puerto Rico's International Migrant Crossroads. (Research Paper No. 7.) Storrs: University of Connecticut, Institute of Puerto Rican and Latino Studies.

Meléndez, E. (1993). *Los que se van, los que regresan: Puerto Rican Migration to and from the United States, 1982–1988* (Political Economy Working Paper Series #1). New York: Centro de Estudios Puertorriqueños, Hunter College.

Migration News. (1997, March). INS: Methodology and State-by-State Estimates. Vol. 4, No. 3. Retrieved from http://migration.ucdavis.edu/mn/pastissues/mar1997mn_past.html.

Mills, C. W., Senior, C., & Goldsen, R. K. (1950). *The Puerto Rican Journey: New York's Newest Migrants*. New York: Harper.

Muñoz Marín, Luis. (1946, September 28). Memorandum to Max Egloff. Foro público sobre el problema poblacional de Puerto Rico. Resumen de las soluciones ofrecidas por los ponentes en la sesión de julio 19, 1946. Section IV: President of the Senate, 1941–1948; Series 2: Insular Government; Sub-series I: Fortaleza; Box 1B: Office of Information; Folder 16. Fundación Luis Muñoz Marín, Trujillo Alto, P.R.

———. (1958). Celebration of the Tenth Anniversary of the Migration Division of Puerto Rico's Department of Labor. Section V: Governor of Puerto Rico, 1949–1964; Series 9: Speeches; Box 13: Status; Folder 8. Fundación Luis Muñoz Marín, Trujillo Alto, P.R.

———. (1960). Discurso a los puertorriqueños en Nueva York pronunciado por el Gobernador Muñoz Marín el 10 de abril de 1960. Section V: Governor of Puerto Rico, 1949–1964; Series 9: Speeches; Box 16: Status; Folder 7. Fundación Luis Muñoz Marín, Trujillo Alto, P.R.

Muschkin, C. G. (1993). Consequences of Return Migrant Status for Employment in Puerto Rico. *International Migration Review, 27*(1), 70–102.

O'Connor, D. J. (1948, August 10). Memorandum to Jesús T. Piñero and others. Mainland Labor Force Needs in 1948–49 and Puerto Rico's Opportunities to Exploit Them. Section IV: President of the Senate, 1941–1948; Series 2: Insular Government; Sub-series 1: Fortaleza; 1C: Office of Puerto Rico in Washington; Folder 18. Fundación Luis Muñoz Marín, Trujillo Alto, P.R.

Olmeda, L. H. (1998). Aspectos socioeconómicos de la migración en el 1994–95. In Junta de Planificación de Puerto Rico (Ed.), *Informe económico al gobernador, 1997* (pp. 1–39). San Juan: Junta de Planificación de Puerto Rico.

Pantojas-García, E. (1990). *Development Strategies as Ideology: Puerto Rico's Export-Led Industrialization Experience*. Boulder, CO: Lynne Rienner; Río Piedras, PR: Editorial de la Universidad de Puerto Rico.

Pascual Morán, V., & Figueroa, D. I. (2000). *Islas sin fronteras: Los dominicanos indocumentados y la agricultura en Puerto Rico*. San Germán, PR: CISCLA/Revista Interamericana.

Pérez, G. (2000). *The Near Northwest Side Story: Gender, Migration, and Everyday Life in Chicago and San Sebastián, Puerto Rico*. Unpublished doctoral dissertation, Northwestern University, Chicago.

Rivera-Batiz, F., & Santiago, C. E. (1996). *Island Paradox: Puerto Rico in the 1990s*. New York: Russell Sage Foundation.

Rodríguez, C. E. (1989). *Puerto Ricans: Born in the U.S.A.* Boston: Unwin Hyman.
Rodríguez-Cortés, C. (1990). Social Practices of Ethnic Identity: A Puerto Rican Psycho Cultural Event. *Hispanic Journal of Behavioral Sciences, 12*(4), 380–396.
Rosario Natal, C. (1983). *Exodo puertorriqueño: Las emigraciones al Caribe y Hawaii, 1900–1915.* San Juan: n.p.
Santiago, C. E. (1993). The Migratory Impact of Minimum Wage Legislation: Puerto Rico, 1970–1987. *International Migration Review, 27*(4), 772–795.
Senior, C. (1947). *Puerto Rican Emigration.* Río Piedras, PR: Social Research Center, University of Puerto Rico.
U.S. Census Bureau. (1913). *Thirteenth Census of the United States Taken in the Year 1910: Statistics for Porto Rico.* Washington, DC: U.S. Government Printing Office.
———. (1921). *Fourteenth Census of the United States: 1920. Bulletin. Population: Porto Rico. Composition and Characteristics of the Population.* Washington, DC: U.S. Government Printing Office.
———. (1932). *Fifteenth Census of the United States: 1930. Agriculture and Population: Porto Rico.* Washington, DC: U.S. Government Printing Office.
———. (1943). *Sixteenth Census of the United States: 1940. Puerto Rico: Population. Bulletin No. 2: Characteristics of the Population.* Washington, DC: U.S. Government Printing Office.
———. (1953a). *Census of Population: 1950. Volume II. Characteristics of the Population. Parts 51–54: Territories and Possessions.* Washington, DC: U.S. Government Printing Office.
———. (1953b). *U.S. Census of Population: 1950. Special Reports: Puerto Ricans in Continental United States.* Washington, DC: U.S. Government Printing Office.
———. (1961). *U.S. Census of Population: 1960. General Population Characteristics, Puerto Rico.* Washington, DC: U.S. Government Printing Office.
———. (1963). *U.S. Census of Population: 1960. Puerto Ricans in the United States.* Washington, DC: U.S. Government Printing Office.
———. (1973). *Census of Population: 1970. Characteristics of the Population. Part 53. Puerto Rico.* Washington, DC: U.S. Government Printing Office.
———. (1982). *Persons of Spanish Origin by State: 1980.* Supplementary Report PC80-S1-7. Washington, DC: U.S. Government Printing Office.
———. (1984). *1980 Census of Population: General Social and Economic Characteristics. Puerto Rico.* Washington, DC: U.S Government Printing Office.
———. (1993). *1990 Census of Population: Social and Economic Characteristics. Puerto Rico.* Washington, DC: U.S. Government Printing Office.
———. (2001a). *The Hispanic Population.* Electronic document. http://www.census.gov./prod/2001pubs/c2kbr01-3.pdf.
———. (2001b). Census 2000 Summary File 1 (SF 1) 100-Percent Data. Electronic document. http://factfinder.census.gov/servlet/DTTable.
———. (2001c). *Current Population Survey, March 2000.* Electronic document. http://www.bls.census.gov/cps/ads/2000/sdata.htm.
———. (2001d). *Profiles of General Demographic Characteristics: 1990 Census of Population and Housing.* Electronic document. http://census.gov/Press-Release/www/2001/tables.
———. (2001e). *Profiles of General Demographic Characteristics: 2000 Census of Pop-*

ulation and Housing. Electronic document. http://ftp2.census.gov/census
_2000/datasets/demographic_profile.

U.S. Commission on Civil Rights. (1976). *Puerto Ricans in the Continental United States: An Uncertain Future*. Washington, DC: U.S. Commission on Civil Rights.

U.S. Department of Justice. (1960–1977). *Annual Report of the Immigration and Naturalization Service*. Washington, DC: U.S. Department of Justice.

———. (1978–2000). *Statistical Yearbook of the Immigration and Naturalization Service*. Washington, DC: U.S. Department of Justice.

Vargas-Ramos, C. (2000). *The Effect of Return Migration on Political Participation in Puerto Rico*. Unpublished doctoral dissertation, Columbia University, New York.

Vázquez Calzada, J. L. (1979). Demographic Aspects of Migration. In History Task Force, Centro de Estudios Puertorriqueños (Ed.), *Labor Migration Under Capitalism: The Puerto Rican Experience* (pp. 223–238). New York: Monthly Review Press.

War Department. (1900). *Report on the Census of Porto Rico, 1899*. Washington, DC: U.S. Government Printing Office.

Whalen, C. T. (2001). *From Puerto Rico to Philadelphia: Puerto Rican Workers and Postwar Economies*. Philadelphia: Temple University Press.

Zentella, A. C. (1997). *Growing Up Bilingual: Puerto Rican Children in New York*. Malden, MA: Blackwell.

13

TANZANIA

To Carry a Heavy Burden in the Heat of the Day—Migration to and from Tanzania

Cassandra Veney

INTRODUCTION

Profile of Tanzania

As a result of the 1884–1885 Berlin Conference, Tanganyika, as it was called then, became a German colony. Germany's defeat in World War I resulted in the loss of its colonies to other European powers. Thus, Tanganyika and the islands of Zanzibar and Pemba became a part of the British Empire and then a trusteeship of the United Nations in 1946. Tanganyika gained its independence in 1961, and in 1963 Zanzibar and Pemba gained their independence. In 1964, Tanganyika and Zanzibar became the United Republic of Tanzania. In 1992, the country held multiparty elections for the first time following independence.

Tanzania is one of Africa's poorest countries. Its economy is heavily dependent on agricultural production (85 percent), and 90 percent of the population is engaged in this sector. The country's 35 million people consist of 120 different ethnic groups. The largest ethnic group is the Sukuma, although no one group is large enough to constitute a majority. In addition, there are people of Asian, Arab, and European descent on the mainland and on the islands of Zanzibar and Pemba. The country's literacy rate is 68 percent—79 percent for males and 57 percent for females. The population on the mainland is 45 percent Christian, 35 percent Muslim, and 20 percent practicers of indigenous religions. Zanzibar's population is 99 percent Muslim.

Vignettes

Refugees in Tanzania. An unnamed woman refugee was forced to flee Burundi in 1972 following another round of ethnic violence and strife. She was resettled and integrated into a local settlement in Tanzania called Rusaba B. Subsequently she gave birth to seven children while living in the country. She encountered few obstacles as a refugee because the government did not have a forced encampment policy, provided the land for the establishment of settlements, and encouraged refugees to become self-sufficient. In fact, the woman was able to obtain access to land where she could produce crops. This woman, along with other refugees, cooperated with her neighbors and helped build schools and other community infrastructures.

However, things began to change for this refugee woman as the government shifted its refugee policies. In November 1997, the Tanzanian army conducted roundups and sweeps that affected her. She was home alone with one of her children while the other children had left for the farm. She begged the army personnel to allow her to collect her other children, but they refused. She was unable to contact her children for two days. She learned that her children were safe, but the government's new encampment policy meant that she was forced to remain in a refugee camp separated from her children. If her children wanted to visit her, they had to secure the financial means. This was no small task for children whose mother was a refugee in one of the world's poorest countries. After 25 years of residing in Tanzania, these actions and others taken against refugees and their relatives were painful and difficult for them to comprehend (Nowrojee, 2001).

Refugees From Tanzania. Juma Mabruk was a 16-year-old who became one of Tanzania's first refugees when he joined a peaceful march organized by the opposition group, Civic United Front (CUF), to call for a rerun of the October 2000 general elections in Zanzibar. The march was violently broken up by the police. It is estimated that as many as 200 people were killed by the police. Mabruk was shot during the demonstration, but he was able to flee with others to Shimoni in Kenya's Coast Province, Kwale District. The Kenyan police took him and 15 others to Msambweni District Hospital where he was admitted for two weeks. In keeping with Kenya's forced encampment policy, the government wanted to relocate the refugees to a camp in its North Eastern Province. This area of Kenya has been adversely affected by the proliferation of arms in the region caused by the civil war in Somalia, Somali refugees, drought, and a lack of economic activity. Therefore, the asylum seekers and the United Nations High Commissioner for Refugees (UNHCR) were opposed to the relocation of the refugees. The Kenyan government finally agreed, and the refugees were allowed to remain (Tanzania: The End, 2001).

Overview of Migration Issues

Tanzania's current refugee crisis (1990–present) consists of individuals who fled from Rwanda, Burundi, the Democratic Republic of the Congo, and Somalia to escape civil war, ethnic strife, and general unrest in their countries of origin. By the end of 2000, Tanzania was host to a total of 540,000 refugees—400,000 from Burundi, more than 100,000 from the Democratic Republic of the Congo, 30,000 from Rwanda, and 3,000 from Somalia. In addition to these refugees, the government claimed that approximately another 470,000 individuals from Burundi resided in the country, consisting of individuals who had fled to Tanzania in the 1970s and 1980s, but who were not granted refugee status. However, their lack of integration into Tanzanian society has left them in a refugee-like situation (United States Committee for Refugees, 1995–2000).

The majority of Tanzania's current refugee population has found refuge in the western regions of the country, which are also the most impoverished parts. Immediately following the April 1994 genocide in Rwanda, approximately a quarter million people entered Tanzania within a 24-hour period. This was the largest and fastest refugee exodus on record. The two regions of Kagera and Kigoma experienced population increases of 50 percent (Refugees International, 2000). It was reported that there were only 40 relief workers on the ground to assist the refugees. In a very short period of time, the country hosted more than 700,000 Rwandans with very little assistance from the international community. Despite the lack of international assistance, the government continued to accept refugees until it closed its borders in March 1995. The government reopened its borders in 1996.

HISTORY OF MIGRATION ISSUES

Following its independence, Tanzania served as a beacon of hope in East Africa due to its political stability in the midst of economic instability. The country's experiment with socialism under its first president, Julius Nyerere, virtually left the economy on the brink of disaster, but the country's various ethnic groups did not turn on each other, the military did not intervene in politics, and civil war was never on the horizon. Thus, Tanzania played the role of a refugee-receiving country and not a refugee-producing country. Tanzania served as a country of asylum for many years prior to the 1990s for thousands of people who fled Rwanda, Uganda, South Africa, Mozambique, Malawi, Burundi, and the former Zaire. The government of Tanzania had generous asylum policies that allowed refugees to be integrated into society, and some refugees were granted citizenship and work permits. The government provided land for the establishment of settlements to achieve the goals of integration and self-sufficiency. For example, settlements were established in 1972 and 1974 for refugees from Burundi who had fled the ethnic strife that occurred there. These settlements had several social facilities, including primary and secondary schools, health centers, a vocational training center, and water wells. Although assistance was provided by the international community, the support Tanzania provided refugees was no small feat for this country considering that it was and still is one of the poorest countries not just on the African continent but in the world.

During the 1960s and 1970s, Tanzania hosted a number of refugees who fled from racist colonial states, particularly South Africa and Mozambique, and who were actively involved in the liberation movements in their home countries. Other refugees fled authoritarian states — the former Zaire, Uganda, and Malawi — where many people had experienced gross human rights violations. The Tanzanian government welcomed these refugees because they were viewed as freedom fighters for democracy, justice, and an end to colonial rule. However, beginning in the 1990s, new political, economic, and social dimensions in the country transformed Tanzania's generous refugee policies from open door to semi-closed (Rutinwa, 1999).

While Tanzania has been a recipient of refugees, it has also produced them. For example, in early 2001, the country experienced its first refugee exodus from the islands of Zanzibar and Pemba to Kenya following a police crackdown on peaceful demonstrators who supported the opposition group, the Civic United Front (CUF). Officials and supporters of the CUF are opposed to the ruling Chama Cha Mapinduzi Party and have called for a rerun of the general elections that were held on the islands in October 2000 (Komba, 2001). Most of the refugees have sought safety in Kenya's Coast Province, although it has not afforded them assistance. The Kenyan government closed all of the camps in this province in 1997 and has no intentions of reopening them for this new group. Therefore, refugees have had to contend with temporary housing and a lack of sanitation facilities.

DIMENSIONS OF MIGRATION ISSUES

Political Dimensions

Tanzania's political system has radically changed from the socialist model that was adopted at the time of its independence in 1961 to the current two-party, democratic one. As the political system was transformed, refugee policies were transformed as well. One can argue that Tanzania's once generous asylum policies toward refugees has shifted from warm and friendly to cold and hostile. The large numbers of refugees who entered Tanzania in the 1990s, in the absence of sufficient international assistance, forced the government to reevaluate its open-door asylum policy (Rutinwa, 1999); it felt that the types of refugees who entered the country needed to be addressed. Previously, the government welcomed refugees whom it viewed as fighters for African liberation, but the new groups of refugees were perceived in a different light. One of the new groups of refugees included thousands of Hutu refugees from Rwanda who were viewed as either the victims or perpetrators of the genocide. The Tanzanian government was vehemently opposed to Hutu refugees residing in the camps who allegedly participated in the 1994 genocide in Rwanda. They were not regarded in a positive light as freedom fighters, but rather as killers and criminals.

Another political dimension to the Rwandan refugee population that affected the shift in the government's policies was the use of the camps for military training and political activity that were banned by the government and the UNHCR. It was an open secret that the former Hutu Rwandan army and militia leaders, *Interahamwe*, were using the camps for military training and that arms were present in the camps (Human Rights Watch/ Africa, 1996). Political activity occurred as well in the form of military incursions over the border into Rwanda. In addition, Hutu leaders in the camps used terror and force to prevent refugees from repatriating (Salter, 1995). To illustrate the shift in refugee policy, consider that the colonial government in Mozambique during the 1960s regularly conducted military incursions across the border into Tanzania in search of guerrilla leaders, and, despite these actions, the Tanzanian government continued to accept refugees from Mozambique. Yet, in response to the perceived threat of armed Hutu militia leaders in the camps, the government demanded the repatriation of all Rwandan refugees by the end of December 1996, although the political climate in Rwanda was still too precarious to guarantee the refugees' safety. Human rights organizations reported police and security personnel using tear gas and sticks to force refugees toward the border. The order to leave Tanzania was targeted at all Rwandan refugees regardless of their legitimate asylum claims.

The government's actions violated international law pertaining to the protection of refugees. Refugees are entitled to due process under the law, which means they should not be forcibly repatriated before their applications for asylum are adjudicated. In a further effort to force the Rwandan refugees out of the country, the government denied the international community and others access to the refugee camps and areas around the camps. This had a detrimental effect on the provision of much-needed relief supplies. All of these actions taken by the government were not totally successful in ridding the country of Rwandan refugees. Shortly after thousands of Rwandan refugees were expelled from Tanzania, other Rwandans began to appear at the border. The international aid agencies were at a loss as to how to assist them because the camps built for them had either been closed or demolished (Tindwa, 1998).

Refugees from Burundi were also accused of using the camps for military activities, as thousands crossed into western Tanzania following the outbreak of ethnic violence in 1993 and 1997. When Tanzanian government officials believe that military and political activities are occurring in refugee camps, they often fear that state sovereignty is being undermined and that refugees are serving as a source of insecurity. The Tanzanian government was concerned that the conflicts that occurred in Burundi, the Democratic Republic of the Congo, and Rwanda would spill over onto its territory, and given these concerns, it enacted a number of refugee policies to address these issues.

First, the government established a forced encampment policy that required all refugees to reside in camps. Furthermore, the government enacted an exclusion zone around the camps—refugees could not travel beyond 2.5 miles of the camps. Clearly, this was in violation of international law, which allows refugees to have free movement in countries of asylum. For those refugees who attempted to avoid the camps, the government conducted a number of police sweeps and roundups in an effort to force all refugees into camps. For example, in 1997 and 1998, the army, under the guise of national security, rounded up refugees from Rwanda and Burundi living outside camps. Many of the refugees had lived in the country for years and were fully integrated into their local communities (United States Committee for Refugees, 1998, 1999). The swiftness of the sweeps did not allow refugees the opportunity to secure their belongings or to locate family members. Under these new policies, life outside the camps for refugees can be characterized as precarious at best as they face hostility and harassment from the police and other security personnel. Moreover, the government's forced confinement policy has been successful because international assistance is only available to refugees who reside in camps (Dodd, 1996).

Finally, the government flexed its political muscles in 1997 when it expelled more than 100 refugees who were from Burundi, claiming that the refugees had participated in criminal activities while in Tanzania. The Burundi army killed several of these refugees upon their return. Again, this action was in violation of international law: Host governments that accuse refugees of violating their laws are obligated to provide them with due process in a court of law instead of forcing them back to their countries of origin, which are often unsafe. In October 1997, approximately 5,000 Burundi refugees, mainly women and children, were forcibly repatriated at a time when Burundi was still experiencing ethnic and civil strife (Foreign Broadcasting Information Service, 1997).

The last political factor that motivated the government to shift its refugee policies was the public's perception of the refugee crisis (Rutinwa, 1999). In other words, public opinion toward refugees had changed considerably. Local communities were no longer tolerant of large numbers of refugees in their midst. The local communities no longer accepted the refugees' dependence on local resources that were already stretched too thin. For example, although Tanzania was very poor in the 1960s and 1970s, it still managed to provide basic services to its citizens such as free education and health care. With the introduction of the Structural Adjustment Programs (SAPs) by the World Bank and International Monetary Fund (IMF), these services were no longer provided free of cost. When refugees are provided these services and more, the local populations begin to resent their presence, believing that host communities should be provided with the same services and compensated by the international community for the use of their hospitals, roads, land, crops, and other property either destroyed or stolen by the refugees (Whitakar, 1999). Because elected officials want to remain in power, they respond to public opinion. Thus, when Tanzanian public opinion turned against the refugees, the government shifted its refugee policies to reflect the new mood.

Social Dimensions

The influx of massive numbers of refugees, coupled with the thousands of refugees already in the country, resulted in numerous social problems for the region. Because Tanzania's refugee population was disproportionately women and children, different kinds of social problems evolved as gender roles and age roles were often restructured and redefined under these conditions. Many refugee women headed households for the first time, and they had to make all decisions concerning finances, education, and health care (Anderson, 2000). Many youths in the refugee camps were able to earn their own money, giving them a new sense of freedom and independence from parents and other elders in the community. However, the refugees were not the only ones facing new social dynamics—host communities were socially affected as well. An increase in crime and banditry was evident in the refugee communities as refugees and Tanzanian citizens robbed and looted villagers for crops, animals, and other items that could be sold. More serious problems became apparent when government officials accused refugees of murdering some local citizens (Amnesty International/Tanzania, 1997).

A number of social problems were manifested in the camps, including theft, drunkenness, prostitution, sexual activities, and sexual violence. Incidents of rape and other forms of sexual violence were perpetrated against women, children, and adolescent female refugees in Tanzania. This refugee population was particularly at risk for beatings, rape, and theft when they left the camps in search of firewood and water. Some of those implicated in the violence included minor and adult refugees, men from the local communities, and police and security personnel. When refugee women are forced to flee alone, they no longer are protected by traditional social systems. This was evident in Tanzania as some refugee women were forced to bribe guards for water, firewood, and other relief supplies, putting them at risk for sexual harassment and abuse (Anderson, 2000). In addition, when women and girls are sexually violated, health problems become social problems with the increase in unwanted pregnancies and sexually transmitted diseases, including AIDS and HIV (Amnesty International/Tanzania, 1997).

While some refugee children in Tanzania have fled with their parents, relatives, and friends, others are unaccompanied. Their experiences in the country have been difficult for several reasons. First, the rains from El Niño affected the distribution of food and other relief supplies, as flooding cut off several roads and railways (Field Notes, 1998).[1] Trucks and other vehicles were not able to reach the remote northwestern part of the country where the refugees resided because the rains made the roads impassable. Therefore, relief agencies reduced refugee rations, putting the children at risk for malnutrition. Second, due to the heavy rains, deadly outbreaks of malaria occurred. Medicines needed to prevent and cure malaria were unavailable due to the transportation problems. Moreover, children who become refugees are often malnourished and sick before they flee, making them particularly vulnerable to parasitic infections and diseases. Relief workers in Tanzania reported that refugee children under the age of five have high morbidity and mortality rates due to poor nutrition and lack of access to proper health care (Field Notes, 1998).

Many children in Tanzania fall into the category of Children in Especially Difficult Circumstances (CEDC) because they witnessed gross human rights violations against members of their families, neighbors, and friends (Amnesty International/Tanzania, 1997). These atrocities have left them emotionally and psychologically traumatized. Also, often the children unaccompanied by adults became victims of rape and other forms of sexual abuse. However, many children lived with foster families in the camps that provided them with security. In addition, during site visits to four refugee camps in the Kigoma District (Nduta, Kanembwa, Mkugwa, and Mtendeli), it was observed that many children and infant refugees were being cared for in the hospital, maternity ward, and in various public spaces (Field Notes, 1998).

It is important to stress that the refugee policies established and implemented by the government have had profound ramifications for refugee women and children. For example, the 1997 forcible repatriation of Burundi refugees targeted women and children. The men were taken to camps while the women and children were involuntarily repatriated—many of them walked for several days without adequate food and water. This action separated families and left women and children without the protection of fathers, husbands, brothers, and other adult male relatives and friends. Similarly, during the 1997 roundups of refugees from Burundi, many children became separated from their parents and relatives.

There has been increasing hostility toward the refugees from the local population and government officials for several reasons. While the local population has lacked access to basic social services, including schools, medical care, and sanitation facilities, these same social services have been available to the refugees in the camps. Local residents feel that they have been more than generous to the refugees in terms of sharing their food and land, and contend that they too should have access to these services.

Other social problems surround the tremendous environmental problems in the region that were present before the refugee influx and exacerbated by the large numbers of new arrivals. Large tracts of forests were destroyed as refugees cut down trees for shelter and cooking, resulting in an increase in the rate of deforestation in the region. Members of the local communities lost their crops and property as refugees trampled across their farms, taking food in the process, and other crops were lost to the construction of roads that were needed to transport food, water, medicine, and other refugee relief (Gaurwa, 1998).

Economic Dimensions

As stated earlier, the most recent refugees from Rwanda, Burundi, and the former Democratic Republic of the Congo crossed the border into the poorest regions of Tanzania. Most people in these regions are engaged in agriculture production, and the majority of the refugees are from rural areas in their homelands—they too were farmers. To better understand the economic dimension of the refugee crisis, the effect of the new arrivals on the host communities will be examined first. Clearly, when refugees looted crops and property during the first phase of the emergency, farmers were economically affected in a negative manner. However, after refugees were settled in camps, they continued to depend on local farmers for staple foods (cassava and bananas) and meat. The United Nations World Food Program (WFP) was responsible for providing and distributing food in the camps. In order to secure additional food and other necessities not contained in the food baskets, refugees had to work, barter, trade, or steal. All of these activities had economic consequences. First, the local farmers realized that they had a willing and able workforce, and many refugees were hired and paid in the form of cash, crops, or other goods. This new cheap source of labor allowed many farmers to expand their productions, and higher yields were achieved although refugees continued to be blamed for the theft of crops. Some farmers put their own families at risk by selling too much of their own food (Whitakar, 1999).

The arrival of relief workers, journalists, international visitors, and Tanzanians who were recruited by the government to work in the camps also affected local communities economically. All of these new arrivals needed places to stay, food to eat, gas for their vehicles, entertainment, and other necessities and amenities. In 1998 the town of Kibondo in the Kigoma region resembled a village that was on the verge of becoming a small town. There were no streetlights, electricity, paved roads, or indoor plumbing, but the era of modernization was on the horizon. The dusty roads were full of four-wheel drive vehicles driven by local Tanzanians, other Tanzanians who had been recruited from other parts of the country, and expatriate staff from other African countries and Europe. The local market sold many varieties of fruits, vegetables, and meats, along with other consumer goods that included pots, pans, tablecloths, batteries, and radios. There was a restaurant (owned by the District Officer's wife), two or three bars, a teashop, a pharmacy, and other shops that sold clothes and household goods. In addition, there was one guesthouse where most of the visitors and relief personnel stayed. Ngara was an even bigger town than Kibondo, and its economic benefits from the refugee influx were evident. The town had several restaurants, guesthouses and hotels, shops, bars, and markets. There was also a barbershop (serviced by a generator) that had the latest rap and hip hop songs blaring from its stereo. Nevertheless, electricity and indoor plumbing were still absent (Field Notes, 1998).

Some Tanzanian citizens saw the arrival of the refugees as an economic plus. Small entrepreneurs were able to secure from the refugees donated food rations and other items such as corn oil, mixed maize, soy flour, biscuits, blankets, and plastic sheeting. These items in turn were sold for a profit. In addition, some members of the local community managed to acquire (illegally) cement, paint, plastic pipes, electric cables, and other goods from the offices of the United Nations and international non-governmental offices. These goods were also sold at a profit, making the refugee influx very lucrative for some local Tanzanians (Gaurwa, 1998).

After refugees were forcibly repatriated, the demolition of refugee camps had an economic downside for some local Tanzanians. Some Tanzanians had been given access to the camps' hospitals and clinics, free of charge. They could also purchase clean water in the camps for lower prices. After the camps were dismantled, they no longer had access to the medical care, and the price of water increased substantially (Gaurwa, 1998).

Finally, the refugee influxes created the need to hire people to fill many positions, including drivers, guards, secretaries, accountants, and administrators. Although Tanzanians hired for these positions were paid much higher wages and given better packages than other Tanzanians, the salaries were much lower than those given to the expatriate staff, especially those from Europe and the United States. Nevertheless, the new workers infused much-needed cash into the local economy.

Prior to the arrival of refugees during the 1990s, the government granted work permits to refugees and allowed them to engage in various economic activities. This is no longer the case. However, refugees have managed to work and to create various economic activities that allow them to obtain cash, food, and other commodities. Rwandan refugees established lucrative trading businesses, along with thriving markets and shops in the camps. The markets were used to sell, among other things, the surplus agricultural products from their farm plots in the camps. The government's political decisions to ban economic activity in camps for Rwandan refugees and to impose an exclusion zone around the camps had economic consequences for the refugees and political consequences for government officials (Dodd, 1996). In addition, the government's new forced encampment policy had economic ramifications.

The ban on economic activity and the exclusion zone were announced immediately following the presidential directive that called for the return of all Rwandan refugees by December 1996. These were political ploys on the part of the government to force the refugees back into Rwanda because the ability to earn cash would no longer be an incentive for them to remain in the country. If refugees were restricted to camps, they would not be able to compete with local citizens for employment and educational opportunities. Moreover, the government would be in a better position to keep track of them, crime would be reduced, and security would return to the communities. The hostility and resentment felt by the local population toward the refugees' economic gains would be reduced and public opinion would once again be on the side of the government. Clearly, the economic dimensions of the refugee influx from Rwanda cannot be separated from the political and social dimensions of the country.

Most of the Rwandan refugees voluntarily or forcibly returned home at the end of 1996, but there are thousands more remaining in the western part of the country—mainly from Burundi. These refugees created and took advantage of economic opportunities whenever possible. For example, they worked on local farms, traded and sold their agriculture surplus from their farm plots, and traded or sold their donated rations from the international community. They also established markets in the camps, along with other businesses and services that catered to other refugees and to the local population.

THE FUTURE

The plight of refugees in Tanzania can be characterized as abysmal and bleak, and yet at the same time there are signs of life and hope. Many of the refugees have escaped certain death in their countries of origin and their wounds have begun to heal with the assistance of the local and international communities. However, unless certain fundamental political issues are resolved in their countries of origin, they will remain refugees and many more will join the exodus. For refugees to discontinue migrating to Tanzania, a concerted effort to resolve the political, economic, and ethnic conflicts in the surrounding countries must be undertaken. In other words, conflict resolution strategies will have to be developed and utilized. These strategies will have to come from various segments of civil society, including politicians, grassroots organizations, bureaucrats, human rights activists, women's groups, religious leaders, journalists, and others committed to ending the human rights violations that often force people to seek safety in Tanzania.

Because many refugees in Tanzania were the victims of human rights abuses or witnessed human rights abuses against family members and friends, this issue must addressed. Human rights must be communicated to people in both the countries of origin and asylum, with the understanding that they are basic rights that extend to all members in society, including women and children.

Also, if the migration of people into Tanzania is to be halted, the perpetrators of human rights violations must be punished. The international community's concepts of voluntary repatriation and local integration as durable solutions for refugee crises cannot be attained as long as human rights violations occur in the countries of origin or asylum. Refugees should not be forced to return home before it is safe, and the Tanzanian government should be reprimanded for encouraging refugees to return to countries that are not safe. To ensure that host communities will continue to accommodate refugees, they, along with their governments, must be assisted. Poor countries, such as Tanzania, should not be expected to shoulder the economic and environmental burden of hosting thousands of refugees without adequate assistance from the international community. However, host communities such as Tanzania must be held accountable for their responsibilities under international law, and these responsibilities must be articulated to the host communities.

The most vulnerable groups in the refugee population—children, the elderly, the disabled, and women—must have their needs addressed. Rape and other forms of sexual violence must be examined, and the victims of such crimes must be provided special services and counseling. It is imperative that refugee women are involved in decisions that affect them in terms of housing, food, fuel, education, income-generating projects, and health care. Currently, decisions about the distribution of relief supplies are made by individuals who are not refugees, Africans, or females—women's voices must be included in every sphere of refugee assistance and protection. The refugee experience is difficult and precarious, but with the proper assistance and cooperation from host communities and the international community, it can lead to empowerment through new economic and educational opportunities.

NOTE

1. Field research was conducted by the author in Kibondo, Kagara Region in March 1998. Interviews were conducted both inside and outside refugee camps with representatives of non-governmental organizations. Personal observations were made while visiting refugee camps and traveling to and from the camps.

BIBLIOGRAPHY

Amnesty International/Tanzania. (1997, January 31–February 3). *Report of the Plight of Refugee Rights: Women and Children Seminar Cum Workshop*. Dar es Salaam, Tanzania: Amnesty International.

Anderson, G. (2000, October 21). Interview with John Guiney, Eastern Africa Province. *America*, *183*(12), 16–21.

Central Intelligence Agency. (2002). *Government Guide—Tanzania*. Retrieved on May 31, 2002 from http://www.governmentguide.com/research_and_education.adp.

Dodd, M. (1996, December 6). Tanzania Piles Pressure on Rwandan Refugees. *Reuters Ltd.*

Foreign Broadcasting Information Service—Africa. (1997, October 23). Burundi—5,000 Refugees Reportedly Expelled From Tanzania.

———. (1998, March 16). Burundi—Over 200 Refugees Return From Tanzania.

Gaurwa, L. (1998, January 28). One Year After the Departure of Rwandese Refugees in Benaco. *Daily News*, p. 1.

Human Rights Watch/Africa. (1996, December 17). Tanzanian Government and UNHCR Must Respect International Law Regarding Refugees. New York: Human Rights Watch.

Komba, A. (2001, February 13). Opposition to Approach UN Security Council. *The Guardian*, p. 2.

Nowrojee, B. (2001). In the Name of Security: Erosion of Refugee Rights in East Africa. *Worldwide Refugee Information*. Retrieved on February 6, 2001 from http://www.refugees.org/world/articles/wrs00_eafrica.htm.

Refugees International. (2000, January 21). Tanzania: Camps Strained Beyond Capacity.

Rutinwa, B. (1996, September). Refugee Protection and Security in East Africa. *Refugee Protection Network*, *22*, 11–14.

———. (1999, May). The End of Asylum? The Changing Nature of Refugee Policies in Africa. *New Issues in Refugee Research* (Working Paper No. 5). Oxford University.

Salter, G. (1995, May/June). Remembering the Dead. *Africa Report*, *40*, 30–33.

Tanzania: The End of the Tanzanian Dream? (2001, February 17). *Africanews*.

Tindwa, P. (1998, February 25). 40 Rwandese Refugees Re-enter Kagara Region Daily. *The African*, p. 2.

United Nations High Commissioner for Refugees. (1997, September). *Milestone*, *1*(2). Dar es Salaam, Tanzania.

———. (1997, December). *Milestone*, *1*(3). Dar es Salaam, Tanzania.

United States Committee for Refugees. (1995). *World Refugee Survey*. Washington, DC: Immigration and Refugee Services of America.

———. (1996). *World Refugee Survey*. Washington, DC: Immigration and Refugee Services of America.

———. (1997). *World Refugee Survey*. Washington, DC: Immigration and Refugee Services of America.

———. (1998). *World Refugee Survey*. Washington, DC: Immigration and Refugee Services of America.

———. (1999). *World Refugee Survey*. Washington, DC: Immigration and Refugee Services of America.

———. (2000). *World Refugee Survey*. Washington, DC: Immigration and Refugee Services of America.

Whitakar, B. E. (1999). Refugees and Host Communities in Western Tanzania. *New Issues in Refugee Research* (Working Paper No. 11). Geneva: Centre for Documentation and Research, United Nations High Commissioner for Refugees.

14

THE UNITED STATES

Immigration to the Melting Pot of the Americas

Rogelio Saenz, Maria Cristina Morales,
and Maria Isabel Ayala

INTRODUCTION

Profile of the United States

With a population of 284.5 million people in mid-2001, the United States is the third largest country in the world, behind China (nearly 1.3 billion) and India (1 billion) (Population Reference Bureau, 2001). The United States is a highly urbanized country with three of every four residents living in an urban area. The five largest cities in the country are New York City (8 million), Los Angeles (3.7 million), Chicago (2.9 million), Houston (2 million), and Philadelphia (1.5 million). Persons 65 years of age and older comprise one of almost every eight people in the country. Female babies born today in the United States can expect to live an average of 80 years while their male counterparts can expect to live 74 years (Population Reference Bureau, 2001). Approximately 7 infants per 1,000 live births died before reaching their first birthday in 2001 (Population Reference Bureau, 2001).

The United States gained its independence from Great Britain in 1776. The country has a democratic form of government. Since World War II, the United States has been viewed as a world leader with respect to political, economic, and military power. The country's Gross National Income Purchasing Power Parity (GNIPPP) per capita value of $31,910 ranks second only to that of Luxembourg ($41,230) (Population Reference Bureau, 2001). Literacy is almost universal, with 97 percent of the population 15 years of age and older being able to read and write (Central Intelligence

Agency, 2001). Nearly three-fifths of workers in the United States are employed in managerial and professional (30.2 percent), technical, sales, and administrative support (29.2 percent) occupations. However, in the recent past major job growth has occurred in high-skilled and high-tech occupations as well as in low-skilled and low-wage occupations (Sassen, 1991).

The country features a highly diverse population. While the majority of the nation's population (56%) is Protestant, significant proportions of the population are Roman Catholic (28%), Jewish (2%), "other" (4%), or hold no religion (10%) (Central Intelligence Agency, 2001). According to the 2000 U.S. census, non-Hispanic whites accounted for 69 percent of the population. The balance were minority group members, with African Americans and Latinos representing the largest minority groups in the country, each accounting for slightly more than 12 percent of the nation's population.

The United States is a nation of immigrants. Over the last four centuries, immigrants have shaped this country. As the renowned historian, Oscar Handlin (1951, p. 3), asserted, "Once I thought to write a history of the immigrants in America. Then I discovered that the immigrants were American history." According to statistics compiled by the U.S. Immigration and Naturalization Service (2000), nearly 65 million immigrants entered the United States on a legal basis between 1820 and 1998. In addition, countless other people entered the country illegally. A historical overview of immigration to the United States reveals significant changes in the composition of immigrant flows. In particular, as shown below, there have been dramatic shifts in the national origins of immigrants who have come to this country at different points in time.

Vignettes

A variety of factors continue to attract immigrants to the United States. While many come with the hopes of achieving the "American dream," their actual experiences often fall short of their expectations. Typically, immigrants find themselves relegated to the bottom of the economic ladder where they work in the least desirable jobs and subsist in meager conditions. For some this represents a temporary situation before they achieve some degree of upward social mobility, while for others this life condition is a more permanent feature. Accordingly, immigrants relay tales describing their experiences and hardships in the United States. The following illustrates the hopes and frustrations of a Taiwanese woman immigrant, who worked in banking in Taiwan before she reluctantly joined her husband in the United States:

I regret very much my migration to the United States. I had a good job and a house in Taiwan. We were so familiar with the environment there. After I came here I could not find a good job because of my language problem. I became like a deaf and blind person. I needed every source of help from my friends. Through a friend's help

I have been working in a knitting factory these past few years. The pay is no good, and we are paid by the hour. How much can I earn in this case? You know that there are more and more knitting factories here, and more and more Chinese are looking for jobs, so the wage does not rise, though inflation does every year. On the contrary, wages sometimes go down. If you do not like the job, the boss does not mind if you leave because there are so many candidates for you. I see some workers who could not even earn a dollar an hour in some jobs in the knitting factory. It is really sad. However, there is also no way for me to go back to Taiwan because I have nothing there now. I cannot find the same job again, and I have no house of my own in Taiwan (Chen, 1992, pp. 136–137).

This Taiwanese immigrant expresses the obstacles, such as cultural and language alienation, wage inequality, and unstable working conditions, that are common to many immigrants.

The Mexican American folksinger Tish Hinojosa gives us a glimpse of the solitary life of Mexican immigrant women in the United States in the mournful song, "Las Marias." The following passage from the song provides an illustration (Hinojosa, 1995; translation from Spanish to English by the authors):

> I am from foreign hands
> My children do not know about me
> Hidden here in the neighborhoods of Americans
> I hide my suffering
> Hidden here in the neighborhoods of Americans
> I hide my suffering

This passage reflects the solitary existence that many immigrant women experience, particularly when they are separated from their children who remain back home. For women whose children were left behind, immigration has transformed "motherhood" (Hondagneu-Sotelo & Avila, 1997). Women who are live-in domestic workers experience additional levels of isolation from the social world around them (Hondagneu-Sotelo, 2001).

Overview of Migration Issues

The Immigration and Naturalization Service (INS) has compiled historical information extending back to 1820 about the volume of immigration to the United States. The latest data compiled by the INS (2000) is based on the 1820–1998 period. Data from this source are used here to provide an overview of the volume and origin of immigration to the United States during this period. It should be noted that these data are based on individuals who immigrated to the United States on a legal basis. As such, people who took other routes (e.g., undocumented immigration, visa overstays, etc.) to come to this country are not included in these statistics.

Nearly 65 million immigrants came to the United States between 1820 and 1998. Table 14.1 shows graphically the fluctuation in the volume of immigration to this country during this time. As can be seen, there have been peaks and valleys in the volume of immigration to the United States. The highest annual volume of immigration occurred during the first two decades and the last two decades of the twentieth century. Immigration to the United States surpassed the 1 million mark in nine years during these decades — 1991 (1,827,167 immigrants), 1990 (1,536,483), 1907 (1,285,349), 1914 (1,218,480), 1913 (1,197,892), 1906 (1,100,735), 1989 (1,090,924), 1910 (1,041,570), and 1905 (1,026,499). Overall, eight decades (1881–1920 and 1961–1998) accounted for about 72 percent of the entire immigration to the United States in this 178-year period. By way of contrast, the lowest levels of immigration occurred in the 1820s, 1830s, 1930s, and 1940s.

The source of immigration has varied over time. As a whole, a dozen countries sent more than 1 million immigrants to the United States between 1820 and 1998 (see Table 14.1). The countries are Germany (7,156,257 immigrants), Mexico (5,819,966), Italy (5,431,454), the United Kingdom (5,247,821), Ireland (4,779,998), Canada and New-foundland (4,453,149), the Soviet Union (3,830,033), Austria (1,842,722), Hungary (1,675,324), the Philippines (1,460,421), China (1,262,050), and Sweden (1,257,133). These 12 countries have accounted for about 68 percent of all immigration to the United States during the 178-year period, yet there are major differences in the timing of immigration across them. We can divide the 12 countries into an "early stage" (Germany, the United Kingdom, and Ireland in the 1840–1890 period), "middle stage" (Italy, Canada/Newfoundland, the Soviet Union, Austria, and Hungary in the 1891–1920 period), and "recent stage" (Mexico, the Philippines, and China in the 1971–1998 period).

While INS data gives us a historical perspective on legal immigration to the United States, data from the March 2000 Current Population Survey (CPS) (U.S. Census Bureau, 2001) help us obtain a broader glimpse of the immigrants in the United States in 2000, regardless of when they arrived and the means (e.g., legal immigration, undocumented immigration, etc.) that they used to enter the country. A total of 28.4 million foreign-born persons were tallied at that time, accounting for one out of every ten inhabitants of the United States. CPS data indicate that one of every two foreign-born persons (51%) enumerated in 2000 was born in Latin America. In addition, persons born in Asia comprised one of every four (26%) foreign-born persons in the country at that time. Individuals born in Europe made up only about one of every 6.5 foreign-born persons (16%) in the country. However, it is clear that the number of Mexican immigrants dominates the national immigrant population. Indeed, nearly 28 percent of all foreign-born individuals in the country are Mexican. This is the largest percentage from

Table 14.1
Top 12 Countries Sending Immigrants (Based on Country of Last Residence) to the United States, 1820–1998

Period	Germany	Mexico	Italy	United Kingdom	Ireland	Canada and New- foundland	Soviet Union	Austria	Hungary	Philippines	China	Sweden
Total Immigrants in 1820–1998	7,156,257	5,819,966	5,431,454	5,247,821	4,779,998	4,453,149	3,830,033	1,842,722	1,675,324	1,460,421	1,262,050	1,257,133
1820	968	1	30	2,410	3,614	209	14	a	a	b	1	c
1821–1830	6,761	4,817	409	25,079	50,724	2,277	75	a	a	b	2	c
1831–1840	152,454	6,599	2,253	75,810	207,381	13,624	277	a	a	b	8	c
1841–1850	434,626	3,271	1,870	267,044	780,719	41,723	551	a	a	b	35	c
1851–1860	951,667	3,078	9,231	423,974	914,119	59,309	457	a	a	b	41,397	c
1861–1870	787,468	2,191	11,725	606,896	435,778	153,878	2,512	7,124	484	b	64,301	c
1871–1880	718,182	5,162	55,759	548,043	436,871	383,640	39,284	63,009	9,960	b	123,201	115,922
1881–1890	1,452,970	1,913	307,309	807,357	655,482	393,304	213,282	226,038	127,681	b	61,711	391,776
1891–1900	505,152	971	651,893	271,538	388,416	3,311	505,290	234,081	181,288	b	14,799	226,266
1901–1910	341,498	49,642	2,045,877	525,950	339,065	179,226	1,597,306	668,209	808,511	b	20,605	249,534
1911–1920	143,945	219,004	1,109,524	341,408	146,181	742,185	921,201	453,649	442,693	b	21,278	95,074
1921–1930	412,202	459,287	455,315	339,570	211,234	924,515	61,742	32,868	30,680	b	29,907	97,249
1931–1940	114,058	22,319	68,028	31,572	10,973	108,527	1,370	3,563	7,861	528b	4,928	3,960
1941–1950	226,578	60,589	57,661	139,306	19,789	171,718	571	24,860	3,469	4,691	16,709	10,665
1951–1960	477,765	299,811	185,491	202,824	48,362	377,952	671	67,106	36,637	19,307	9,657	21,697
1961–1970	190,796	453,937	214,111	213,822	32,966	413,310	2,465	20,621	5,401	98,376	34,764	17,116
1971–1980	74,414	640,294	129,368	137,374	11,490	169,939	38,961	9,478	6,550	354,987	124,326	6,531
1981–1990	91,961	1,655,843	67,254	159,173	31,969	156,938	57,677	18,340	6,545	548,764	346,747	11,018
1991–1998	72,792	1,931,237	58,346	128,671	54,865	157,564	386,327	13,776	7,564	433,768	347,674	10,325

Notes: (a) Data for Austria and Hungary not reported until 1861; (b) Prior to 1934, Philippines recorded as insular travel; (c) Data for Norway and Sweden not reported separately until 1871.

Source: Immigration and Naturalization Service (2000), Table 2.

any single country since the 1830 decennial census when 30 percent of the foreign-born population was from Germany. These data confirm that contemporary immigration in the United States is primarily Latin American and Asian in nature.

Results from the March 2000 CPS (U.S. Census Bureau, 2001) provide additional information that allows us to assess demographic patterns of the immigrant population. The data show that immigrants are highly concentrated, with 70 percent living in six states, each of which has more than 1 million immigrants: California (8.8 million), New York (3.6 million), Florida (2.8 million), Texas (2.4 million), New Jersey (1.2 million), and Illinois (1.2 million). One-fourth of Californians are immigrants as are one-fifth of New Yorkers. The Los Angeles and New York metropolitan areas (MAs) each contain 4.7 million immigrants; together these two MAs account for one-third of the nation's immigrant population. Furthermore, immigrants account for 43 percent of the population of the Miami MA population, while they make up 30 percent of the populations of the Los Angeles and San Francisco MAs.

Now that we have provided an overview of the magnitude of immigration to the United States and some basic demographic information about the current immigrant population, we turn our attention to a discussion of the four major eras of immigration to this country.

HISTORY OF MIGRATION ISSUES

A historical overview of immigration to the United States reveals four major eras that have witnessed major flows of immigration, with each of the eras comprised of different nationality groups. A brief overview of each of these eras follows, with special attention paid to the most prominent groups and events associated with each of the eras.

First Immigration Era: 1607–1820

The first era of immigration began with the settlement of Jamestown in 1607 and continued to the early part of the nineteenth century. Heavy exploration by various European groups occurred in the United States. The population of the colonies expanded tremendously with the arrival of countless immigrants from Europe, many of whom came as indentured servants, as well as large numbers of African slaves. While European indentured servants experienced harsh conditions under servitude, their experiences were mild compared to the intolerable conditions that African slaves had to endure. The first Africans, consisting of a group of 25, arrived in Jamestown as indentured servants, but the institution of slavery blossomed within a few decades. The development of the plantation system in the Southern colonies brought numerous slaves to the American colonies. Kivisto (1995), using estimates developed by Curtain (1969), reports that about 480,000 slaves were brought to the United States. The African American population stood at approximately 757,000 in 1790 and expanded to nearly 1.8 million by 1820.

Despite the presence of numerous nationalities in the American colonies, the English emerged as the dominant group in the United States, accounting for 82 percent, or 2.6 million, of the European-origin population in the United States in 1790 (Kivisto, 1995). The largest other European groups included the Scots (221,562), Germans (176,407), Dutch (78,959), Irish (61,534), French (17,619), and Jews (1,243). As the dominant group, the English shaped societal institutions and social life in the United States.

Furthermore, the British shaped the standards by which different racial and ethnic groups would be judged for inclusion in all segments of life in the country. Based on these standards, there was a clear racialized stratification system: the English occupied the most elevated position in the social and economic hierarchy, followed by other Europeans; Native Americans (Indians) and African Americans were the lowest in the hierarchy. Individuals who deviated greatly from the English in terms of skin color, culture, religion, and language tended to experience the greatest amount of prejudice and discrimination and occupied the lowest positions on the social and economic ladder.

Second Immigration Era: 1820–1890

The second immigration era saw significant increases in immigration to the United States. The most prominent groups in this era originated from northern and western Europe. In particular, Germany (4,505,096), Ireland (3,484,688), and the United Kingdom (2,756,613) sent the most immigrants to the United States during this period (see Table 14.1). Together, these three countries accounted for 10.7 million of the 15.4 million immigrants who entered the United States between 1820 and 1890. As such, seven of every ten immigrants came from Germany, Ireland, and the United Kingdom, and one of every two (51%) immigrants came solely from Germany and Ireland.

The movement of Germans and Irish to the United States was stimulated by a number of forces including massive population growth, upheavals associated with industrialization, economic problems, and, in the case of the Irish, the potato famine. The United States, with its vast amounts of land and economic opportunities, represented an ideal safety valve for the burgeoning populations of these two countries. Still, both Germans and Irish experienced a harsh reception upon their arrival in the United States (Dinnerstein, Nichols, & Reimers, 1990). For example, Germans were perceived as clannish and political radicals. The Irish were disparaged as rogues, troublemakers, and drunks. The acceptability of the Irish was further diminished by their Catholicism, which contrasted with the Protestantism of the mainstream population.

It is important to point out that an immigration policy did emerge by the mid-1870s to bar certain individuals from immigrating to the United States. For instance, immigration legislation was established during this period to curb the flow of immigrants with attributes deemed undesirable by the mainstream population (e.g., criminals, prostitutes, those likely to become public charges, and those with physical and mental health problems). The Chinese Exclusion Acts of 1882 and 1892 were enacted to bar Chinese from entering the country. Furthermore, a series of Alien Contract Labor Laws were designed to keep out people who tried to come to this country under labor contracts arranged before arriving here. These policies suggest that Americans had concerns not only with respect to the volume of immigration, but also regarding the types of individuals who were coming to the United States.

The last decade of the second immigration era witnessed major increases in the volume of immigration from northern and western European countries. The three countries sending the most immigrants to the United States experienced significant increases in the volume of immigration in the 1881–1890 period compared to that of the 1871–1880 period (see Table 14.1). The immigration flow from Germany increased by 102 percent between these two decades, while Ireland's flow rose by 50 percent and the United Kingdom's flow increased by 47 percent. Several other countries in the region also increased their volume of immigration to the United States dramatically between the decade of the 1870s and the 1880s — Sweden (increase of 238%), the Netherlands (225%), Switzerland (190%), Belgium (179%), Denmark (177%), and Norway (85%). In fact, six northern and western European countries (Denmark, Germany, the Netherlands, Sweden, Switzerland, and the United Kingdom) peaked in their volume of immigration to the United States in the decade of 1881–1890.

However, it was clear that change was in the air. During the same period, a number of southern and eastern European countries experienced a tremendous surge in their volumes of immigration to the United States (see Table 14.1). For example, compared to the volume of immigration that occurred during 1871–1880, the flow of immigration during 1881–1890 increased dramatically for Hungary (the immigration flow increased 13-fold), Greece (11-fold), Italy (about five-fold), the Soviet Union (about five-fold), Poland (four-fold), and Austria (3.5-fold), marking the beginning of the next immigration era.

Third Immigration Era: 1890–1924

The emergence of southern and eastern Europeans among immigrants coming to the United States in the 1880s represented a harbinger of the changes to come in the composition of immigrants entering the country. In the 1890s, the first decade of this immigration era, there were major declines in the flow of immigrants from the three countries that had sent the most immigrants to American shores in the second immigration era (see Table 14.1). The volume of immigration from the United Kingdom in 1891–1990 compared to the volume in 1881–1890 declined by 66 percent. For Germany it dropped by 65 percent and for Ireland it fell by 41 percent. This pattern was also evident for other northern and western European countries — Switzerland (−62%), the Netherlands (−50%), Norway (−46%), Denmark (−43%), Sweden (−42%), France (−39%), and Belgium (−10%). During the same period, in contrast, southern and eastern European countries experienced significant increases in their volume of immigration to the United States — Greece (an increase of 592% in the flow of immigrants between the 1881–1890 and 1891–1900 periods), the Soviet Union (137%), Italy (112%), Romania (101%), Spain (98%), Poland (87%), Portugal (62%), and Hungary (42%).

Thus, a major shift occurred over a short period of time in the source of immigration to the United States, changing from a prominence of immigrants from northern and western Europe to immigrants from southern and eastern Europe. This third immigration period saw major increases in the overall volume of immigration to the United States. For example, 18.2 million immigrants came during 1891–1920 compared to 10.4 million during 1861–1890. The four most prominent countries from which immigrants originated during this era included Italy (3,807,294 total immigrants between 1891–1920), the Soviet Union (3,023,797), Hungary (1,432,492), and Austria (1,355,939) (see Table 14.1). Together these four countries accounted for one of every two (53%) of all immigrants coming to the United States between 1890 and 1920, with Italy alone accounting for one of every five (21%) immigrants during the period.

Southern and eastern European immigrants were motivated to come to the United States by forces similar to those propelling their northern and western European counterparts in the earlier immigration era. At this time, many southern and eastern European countries were experiencing significant industrialization, major population growth, economic problems, and political upheavals. The United States represented an appealing destination for immigrants seeking a better life at this time. Yet, southern and eastern European immigrants experienced a harsh reception filled with prejudice and discrimination (Dinnerstein et al., 1990). While earlier immigrants faced hostility in the United States, southern and eastern European immigrants experienced even harsher treatment because they were different from the mainstream population in so many ways, including their physical characteristics (darker skin), religion (many were Catholics and Jews), culture, and language. The newcomers were quickly marked as the "other" — people who did not meet the standards of being "American." Incidentally, the arrival of southern and eastern European immigrants occurred at a time when "scientific racism" (i.e., the use of scientific instruments to account for racial differences in intelligence) and the "eugenics movement" (i.e., concern for creating a genetically ideal population) were in vogue. In this environment, southern and eastern European newcomers were viewed as physically and intellectually inferior to the mainstream population. Indeed, many Americans feared that southern and eastern Europeans would intermix with the American population, and thus "contaminate" the American race. One of the most prominent proponents of this position was Madison Grant (1916), author of the book *The Passing of the Great Race*.

Given this social environment and the increasing volume of immigration, it is not surprising that many Americans called for significant reforms to curb the flow of immigrants, and, more specifically, the flow of those originating from southern and eastern Europe. To deal with the immigration issue, Congress established the Dillingham Commission in 1907. In 1911, the commission issued a 41-volume report warning about problems associated with this "new" group of immigrants that was seen as incapable of assimilating into America's ways. The commission recommended measures to curb the flow of undesirable immigrants, with the most prominent measures being the establishment of a literacy requirement and immigration quotas. These recommendations were influential in the formation of immigration policies that would emerge over the next 13 years. The Immigration Act of 1917 required immigrants entering the United States to pass a literacy test. The act also expanded the list of people excluded from gaining entry into the United States to those unable to meet established physical, mental, moral, and economic standards, as well as to Asians, anarchists, and subversives. The Immigration Act of 1921 imposed immigration quotas, with countries being allocated an immigration quota equivalent to 3 percent of the population of a given nationality living in the United States in 1910. Given the recent arrival of southern and eastern Europeans in the United States, this measure placed severe caps on the number of immigrants from southern and eastern Europe that would be allowed to enter the United States. Indeed, the measure favored immigration from more established groups (i.e., those from northern and western Europe).

Yet, the quotas created by the Immigration Act of 1921 were not restrictive enough for opponents of immigration, resulting in the Johnson-Reed Act of 1924. According to this act, countries would receive immigration quotas that were equivalent to 2 percent of the population of a given nationality residing in the United States in 1890. This change placed an even more severe limitation on the numbers of southern and eastern Europeans that were allowed to enter the country. It should be mentioned that the quota acts exempted nations in the Americas from quotas and essentially barred immigration from Asia.

The quotas were extremely effective in altering the composition of immigrants. For example, while immigrants from Italy, the Soviet Union, Hungary, and Austria accounted for 53 percent of all immigrants who came to the United States in the 1891–1920 period, they comprised only 14 percent of those arriving in the 1921–1930 period. Indeed, numerous southern and eastern European countries experienced significant drops in the number of immigrants that came to the United States between the 1911–1920 and 1921–1930 periods—the Soviet Union (−93%), Hungary (−93%), Austria (−93%), Greece (−72%), Portugal (−67%), Italy (−59%), and Spain (−58%). In contrast, during this period, the number of immigrants from Germany increased by 186 percent and the number from Ireland rose by 45 percent.

Over the course of the third immigration era, the United States experienced unprecedented levels of immigration that created a major shift in its ethnic mosaic. This level of immigration would not be seen for decades. Indeed, the volume of immigration (8.8 million) that occurred in 1901–1910 was greater than the volume (7.4 million) that took place in 1931–1970 (see Table 14.1). Nevertheless, by the mid-1960s, there began the rise of another significant immigration era that further altered the racial and ethnic face of the United States.

Fourth Immigration Era: 1965–Present

The United States experienced another dramatic shift in the composition of immigrants arriving during the 1960s. While the number of European immigrants declined by 15 percent between the 1951–1960 and 1961–1970 periods, the number of Asian (179% increase) and Latin American (130%) immigrants more than doubled. Moreover, the share of Europeans among all immigrants coming to the United States dropped from 56 percent in the 1931–1960 period to 34 percent in the 1961–1970 period, while the share of Latin Americans (19% in the 1931–1960 period; 39% in the 1961–1970 period) and Asians (5%; 13%) increased dramatically over the same period. Latin American and Asian immigrants together comprised the majority (52%) of all immigrants that entered the country in the 1961–1970 period. More telling, however, was the 1981–1990 period, during which Latin American and Asian immigrants accounted for more than four of every five (84%) immigrants who came to the United States. During the latest time period for which there is data (1991–1998), Latin American immigrants accounted for almost one of every two immigrants (48%) who entered the country, Asian immigrants for nearly one of every three (31%), and European immigrants for about one of every 6.5 (15%) entering the nation.

The volume of immigration to the United States over the last four decades (1961–1998) has been quite impressive. Indeed, immigrants who came to this country in this period account for approximately 35 percent of all immigrants who came to the United States between 1820 and 1998. The ten countries that have sent the most immigrants to the United States during the 1961–1998 period are Mexico (4,681,311), the Philippines (1,435,895), Canada/Newfoundland (897,751), China (853,511), the Dominican Republic (793,527), Korea (772,561), Cuba (754,688), India (737,742), Vietnam (699,583), and the United Kingdom (639,040). More broadly, immigrants from the eight Latin American and Asian countries listed among the top ten senders of immigrants to the United States during this period accounted for nearly one in two immigrants (46%) who came to the nation during the period. It should be noted that these numbers underestimate the actual flow of immigrants from these countries, as they do not account for the large volume of undocumented immigration.

DIMENSIONS OF MIGRATION ISSUES

Economic Dimensions

While European immigrants experienced prejudice and discrimination in the United States, within three or so generations many had become integrated into all segments of life in this country (Lieberson & Waters, 1988). It is not clear that today's immigrants will become integrated as quickly. Some Asian groups have attained a rapid rise in their socioeconomic standing in the United States due to the high levels of human capital (e.g., education, skills, job experience) they brought with them from their home countries. On the other hand, Mexican, Caribbean, and Central American immigrants continue to occupy extremely low positions on the social and economic ladders of the United States. Particularly telling is the case of Mexicans. Despite the group's long presence in the United States, native- and foreign-born persons of Mexican origin continue to be ranked among the lowest levels on a wide variety of social and economic indicators (Saenz, 1999).

Data from the March 2000 CPS (U.S. Census Bureau, 2001) are available to assess the socioeconomic standing of various groups of immigrants on several socioeconomic dimensions in 2000. Table 14.2 provides basic information on five socioeconomic dimensions for foreign-born individuals by region of birth. These data show that four-fifths or more of African (95%), Northern American (86%), Asian (84%), European (81%), and South American (80%) foreign-born persons 25 years of age or older have at least completed a high school education. These groups are also the most likely to have at least a bachelor's degree as well, with African immigrants leading the way with about half having a college degree. In contrast, Mexican (34%) and Central American (37%) immigrants are the least likely to hold a high school diploma. Only a very small percentage of members of these groups are college graduates.

Despite the low levels of education among Mexican and Central American immigrants, these groups have the highest levels of labor force participation

Table 14.2
Socioeconomic Indicators for the Foreign-Born Population in the United States by Region of Birth, 2000

Socioeconomic Indicator	Europe	Asia	Africa	Latin America	Caribbean	Central America	Mexico	Other Latin America	South America	Northern America
Educational Attainment (Age 25 and Older)										
Pct. High School Graduates or Higher	81.3%	83.8%	94.9%	49.6%	68.1%	37.3%	33.8%	50.8%	79.7%	85.5%
Pct. Bachelor's Degree or Higher	32.9%	44.9%	49.3%	11.2%	19.3%	5.5%	4.2%	10.5%	25.9%	36.2%
Labor Force Participation (Age 25–64)										
Pct. Males in Labor Force	93.1%	91.4%	dna	93.5%	90.8%	94.5%	94.4%	94.7%	91.7%	dna
Pct. Females in Labor Force	73.8%	68.9%	dna	63.4%	73.9%	58.1%	55.1%	68.5%	73.0%	dna
Occupational Attainment (Workers 16+)										
Pct. Workers Employed in:										
Managerial and Professional	38.1%	38.7%	36.5%	12.1%	22.6%	7.0%	6.3%	9.4%	23.2%	46.3%
Technical, Sales, & Administrative Support	23.9%	27.5%	22.1%	16.5%	25.1%	12.7%	11.2%	17.7%	24.0%	24.9%
Service	15.0%	15.0%	19.6%	22.9%	22.6%	22.9%	21.8%	26.7%	23.0%	8.3%
Precision Production, Craft, & Repair	12.2%	5.9%	4.2%	15.9%	9.0%	18.3%	19.2%	15.2%	13.7%	9.3%
Operators, Fabricators, & Laborers	10.2%	12.0%	17.1%	24.8%	19.9%	28.1%	28.6%	26.5%	15.2%	9.5%
Farming, Forestry, & Fishing	0.6%	0.8%	0.5%	7.8%	0.8%	11.1%	12.9%	4.5%	0.9%	1.7%
Earnings in 1999 (Full-Time, Year Round Workers)										
Median Earnings of Males	$44,990	$36,911	dna	$20,974	$26,971	$19,499	$19,181	$20,801	$27,502	dna
Median Earnings of Females	$28,319	$29,662	dna	$17,213	$21,255	$15,346	$15,149	$15,857	$23,080	dna
Poverty in 1999										
Pct. of Persons in Poverty	9.3%	12.8%	13.2%	21.9%	20.6%	24.2%	25.8%	17.8%	11.5%	7.4%

Notes: "dna" indicates that "data are not available"; the "Latin America" region includes the Caribbean, Central America, Mexico, South America, and Other Latin America; Northern America includes Canada, Bermuda, Greenland, and two islands governed by France (St. Pierre and Miquelon).

Source: U.S. Census Bureau (2001). The data used to generate this report are from the March 2000 *Current Population Survey*.

among males 25–64 years of age. Approximately 95 percent of Central American, Mexican, and other Latin American immigrant men are labor force participants. In contrast, among female immigrants 25–64 years of age, Caribbean, European, and South American immigrant women exhibit the highest levels (nearly 75%) of labor force participation.

There are also marked differences between Latin American immigrants and their counterparts from elsewhere with respect to the occupations they hold. For instance, Northern American (71%), Asian (66%), European (62%), and African (59%) immigrants are the most likely to be employed in the two occupations that are associated with relatively high pay and favorable working conditions (managerial and professional; and technical, sales, and administrative support). In contrast, Latin American immigrants, particularly those from Mexico (18%) and Central America (20%), are significantly less likely to be working in these occupations and are the most likely to be working in the remaining four occupations (service; precision production, craft, and repair; operators, fabricators, and laborers; and farming, forestry, and fishing), which tend to have relatively lower pay and more difficult working conditions. Particularly noticeable is the fact that Mexican and Central American immigrants are far more likely than other immigrants to be working in farming, forestry, and fishing occupations.

Data for job earnings in 1999 among full-time, year-round workers are also presented in Table 14.2. (Note that data are unavailable for African and Northern American immigrants.) European and Asian immigrants have the highest median earnings among the different immigrant subgroups—European men ($44,990), Asian men ($36,911), Asian women ($29,662), and European women ($28,319). South American and Caribbean immigrants occupy a middle position with respect to their median earnings—South American men ($27,502), Caribbean men ($26,971), South American women ($23,080), and Caribbean women ($21,255). Central American, Mexican, and other Latin American immigrants have the lowest median earnings, with Mexican women having the lowest median earnings ($15,149) of any group.

By and large, the patterns associated with poverty tend to reflect the patterns described above. The lowest poverty rates occur among Northern American (7%), European (9%), South American (12%), and Asian (13%) immigrants. In contrast, approximately one of every four Mexican (26%) and Central American (24%) immigrants is poor.

Social Dimensions

As illustrated above, immigrants who have come to the United States have encountered prejudice, discrimination, and a general lack of acceptance into the host society. Sociological knowledge suggests that several factors are related to the extent to which minority groups, including immigrants, are accepted and integrated into the larger society. These include the size of the group, the level of the group's concentration, the timing of the group's arrival in this country, and the degree of the group's ethnic and racial distinctiveness from the majority group (McLemore & Romo, 1998). Accordingly, immigrant groups that are less likely to gain acceptance include those that have large immigrant populations, those that are geographically concentrated, those that arrived in poor economic times, those that have cultures and customs that are distinct from the majority group, and those that are non-white.

In the discussion below, we focus on three social dimensions—social distance, residential segregation, and intermarriage. Unfortunately, much of the existing information on these topics focuses on racial and ethnic groups rather than specifically on immigrant groups.

Social distance represents the feelings and attitudes that people have of various racial and ethnic groups. Using data from the 2000 General Social Survey, Smith (2001) provided a wealth of information regarding the manner in which people in the United States view five groups—whites, African Americans, Asians, Latinos, and Jews. As a whole, Smith's analysis indicates that there is a social hierarchy, with whites being viewed the most positively, followed closely by Jews. In contrast, African Americans are viewed the least favorably, with Asians and Latinos viewed somewhat more favorably. For example, few non-whites expressed objection to a close family member marrying a white individual (9%) or living in a neighborhood where whites represented the majority group (6%). Similarly, few non-Jewish respondents objected to having a close relative marrying a Jewish individual (13%) or living in a neighborhood comprised of a Jewish majority (9%). Asians and Latinos lag somewhat behind whites and Jews with respect to people not objecting to close contact. Approximately one-fifth of non-Asians and non-Latinos objected to having a close family member marrying an Asian or Latino individual, although relatively lower proportions objected to living in a majority-Asian (18%) than in a majority-Latino neighborhood (27%). Finally, people tended to want the least amount of contact with African Americans. Approximately one-third of non-African Americans objected to having a close relative marry an African American individual while three-tenths objected to living in a neighborhood where African Americans represented the majority group.

Respondents in the 2000 General Social Survey were also asked about their views toward immigration. Whites were the most likely to hold anti-immigration views while Asians and Latinos were the least likely to hold such views, and a significant portion of respondents had deep concerns regarding the impact of immigration: ". . . 70 percent think that crime rates will rise, 57 percent feel that native-born Americans will lose jobs, and 53 percent believe that immigrants will make it 'harder to keep the country united'" (Smith, 2001, p. 17).

We now shift our discussion to residential segregation, or the degree to which racial or ethnic groups live in different areas (often census tracts) within cities. Demographers frequently use the index of dissimilarity (denoted as D) to measure the extent to which two given groups live apart within a given city. The D ranges from 0 to 100, with a score of 0 indicating that members of each group live in the same areas of the city (no segregation) and 100 indicating that the members of the two groups live in totally different areas of the city (complete segregation). D can be interpreted as the percentage of members of one of the two comparison groups that would need to move to other parts of the city for the two groups to have the same geographic distribution. The Lewis Mumford Center (2001) report observed that African Americans continue to be the most segregated from the white population (average D of 65 across metropolitan areas of the country), while Latinos have the second highest levels of segregation from whites (average D of 52) and Asians have the lowest level of segregation from whites (average D of 42). To illustrate with the case of African Americans, on average, about two-thirds of African Americans would need to relocate to other parts of the city in order for the African American and white populations to have the same geographic distribution patterns.

Whites and various minority populations have completely distinct experiences with respect to the racial and ethnic composition of the places where they live. The Lewis Mumford Center (2001, p. 3) report illustrates this reality:

Stark contrasts are readily apparent between the typical experiences of whites versus that of each minority group. The typical white lives in a neighborhood that is 80.2% white, 6.7% black, 7.9% Hispanic, and 3.9% Asian. The experience of minorities is very different. For example, the typical black lives in a neighborhood that is 51.4% black, 33.0% white, 11.4% Hispanic, and 3.3% Asian. The typical Hispanic lives in a neighborhood that is 45.5% Hispanic, 36.5% white, 10.8% black, and 5.9% Asian. The typical Asian lives in a neighborhood that is 17.9% Asian, 54.0% white, 9.2% black, and 17.4% Hispanic.

Under these residential arrangements, the social, economic, and political lives of whites and minorities vary tremendously. Indeed, people's life chances, their access to societal resources, and their access to the opportunity structure are related to the places where they live.

Intermarriage is often seen as the most prominent indicator of assimilation. Intermarriage involves people marrying outside their own racial or ethnic group. The white population has experienced such a significant amount of intermarriage, much of this involving whites marrying other whites from other nationality groups, that some observers have suggested that whites are experiencing an "eclipse in ethnicity" (Alba, 1985). Others have also noted the difficulty that whites have with respect to their ethnic identification due to the high levels of intermarriage within the racial group (Waters, 1990). Intermarriage for other groups, however, has varied tremendously. By and large, among the three other major racial/ethnic groups, Asians have the highest levels of intermarriage, followed by Latinos and then African Americans, who are the least likely to marry outside of their group (Huntington, 2000). Native-born individuals have higher intermarriage rates than their foreign-born counterparts (Qian & Lichter, 2001).

The discussion of social dimensions associated with immigration for the most part shows a social hierarchy that is similar to the economic hierarchy described earlier. On a wide variety of social indicators, whites are positioned at the top, followed by Asians, Latinos, and African Americans. While the social indicators presented in this section tend to be based on entire racial or ethnic groups, it is certain that the social position of immigrants is lower than that of their native-born counterparts within each racial or ethnic group.

Population projections suggest that much of the population growth in the coming decades will be driven primarily by growth in the Latino and Asian populations. Furthermore, as did their earlier immigrant counterparts, Latin American and Asian immigrants have experienced a significant amount of prejudice and discrimination. Such treatment has been exacerbated by their distinct differences from the mainstream population with respect to race and phenotype, culture, and language, as well as because of the large-scale nature of immigration. Immigrants have been viewed as scapegoats for a variety of social and economic ills. In the last few decades there have been state initiatives to declare English as the official language, eliminate bilingual education, and restrict immigrants from gaining access to social and economic benefits.

Moreover, hidden in the social indicators presented earlier are the more arduous hardships that immigrants encounter on a personal basis, many of these propagated by the rise of anti-immigration hostilities. These include being victims of violence, direct prejudice and discrimination, harassment, racial profiling, or so forth. It is reported that in 1998 African Americans were the victims of two-thirds of hate crimes associated with race while Latinos were the victims of nearly two-thirds of hate crimes associated with ethnicity or national origin (Civilrights.org, 2002). Immigrants have experienced violence not only from racist hoodlums but also from law authorities, as exemplified by such high-profile cases involving the savage beating of Haitian immigrant Abner Louima and the senseless death of Amadou Diallo at the hands of the New York City police as well as the savage beatings of a Mexican man and woman by Riverside, California sheriff's deputies.

Political Dimensions

The fourth immigration era, from 1965 to the present, has been associated with a period of liberalization of immigration policy (Easterlin, Ward, Bernard, & Ueda, 1980; Lee, 1999), beginning with the passage of the Hart-

Cellar Act of 1965. This act included several key provisions that stimulated immigration from Latin America and Asia (Lee, 1999). First, the act eliminated the national origins quota system and the severe restrictions on Asian immigration. The act elevated the number of immigrants that was allowed to enter the country annually to 290,000. A cap of 120,000 visas was placed on western hemisphere countries without a limitation on any particular country, while eastern hemisphere countries had a limit of 170,000 visas with no country being allowed more than 20,000 (Easterlin et al., 1980). Second, the act contained a preference for "family reunification," in which U.S. citizens can petition to sponsor close relatives to be allowed to immigrate to the United States. It has been reported that 74 percent of all visas during the period were associated with family reunification (Briggs, 1996). Third, the act exhibited a preference for other groups, such as high-skilled workers and refugees (Briggs, 1996). Many Asians immigrated as high-skilled workers, creating a "brain drain" for their home countries. Furthermore, many Indochinese refugees came to the United States after the Vietnam War.

The refugee issue attracted much attention toward the late 1970s. The first act to address systematically the admission and incorporation of refugees based on humanitarian need was the Refugee Act of 1980 (Immigration and Naturalization Service, 2001). The act reduced the worldwide quota to 270,000 but excluded refugees from the numerical limitation. Additionally, it allowed for the permanent resident status of refugees who had been physically present in the United States for at least one year and for asylees one year after asylum was granted (Immigration and Naturalization Service, 2001). Following the passage of the Refugee Act of 1980, 125,000 Cubans came as refugees, a group that has been called *Marielitos* due to the location, Mariel Bay, from which they departed Cuba.

In the 1970s and 1980s there was much debate regarding the large flow of undocumented immigration to the United States, especially in the case of Mexico. Proponents of immigration control expressed concern that the country could not control entry through its southern border. Furthermore, public panic surged suggesting that undocumented immigrants were taking jobs from U.S. citizens and draining the welfare system. The Immigration Reform and Control Act (IRCA) of 1986 represented a balance between opposing forces—nativists and labor unions on the one hand and employers who rely on undocumented workers and immigration advocates on the other—in the immigration debate. IRCA had three major provisions. First, it created sanctions in the form of fines and/or jail for employers who knowingly hire undocumented workers. Previously, in an ironic fashion, it had been illegal to be an undocumented worker while at the same time it was not illegal to hire one (Bustamante, 1972). Second, IRCA created an amnesty program that offered amnesty to undocumented immigrants who had lived in the United States on a continuous basis since January 1, 1982. Third, the act provided a special amnesty program for seasonal agricultural workers (SAWs) who had worked in agriculture for at least 90 days between May 1985 and May 1986. Moreover, it allowed for the possibility of letting immigrants enter the country on a temporary basis to work in agriculture (a group called "replacement agricultural workers," or RAWs) in the event that the industry had a shortage of workers. Approximately 1.7 million people were granted legal status through the general amnesty program, while an additional 1.3 million obtained such status through the SAW program (Woodrow & Passel, 1990). Of the 3 million who gained legal status through IRCA, approximately three-fourths were Mexican (Chavez, 1996).

Further immigration policies surfaced in the 1990s. The Immigration Act of 1990 provided a major overhaul to immigration law, setting current categories and numerical limitations for immigration to the United States (Immigration and Naturalization Service, 2001). The act raised the cap of annual immigration to 675,000, of which 480,000 was to be family-sponsored, 140,000 employment-based, and 55,000 diversity immigrants. In addition, the Immigration Act of 1990 provided temporary status to undocumented people from certain countries that faced armed conflict and natural disasters, placed a limitation on the number of people who can be issued temporary work visas, revised naturalization requirements, imposed new legal restrictions on aliens convicted of crimes, recodified grounds for exclusion, and increased funding for Border Patrol personnel.

During the 1990s, the U.S. government spent millions of dollars on increased Border Patrol surveillance and on the construction of walls and fences along the U.S.-Mexico border designed to make it harder for undocumented immigrants to enter the United States (Weeks, 1999). In 1994, the INS implemented the agency's first national Border Patrol strategy to increase staffing and obtain new resources. Other border-control strategies include "Operation Gatekeeper" in San Diego, CA, "Operation Safeguard" in Tucson, AZ, "Operation Hold the Line" in El Paso, TX, and "Operation Rio Grande" in McAllen, TX.

The latest immigration policy, the Illegal Immigration Reform and Immigrant Responsibility Act of 1996 (IIRIRA), was established alongside other reform efforts in the United States, most notably welfare reform and Proposition 187 in California, which attempted to prevent immigrants from drawing a variety of social and economic benefits. The IIRIRA increased penalties for immigrant-related offenses, increased enforcement personnel, and enhanced enforcement authority. Further, it included restrictions on the eligibility of undocumented immigrants for public benefits, such as welfare, Social Security, and higher education assistance.

THE FUTURE

This chapter has provided a broad historical overview of immigration in the United States. The overview describes a nation that has historically been enmeshed in disputes over which groups are welcomed and which should be excluded from entering the country. Americans have a history of having a love/hate relationship with immigrants (see Newman, 2000). During good times immigrants are welcomed to fill the need for cheap labor. During bad times or when political alliances shift, however, immigrants are blamed for the nation's social and economic ills. With the United States' new war on terrorism, it is not clear the direction that immigration legislation will take in the near future. Nevertheless, it is likely that economic, political, and social forces will continue to spawn major flows of immigrants to the United States. The movement of people to this country is so well established, especially in the case of some countries such as Mexico, that it is difficult to halt (Massey & Espinosa, 1997). However, only time will tell which immigrants will be welcome and what will happen to those already here with respect to their social, economic, and political standing. In particular, the most recent changes in immigration policy will undoubtedly affect the degree and speed in which immigrants will be integrated into the larger society. Such policies are detrimental to the most economically and politically vulnerable segments of the immigrant population—those with little human capital; those who are in the country illegally; and those working in low-wage, dead-end jobs that offer few, if any, benefits. While this profile describes many immigrants in this country, our examination of social and economic data above shows that it is especially descriptive of Latin American immigrants, especially those coming from Mexico, Central America, and the Caribbean. It is these groups that are likely to face the greatest hardships in gaining access to the American dream, which continues to lure many immigrants to this country.

BIBLIOGRAPHY

Alba, R. D. (1985). *Italian Americans: Into the Twilight of Ethnicity.* Englewood Cliffs, NJ: Prentice-Hall.

Briggs, V. M., Jr. (1996). Immigration Policy and the U.S. Economy: An Institutional Perspective. *Journal of Economics Issues, 30*(20), 371–389.

Bustamante, J. A. (1972). The Wetback as Deviant: An Application of Labeling Theory. *American Journal of Sociology, 77,* 706–718.

Central Intelligence Agency. (2001). *The World Factbook 2001.* Washington, DC: Central Intelligence Agency. http://www.cia.gov/cia/publications/factbook/.

Chavez, L. R. (1996). Borders and Bridges: Undocumented Immigrants from Mexico and Central America. In S. Pedraza & R. G. Rumbaut (Eds.), *Origins and*

Destinations: Immigration, Race, and Ethnicity in America (pp. 250–262). Belmont, CA: Wadsworth.

Chen, H. (1992). *Chinatown No More: Taiwan Immigrants in Contemporary New York*. Ithaca, NY: Cornell University Press.

Civilrights.org. Cause for Concern. Retrieved 2002 from http://www.civilrights. org/publications/cause_for_concern/p9.html.

Curtain, P. (1969). *The Atlantic Slave Trade*. Madison: University of Wisconsin Press.

Dinnerstein, L., Nichols, R. L., & Reimers, D. M. (1990). *Natives and Strangers: Blacks, Indians, and Immigrants in America* (rev. ed.). New York: Oxford University Press.

Easterlin, R. A., Ward D., Bernard, W. S., & Ueda, R. (1980). *Immigration: Dimensions of Ethnicity*. Cambridge, MA: Belknap Press of Harvard University Press.

Fischer, D. H. (1989). *Albion's Seed: Four British Folkways in America*. New York: Oxford University Press.

Grant, M. (1916). *The Passing of the Great Race*. New York: Charles Scribner's Sons.

Handlin, O. (1951). *The Uprooted: The Epic Story of the Great Migrations that Made the American People*. Boston: Little, Brown and Company.

Hinojosa, Tish. (1995). Las Marias. On *Frontejas* [CD]. Cambridge, MA: Rounder Records.

Hondagneu-Sotelo, P. (2001). *Domestica: Immigrant Workers Cleaning and Caring in the Shadows of Affluence*. Berkeley: University of California Press.

Hondagneu-Sotelo, P., & Avila, E. (1997). "I'm Here, but I'm There": The Meanings of Latina Transnational Motherhood. *Gender and Society, 11*(5), 548–571.

Huntington, S. P. (2000). Reconsidering Immigration: Is Mexico a Special Case? *Center for Immigration Studies Backgrounder Report*. Washington, DC: Center for Immigration Studies. http://www.cis.org/articles/2000/back1100.html.

Immigration and Naturalization Service. (2000). *1998 Statistical Yearbook of the Immigration and Naturalization Service*. Washington, DC: U.S. Department of Justice.

———. (2001). *The INS Online, 2001*. Retrieved June, 25, 2001 from http://www.ins.usdoj.gov/graphics/index.htm.

Kivisto, P. (1995). *Americans All: Race and Ethnic Relations in Historical, Structural, and Comparative Perspectives*. Belmont, CA: Wadsworth.

Lee, Erica. (1999). Immigrants and Immigration Law: A State of the Field Assessment. *Journal of American Ethnic History, 18*, 85–114.

Lewis Mumford Center. (2001). *Ethnic Diversity Grows, Neighborhood Integration Lags Behind*. Albany, NY: Lewis Mumford Center for Comparative Urban and Regional Research, University of Albany. http://mumfordl.dyndns.org/cen2000/report.html.

Lieberson, S., & Waters, M. C. (1988). *From Many Strands: Ethnic Groups in Contemporary America*. New York: Russell Sage Foundation.

Los Tigres del Norte. (1995). Jaula de Oro. On *Jaula de Oro* [CD]. Van Nuys, CA: Fonovisa Records.

Massey, D. S., & Espinosa, K. E. (1997). What's Driving Mexico–U.S. Migration? A Theoretical, Empirical, and Policy Analysis. *American Journal of Sociology, 102*, 939–999.

McLemore, S. D., & Romo, H. D. (1998). *Racial and Ethnic Relations in America* (5th ed.). Boston: Allyn and Bacon.

Newman, D. M. (2000). *Sociology: Exploring the Architecture of Everyday Life* (3rd ed.). Thousand Oaks, CA: Pine Forge Press.

Population Reference Bureau. (2001). *2001 World Population Data Sheet*. Washington, DC: Population Reference Bureau. http://www.prb.org/.

Qian, Z., & Lichter, D. T. (2001). Measuring Marital Assimilation: Intermarriage Among Natives and Immigrants. *Social Science Research*, *30*, 289–312.

Saenz, R. (1999). Mexican Americans. In A. G. Dworkin & R. J. Dworkin (Eds.), *The Minority Report: An Introduction to Racial, Ethnic, and Gender Relations* (3rd ed., pp. 209–229). Fort Worth, TX: Holt, Rinehart, and Winston.

Sassen, S. (1991). *The Global City: New York, London, and Tokyo*. Princeton, NJ: Princeton University Press.

Smith, T. W. (2001). *Intergroup Relations in a Diverse America: Data from the 2000 General Social Survey*. New York: The American Jewish Committee. http://www.ajc.org/InTheMedia/Publications.asp?did=439.

U.S. Census Bureau. (2001). *Profile of the Foreign-Born Population in the United States*. Current Population Reports, No. P23–206. Washington, DC: U.S. Government Printing Office.

Waters, M. C. (1990). *Ethnic Options: Choosing Ethnic Identities in America*. Berkeley: University of California Press.

Weeks, J. R. (1999). *Population: An Introduction to Concepts and Issues* (7th ed.). Belmont, CA: Wadsworth.

Woodrow, K. A., & Passel, J. S. (1990). Post-IRCA Undocumented Immigration to the United States: An Assessment Based on the June 1988 CPS. In F. D. Bean, B. Edmonston, & J. S. Passel (Eds.), *Undocumented Migration to the United States: IRCA and the Experience of the 1980s* (pp. 33–75). Washington, DC: The Urban Institute Press.

INDEX

ABOUT THE EDITORS
AND CONTRIBUTORS

NOBUKO ADACHI is a research adjunct in anthropology at Illinois State University and is co-editor of *Pan-Japan: The International Journal of Japanese Diaspora*.

MARIXSA ALICEA is Associate Professor at the School for New Learning at DePaul University. She is co-author of *Surviving Heroin: Women Heroin and Methadone Users*. She has also published numerous articles concerning the Puerto Rican migration experience, the U.S. Latina experience, and multicultural teaching practices.

MARIA ISABEL AYALA, a graduate student in the Department of Sociology at Texas A&M University, is conducting research in the areas of international migration and gender.

JORGE DUANY is Professor of Anthropology at the University of Puerto Rico, Río Piedras. His latest book is entitled *The Puerto Rican Nation on the Move: Identities on the Island and in the United States* (2002).

JEREMY HEIN is Professor of Sociology at the University of Wisconsin–Eau Claire. He has expertise in the areas of race and ethnicity, international migration, and comparative sociology.

TWANNA A. HINES is a graduate student at the University of Amsterdam.

GRAEME HUGO is Professor of Geography and Director of the National Centre for Social Applications of GIS at the University of Adelaide, Australia. His main research interests include the impact of development on economic and social well-being in Southeast Asia and population trends and their implications in Australia.

SEAN KENNY is an Irish author whose novels *The Hungry Earth* and *Celtic Fury* explore the spiritual roots of modern Irish society. His latest novel, *The Memory Trap*, looks at the social problems of Silicon Valley, a society made up entirely of recent migrants.

FELIX MASUD-PILOTO is Associate Professor of History at DePaul University and the Director of the Center for Latino Research. He has published numerous articles about Cuban migration to the United States and is the author of *From Welcomed Exiles to Illegal Immigrants: Cuban Migration to the United States, 1959–1995.*

MARIA CRISTINA MORALES is a doctoral student in the Department of Sociology at Texas A&M University and is conducting research in the areas of immigration, labor, and social inequality.

JOSEPH R. OPPONG is Associate Professor of Geography at the University of North Texas, Denton, Texas. His research interest focuses on the geography of disease and health services, and the application of geographic information systems to disease and health care.

ROGELIO SAENZ, Professor of Sociology and head of the Department of Sociology at Texas A&M University, has published extensively in the areas of demography and social inequality.

JAMES STANLAW is Associate Professor of Anthropology at Illinois State University. He specializes in linguistics and Japanese studies.

MAURA I. TORO-MORN is Associate Professor of Sociology at Illinois State University. She is the author of numerous articles focusing on the gender and class dimensions of Puerto Rican migration to the United States. She teaches about race, class, and gender inequality in the United States.

JAMES A. TYNER is Associate Professor of Geography at Kent State University. His research interests include migration, social geography, and Southeast Asia.

CASSANDRA VENEY is Associate Professor and Director of the Unit for African Studies in the Department of Politics and Government at Illinois State University. Her research interests include the plight of African refugees, human rights, and internal displacement in East Africa.

PATRICIA ZAMUDIO works at the Center for Research and Graduate Studies in Social Anthropology in Xalapa, Veracruz and is studying Mexican international migration from Veracruz—a new state of origin of migrants—to the United States.

YU ZHOU is Associate Professor in the Department of Geography at Vassar College. Her research has been on Chinese transnational migrants and urban economic development in China.